For Mickey — With ... spirits in the love ♡ admiration for the women pilots who flew in World War II — Honoring a memory and leaving a legacy — Evelyn's "glorious summer will not fade"

Sharpie

The Life Story of Evelyn Sharp
Nebraska's Aviatrix

Diane Ruth Armour Bartels

Diane Ruth Armour Bartels

Dageforde Publishing

ISBN: 1-886225-16-8
Library of Congress Catalog Number: 96-85189

Cover Art by Angie Johnson Art Productions
Cover Photo courtesy Mary Farmer Palmer

The icon represents Evelyn Sharp's personal comments written on the back of certain photographs.

Grammatical and spelling errors found within primary sources have been included in their unaltered form.

Printed in the United States of America.

Dageforde Publishing
941 'O' Street, Suite 728
Lincoln, Nebraska 68508-3625
(402) 475-1123; e-mail dageforde.lnk@ispi.net
www.dageforde.com

Dedication

Dedicated to those people who lead their lives in such a manner as to bring honor to past generations and leave a legacy of perseverance and goodwill to the generations that are to follow.

Table of Contents

Foreword

*A*ccording to *Webster's Dictionary*, a pioneer is "one who goes before and prepares the way for others." By that definition, Evelyn Sharp was a pioneer. As this book will prove, she was an extraordinary pioneer at that.

Here is the story of a woman who was determined to fly. She faced many obstacles. Conventional wisdom of the early 1900s had it that women were neither physically nor psychologically equipped to fly airplanes. Evelyn, and many other courageous women of her generation, challenged these assumptions and proved the pundits (who were mostly male) wrong.

This is also the story of Ord, Nebraska, the town where Evelyn grew up and where she learned to fly. Ord was an uncommon town with uncommon leaders, like Dr. Glen Auble, who gave Evelyn the support she needed both literally and figuratively to get off the ground.

Born in 1919, Evelyn Sharp came of age during the Great Depression. The description of her efforts to obtain money to pay for flying lessons hit me hard, for I grew up in a Chicago suburb during the Depression and my great passion was airplanes. Whenever my mother turned her back, I jumped on my bicycle and peddled twelve miles to the local airport. Unlike Evelyn, I had no dreams of flying. I wanted to design airplanes. So, I sat in the shade of a hangar, hour after hour, and traced on paper the sleek lines of the planes that rested along the fringes of the grass field.

I think it is fair to say that my generation was obsessed with airplanes. Often, there would be a dozen or more young persons standing around the airport, and I remember that there were always two or three girls in the crowd. They were as enthusiastic about airplanes as we boys were. We watched breathlessly as devil-may-care men climbed into open cockpits, as mechanics spun propellers, and as frail crafts fashioned of wire, fabric, and plywood bounced down the rough runway, lurched into the air, and soared into the clouds.

Although we young people remained on the ground, we were nevertheless liberated by watching these planes rise into the sky. I think we sensed that, one day, we too would find ways to escape the earthly despair and despondency of the Depression and, like the pilots we envied, take off into the future! In short, airplanes pointed us to what lay ahead—we learned to think about what we could do; we considered possibilities, not reality as we knew it.

I stayed on the ground. Evelyn Sharp took to the air. She fulfilled her dream. She earned a place in the pantheon of women aviation pioneers—Amelia Earhart, Florence Barnes, Ruth Elder, Louise Thaden, and Jacqueline Cochran.

But this book is more than the story of women taking their rightful places in the world of aviation. Evelyn and her friends smashed traditions which ignored and diminished the enormous talent which women possessed. Here was a pool of talent which had never been tapped. Here were women who wanted to fly; who wanted to take their places in the sky alongside men; and who, when fate decreed, were willing to give their lives for their country.

As you read this book, you will relive the early days of aviation—the days of "seat-of-the-pants" flying with nary a computer in sight. Here is the story of a woman, one of many, who prepared the way for others.

All honor to the pioneers!

Robert N. Manley
Nebraska Historian
Gardner, Kansas

*D*iane Bartels' biography of the life of the young aviatrix Evelyn Sharp is a contribution to the history of American aviation and to women's history. It is also a dramatic and touching story. Bartels relates how a small-town Nebraska girl resolved to become a flier in the 1930s when few women won wings. With diligence and determination she attained her goal.

In 1942, the United States War Department organized the Women's Auxiliary Ferrying Squadron to pilot planes where they were needed. Evelyn became the seventeenth woman accepted in the WAFS. Exuberant about her acceptance, a warm-hearted patriot, she served her country until, on April 3, 1944, the P-38 she was to ferry from the New Cumberland Air Depot in Pennsylvania to Newark, New Jersey, crashed soon after takeoff. The twenty-four-year-old Sharpie had given her life for her country—a war heroine.

Drawing on the youthful pilot's letters, oral interviews, and tireless reading of newspapers, Bartels has produced a lively and fascinating book.

James A. Rawley
University of Nebraska-Lincoln
National Endowment for the Humanities Teacher-Scholar Mentor

But thy eternal summer shall not fade,
Nor lose possession of that fair thou ow'st,
Nor shall death brag thou wandr'st in his shade,
When in eternal lines to time thou grow'st,
So long as men can breathe or eyes can see.
So long lives this, and this gives life to thee.

—William Shakespeare

A prime characteristic of the beings we call "human" is their consciousness that their life span is limited, that they will die. That realization, whether it occurs gradually or with traumatic suddenness, colors our whole search for meaning in life. Indeed, it may be the primary source for the demand that such a meaning exists. The foreshadowing of our death also gives rise to the contrary notion that we must be, in some sense, immortal. Not only do most religions teach that a spark of life continues when the body dies, but we strive to leave earthly evidence that we have lived. The few do great deeds, erect massive monuments, begin lasting institutions, or create noble works of art. The rest of us must be content with more primal activities—fathering and mothering children, scratching a small piece of the earth's soil, touching the lives of those around us. But Time is the great enemy, not only of the body, but of human memory as well. Even institutions decay, monuments crumble, and art is lost to the vagaries of chance or the ravages of war. Remembrances fade, stories are forgotten, letters thrown out with the trash.

Of all the perishable works of man and woman, however, the

printed word endures with amazing persistence. Those people fortunate enough to have their lives preserved in writing cheat death of even its corporeal victory. How else would we know, as if she were with us now, Evelyn Sharp, this skillful and courageous young woman who lived most intensely in the trackless silver ocean of the sky? Had not Diane Bartels researched and written this biography, with tenacity and skill equal to her subject's, Evelyn would have faded forever into the sunset of her peers and dusty government and newspaper archives.

Still, it is not unfair to say that Evelyn earned her luck in death as she surely did in life, for these pages glow with the love that this vibrant woman inspired in all who knew her. Her peers, her elders, her comrades in flight obviously found her irresistible; and the warmth of their memories have kept her alive. Her maturity, bravery, charm, wit, energy, and goodness (what a quaint word in our cynical times!) are traits of a storybook character; but Diane establishes indisputably that they were altogether real. Diane, too, was drawn to this project by love. Her love of teaching led her to the National Endowment for the Humanities Summer Institute in which this biography was begun. Her own love of flying gave her the expertise and insight to understand Evelyn's accomplishments. And her love of this soul-mate from the past gave her the strength to bring this book to life. As a result, Evelyn Sharp's glorious summer will not fade, and she will grow to time in eternal lines for new generations of humans who look to the sky and dream of flight.

Robert Bergstrom
University of Nebraska-Lincoln
National Endowment for the Humanities Teacher-Scholar Mentor

Acknowledgments

*H*illary Rodham Clinton has recently written a book entitled *It Takes A Village*. The premise lies in her strong belief that it takes more than a mother, a father, or a grandparent to bring up a child. It requires nurturing, discipline, and unconditional love from neighbors next door, the community, and indeed, society itself.

This concept of "village" has taken on a kindred meaning in my pursuit as a biographer. I could never have written *Sharpie* without those of you listed below. You have been my "village," perhaps without realizing it. There are no words to adequately express the appreciation and emotional fulfillment I feel within my heart. With profound humility, I can simply say thank you for helping me to share the life story of Evelyn Genevieve Sharp, who herself was a product of the "village" in another day and another time.

NEBRASKA

Irene Auble Abernethy, Norma Ackles, Tom Anderson, Glen D. Auble, Al Baeder, Rich Baeder, Maurice & Anne Baker, Doug Barber, Wayne & Ramona Barclay, Robert E. Barrett, Steven Scott Bartels, Kaye Diane Bartels-Eiland, Urcell Baer Bartruff, Jerry Bauer, Victor Beck, Robert Bergstrom, Arvine Bierman, Don Blaha, Roger Boerkircher, Bert C. Boquet, Jr., Dean Bresley, Heloise Christensen Bresley, Linda Johnson Brown, Eldon Buoy, Richard Burrows, Dorothy Piskorski Butts, Christine Marie Carbon, Maxine Waters Carlson, Ella Marie Carson, Elizabeth Easily Cass, Gary P. Cassell, Wanda S. Caswell, Elsie Cecrle, Sylvia Chalupsky, Alice Chrastil, Jeff Clausen, Dean & Ruth Clawson, John A. Clinch, Ruby Coleman, Wilfred Cook, Helen G. Crosswait, Ella May Daake, Linda J. Dageforde, Graydon Dill, Harry, Jr. & Sandy Dingman, Leonard Dlugosh, J. L. Doksansky, LaVern Duemey, Christine Dunbar, Lois Durham, Arthur Dye, Betty J. Edison, Maxine Severns Eacker,

Christopher Paul Eiland, Bill Farnham, Kara Fischer, The Florette Flower Shop, Shirley Friink, Dave Fritz, Phyllis Garnick, Clyde W. Gewacke, Patricia M. Grove, Jeneatte Waters Hall, Claire Hansen, Don Heath, Don Heinrichs, Jim Helm, Chelys Mattley Hester, Jack Hoehne, Karen Hoffman, Alice Howell, Joyce Huffman, Robert Hurst, Jon Ihrig, Angie Johnson, Dan Johnson, Ray A. Johnson, Wilma Krikac Johnson, Patricia K. Jones, Wayne V. Jorgensen, Spud Kaputska, Dorette Hoehne Kleinkauf, Virginia Clark Knecht, Bill Knoll, Alton L. Kraft, Jerry A. Kroeger, George Kruml, John Kurtz, Barbara Dale Lahr, Mary Larson, Kenny Leach, Kerry Leggett, Eleanor A. Lilienthal, Lincoln Public Schools, Victor E. Lofgreen, Belva Lowery, Florence Boring Lueninghoener, Stanley Lumbard, Margaret Malicky, Eugene H. Masters, Roy L. Maxson, Mearl McNeal, Deb McWilliams, Evelyn L. Mersch, Patsy L. Meyer, Shannon Masters Meyer, Sharon K. Meyer, Marty Miller, Dr. Samuel D. Miller, Vernon Miserez, Dean Misko, Ellen Servine Misko, Ralph Misko, Helen Moore, Lynn L. Mortensen, Nebraska Chapter Ninety-Nines, Inc., Irene Schmale Nesiba, Darrell Noll, Randy O'Brien, Ord Airport Authority, Frank Osentowski, Helen Osentowski, Douglas F. Otoupalik, Donald Patrick, Carol Philbrick, Dale A. Philbrick, Robert & Norma Philbrick, Marsha Plugge, Diane Proskocil, Jack Rathjen, James A. Rawley, Edna Osgood Reiber, Betty Rieker, Russell Roberts, Roscoe & Norma Roeder, Susan J. Rosowski, Archie Rowbal, Ken Ruhnke, Lawrence Rushenberg, Evelyn Skala Rybin, Benita Schmidt, Lillian Setlik, Adolph Sevenker, Velma Shafer, Wilson Shafer, Cathlin Shuster, Ted Slobaszewski, Diana L. Smith, Margaret Lewis Snyder, Leonard Sobon, Stella Nielsen Stanley, Marguerite Stark, David F. Stevens, Donna Stevens, Irma Leggett Sullivan, Don Sutton, Charles E. Taylor, Carroll Tetschner, Bernerd L. Thompson, Lucile G. Tolen, Tom Tolen, Dillo Troyer, Patricia J. Turek, Thomas J. Umberger, Regis F. Urschler, Sally VanZandt, Sally Wagner, Lyda Walters, Dave Williams, Marlene Williams, Thomas Williams, Bess Wilson, Dennis Wohlers, Maxine Wood, Olive Miller Yates, Charles B. Zangger, Elno Zikmund

ALABAMA

Nancy Batson Crews

ARIZONA

Don Downie, Verley Hansen, Ruth Helm, Virginia DeHart Lofflin, Ralph Tuttle

CALIFORNIA

Elsie Ayers, William Bauer, George Brown, H. Glenn Buffington, Iris Cummings Critchell, Virginia Klein Cruce, Jean E. Davis, Edward H. Ellington, Barbara Towne Fasken, Zona Gale Forbes, Betty Huyler Gillies, Patricia Thomas Gladney, Rita Gladney, Barbara Nay Gleason, Dave Holland, Lillian Kusek Hominda, Howard E. Jones, Roy Joseph, Norma Mae Snell Kaufman, Earl J. Klein, Fred Kuster, Helen Kuster, William R. Lachenmaier, Jean Landis, Barbara Erickson London, Gus Marsh, Jr., Gale Mathews, Frank R. Moore, Mary Lou Kolbert Neale, William Orcutt, Yvonne C. Pateman, Brian F. Pemberton, Eleanore Perlinski, Martha Wagensell Rupley, Winifred Schachterle, Sam Stevens, Don Tunnicliff, Mae Klein Wakefield, Verna West, Shirley White

COLORADO

Ruth Lake Armour, Rosanne Perlinski Bax, Mary Beranek Bradley, Robert Brisbon, Hugh Greenwood, Duane Reed, Julie Beth Armour Thornton, Donald Vasicek

DISTRICT OF COLUMBIA

Deborah G. Douglas, Melissa Keizer, National Endowment for the Humanities

FLORIDA

James Austin, Claire Callaghan, Bernice Falk Haydu, Teresa James, Gertrude Meserve Levalley

HAWAII

Wendell Harding

ILLINOIS

Dorothy Auble Hardisty, Jim Haynes, Peggy Nigra, Dick Snow, Verna Nielsen Wilson

INDIANA

Marty Wyall

IOWA

T. Bruce Farmer, Theron Lessor, Eric Palmer, Mary Farmer Palmer, Ralph Smith, Russell & Dolly Zangger

KANSAS

Mildred D. Axton, Robert N. Manley, Jim Peterson, Robert K. Vasey, Lucille Doll Wise

MASSACHUSETTS
Grace Corrigan
MICHIGAN
John B. Bergeson
MINNESOTA
Milo W. Bresley, Richard & Carol Stucky, Cheryl Young, Lydia Zetzman
MISSOURI
James Burson, Francie Meisner Park, Adela Riek Scharr, Retta Whinery
MONTANA
Phyllis Adolph, Norma Berry, Edward Crouse, Bonnie Dawson, Mildred Foote, Sharon Foote, Robin Gerber, Ethel Hamilton, Mary Harvey, Mary R. Haughian, Mary Heins, Jack & Ilene Jennings, Eloyce Hubbard Kockler, Allie LaFont, Cindy McCaffree, Rae McLaughlin, Louise Rasmussen, Mary Rasmussen, Nina Rodgers, Jane Ferguson Schultz, Karen D. Stevens
NEW JERSEY
Kittie Leaming King, Samuel S. Parker
NEW MEXICO
Janet Beran Littleton
NEW YORK
DeWitt Wallace Trust Fund/Reader's Digest, Kathryn Bernheim Fine, Sally VanWagenen Keil
NEVADA
G. L. Buchner
NORTH DAKOTA
Beth H. Bauman
OHIO
Meigs K. Adams, Clarice I. Bergemann, Phyllis Burchfield Fulton, Jeffrey D. Joy, Mary Frances Joy, George Kirkendall, Sr., Carl Nicholson
OKLAHOMA
The Ninety-Nines, Inc.
OREGON
Mildred Millard Arvidson, Bernice I. Batten, Sandy Bennett, Mae Lee Misko, Gerald Severson, Joan Jacobs Shuey
PENNSYLVANIA
Nancy & Alan Abt, Carroll Buckingham, Ruth Coble, Orres

Greenwood, Randy Hicks, John W. Macfarlane, Jack Shambaugh, Patricia H. Vance, Janet Wright

SOUTH DAKOTA

Arden Clark, Howard Kennedy, Raymond Kolb, Allen Marek, Herma Marsden, Kenneth Charles Marsden, Warren O'Connell, Lloyd L. Petersen, Don Young

TEXAS

LaVerne Lakin, Lois Woodworth Taylor, Marianne Verges, Florene Miller Watson, I. H. Young

VIRGINIA

Barbara Donahue Ross, Crystal Thode Thompson

WASHINGTON

Charles Cetak, Tamara Keeton

WISCONSIN

Tammy J. Cuddy, Thelma Hilts, Cecelia M. Loken, Jim Ollis, Edward Piskorski, Betty Schindler, Jean C. Smith, Margaret Terry, Henrietta Voechting, Marion Westphal, Gertrude Ziemann, Gretchen Ziesmer

WYOMING

Clyde Ice, Howard W. Ice, Georgia M. Ratigan, John Ratigan, Irene Whiting

Introduction

*O*nce again I have returned to the North Loup Valley which lies at the eastern edge of the Sandhills in north central Nebraska. This is where Evelyn Genevieve Sharp spent most of her growing-up years, assimilating the values and character traits which define this woman who has been referred to as Nebraska's best-known aviatrix. It is here along the gently flowing waters of the North Loup River that I feel most connected with the persona of a woman I have never met, yet have grown to love and admire.

There has never been a time in my life when I do not remember wanting to fly. As a young girl, walking the bean fields on the family farm, I watched military planes make their approaches into the nearby air base and listened to my father tell stories of Nebraska's triangular airfields, where thousands of young pilots and their crews prepared for the Second World War. I remember reading books which told of the decisive role aviation played in the war's land and

Nebraska's 1991 Teacher-Scholar National Endowment for the Humanities/Reader's Digest Award:
Diane Ruth Armour Bartels

sea battles. Those volumes now occupy a special place on shelves in my library.

In the 1950s, Grosset & Dunlap, publisher of the Signature Book Series, introduced me to a world where women made a difference. The first book my mother gave me was entitled *The Story of Amelia Earhart*. I read it and reread it, absolutely fascinated that a young girl from Atchison, Kansas, could grow up to be a world famous pilot. I wanted to be just like her.

It wasn't until I graduated from the University of Nebraska in 1964 that I began to think about getting a pilot's license. My only experience in a small plane had been on those yearly outings when the Soil Conservation Service hired local pilots to take up farmers in order to survey conservation practices in the county. I do not remember how he did it, but my dad always managed to get my sister and me aboard. I never forgot that sense of freedom, the absolute beauty of what I already knew was an imperfect world below, and the feeling I was spiritually closer to that which was good and true.

In the summer of 1966, I closed the door to my elementary classroom and took up flying at the Lincoln Aviation Institute in Lincoln, Nebraska. It was wonderful. For two months, I flew every day the weather permitted and, on August 12, Thomas J. Umberger, an FAA flight examiner, "signed off" my logbook. My dream had come true. I was just like Amelia.

A small piece of paper, officially recognizing me as a licensed private pilot, created a dimension to my life with no comparable parallel. It eventually brought me to the 1973 Nebraska State Air Show in Ord, and to a young woman named Evelyn Sharp. Fascinated by history and especially the role women played, I was immediately attracted to an old card table in the corner of a large hangar. On its well-worn surface, someone had carefully arranged black and white photographs of a young girl standing beside an airplane of a much-earlier day. As I began reading the related newspaper clippings, faded and yellowed with age, I sensed someone standing beside me. I looked up to see this older man, bespectacled and gray, peering at me intently over the top of his glasses. He spoke first, wondering if I *knew* about Evelyn. Dr. Glen Auble had been a friend and mentor to Evelyn Sharp and it was his mission that she not be forgotten. I have often wondered if he saw me as just one more person to tell, or if he sensed I would fulfill his dream to have her life story written.

On the flight back to Lincoln that afternoon from Ord, I made a commitment to do whatever I could to save the primary research materials which documented her life. I, too, did not want Evelyn Sharp to be forgotten. For the next eighteen years, I intermittently acquired any piece of memorabilia with which one was willing to part. I maintained a correspondence with Dr. Auble until his death in 1986, made arrangements for dedicatory plaques to be hung at the Grand Island and Ord airports, and submitted biographical data for Evelyn's acceptance into the Women of Nebraska Hall of Fame sponsored by the Nebraska International Women's Year Coalition.

Presented to the Community of Ord
in recognition of their support of

EVELYN SHARP
1919 - 1944
by the Nebraska Chapter of the Ninety-Nines
International Organization of Licensed Women Pilots
on the occasion of the
Fiftieth Anniversary of the Chapter
June 6, 1987

Dedicatory plaque, November 7, 1987, Ord, Nebraska

In the summer of 1988, I was selected to participate in the National Endowment for the Humanities Institute, "The Struggle for Freedom and Equality: Life Stories of Great Americans." I chose Evelyn Sharp as the biographical subject for my final project. When I finished my presentation in the East Senate Chamber of Nebraska's State Capitol Building, there were tears in the eyes of several colleagues, my own included. They encouraged me to continue my research and finish the manuscript.

In May of 1990, I was persuaded by the Institute's project director, Lynn L. Mortensen, to apply for the National Endowment for the Humanities/Reader's Digest Teacher-Scholar Award. It carried a stipend which would nearly match my teaching salary and allow me a year's leave of absence from my professional responsibilities. That March, I was officially recognized as Nebraska's 1991 Teacher-Scholar at ceremonies in Washington, DC. On the flight home, I reflected on the conversation with Dr. Auble in the Ord airport hangar nearly eighteen years earlier. Perhaps he was more perceptive than I had realized.

As I began reading Nebraska newspapers at the State Historical Society Archives and interviewing Evelyn Sharp's contemporaries, it soon became apparent that her presence had created lasting impressions. Autographed picture postcards of herself and her dog, Scottie, ticket stubs for a sky-ride, newspaper articles, photos, and personal correspondence found their way out of old trunks in an attic, torn, yellowed pages of scrapbooks, and special drawers in a bureau. Men and women remembered her skill as a pilot, but spoke of a genuineness and an unassuming friendliness which seemed to epitomize Nebraska's "Queen of the Air."

In this biography, I have written the life story of a very special and unique woman as well as the human history of a place and a time. A time not perfect, yet a period in our nation's history when a strong sense of community, perseverance, and commitment was honored and acted upon.

I have laughed, shared tears, and put my arms around those who knew and remembered her, and those who have only heard the stories about this young aviatrix. The persona of Evelyn Sharp has left "indelible footprints" on their hearts as well as mine.

Diane Ruth Armour Bartels
Lincoln, Nebraska
August 1996

Hard Right Rudder

*E*velyn reached up. She ran her fingers along the edge of the steel, red-tipped propeller blade. It felt cold. Somehow colder than the thirty-one degree temperature the Weather Bureau had reported at ten o'clock that morning. An eleven-mile-per-hour wind, blowing from the north-northwest, made her cheeks cold.[1] Evelyn pulled the fur-lined WASP (Women Airforce Service Pilots) flight jacket a little closer around her neck and finished her visual pre-flight.

No excess oil beneath the turbocharger's cooling system.

Gear struts looked good.

Tire pressure seemed okay, too.

Hunching over, she walked into the open space between the twin-tail booms of the P-38 and straightened up. With a final cinch on the straps of her seat-type parachute, she climbed the retractable three-rung ladder and stepped onto the wing behind the cockpit. Today she would deliver this sleek, fighter aircraft and perhaps be back in Long Beach, California, tonight.

Evelyn swung her right leg over the edge of the cramped cockpit, stepped onto the seat, and eased herself in. There was not a lot of room in these pursuits. As she reached up to pull the canopy down, she sensed someone beside her. One of the ground crew mechanics was lowering it into place. Evelyn looked up and smiled. He nodded, returning the smile.

Out of the wind and with the sun shining through a nearly cloudless sky, Evelyn unzipped her flight jacket. Then, with an experience of some nine years of flying and over 3,500 hours of logged flight time, she pulled out her checklist. In a methodical manner, she turned knobs, flipped switches, tested warning lights, and noted the movement and reading of various dials and gauges. With her left hand, she pushed both throttles one-tenth open. With her right hand, she flipped the ignition master up and left ignition switch to BOTH. Repositioning the fingers of her right hand along the main switch box, Evelyn pushed the engage switch, still holding the starter switch to LH (left hand). With a shot of prime, the P-38's left engine fired and she shoved the mixture control to AUTO RICH. She glanced at the oil pressure gauge. It was coming up. Repeating the procedure for the right engine, Evelyn soon had both counter-rotating 1,425 hp Allison engines running. The left one was not idling as smoothly as the right, but neither was warmed up yet. She would keep the rpm below 1400 until the oil temperature reached forty degrees Centigrade or showed a definite increase of ten degrees. In the meantime, she tested her radio communication equipment with a transmission to the Harrisburg Control Tower.[2]

Cleared to taxi from the Navy's long hangar on the north side of the field, Evelyn released the parking brake. The idling props eased the P-38 ahead. An Army guard from the nearby New Cumberland Air Depot held both hands overhead, motioning her forward. Then, raising his left arm over his head, and with the right arm extended at shoulder height, he pointed the way to the taxi-strip. Evelyn advanced the right throttle, swinging the plane to the left. The pretty, young woman gave a "thumbs up" as her P-38, with the eerie whine of its superchargers, taxied by. The soldier snapped to attention and saluted.

As Evelyn made her way to the departure end of Runway 30, perhaps she thought about some of the engine problems P-38 pilots talked about over drinks at officers' clubs. What options did she have if she lost an engine on takeoff? The borough of New Cumberland, the Susquehanna River, and the city of Harrisburg, Pennsylvania, were on her flight path, both ahead and to the right. Also ahead and to her left was Beacon Hill, with an elevation some 150 feet higher than the airport.

Evelyn's thoughts returned to ground-check procedures as she entered the warm-up area on the southeast end of the runway. By this time, the oil temperature gauge of each liquid-cooled engine registered normal. Once again, she referred to the checklist.

Flaps, extended and retracted.

Normal fuel pressure.

Increasing the rpm to 2300, she checked the propeller control levers and the propeller selector switches. Both left and right magnetos were operating in the maximum one-hundred-drop limit. Adequate charges on the voltmeter and ammeter were noted. Evelyn moved the intercooler flap controls to OPEN to check the operation of the turbochargers. Everything seemed to check out.

With the top hatch locked in place, and the side windows cranked and closed, Evelyn fastened her safety harness and checked to make sure it was secure. Army 43-28750 was ready to go.

Cleared by the Tower for takeoff, she rolled onto the runway, lining up the nose wheel with the center line. With unlimited visibility and no ceiling reported, Beacon Hill was clearly visible, less than a mile from the end of the runway. Most of the trees on the hill were deciduous, and thus, on this third day in April 1944, were still without leaves. She thought she could see one of the radio towers, or perhaps the transmitting tower, just over the top, but wasn't sure. The brownish-gray of individual trunks and limbs blended together in the distance.

Scanning the instrument panel for one last look, Evelyn took a deep breath, positioning herself in the seat. She reached up with her left hand and advanced both throttles simultaneously.

2000 rpm
2500
3000

With brakes on, the Fork-Tailed Devil sat there, shuddering and eager to fly. The six-foot-long, three-bladed props thrust volumes of air over the wings. With forty-six inches of manifold pressure, Evelyn released the brakes. The fighter plane surged ahead. It rolled quickly down the runway, gaining speed. As acceleration established itself, Evelyn glanced down at the coolant temperature gauges and then quickly refocused her attention on the outside runway alignment. Approaching an airspeed of seventy, she gently, but firmly began to ease the control column back. With one more glance inside to check temperatures and verify critical airspeed, Evelyn pulled back on the control, rotating the nose wheel off. In another hundred yards, the P-38 lifted clear of the runway. The time was 10:29 a.m.

Evelyn did not need to see the black smoke belching from behind her left engine to know she did not have full power. Back on the tarmac, Pvt. Frank J. Dougherty and Pfc. Mike E. Lawrence, Military Police Section of the 3384th SU watched in horror as the plane struggled into the air.[3]

Inside the plane, Evelyn knew she was in trouble, serious trouble. Reducing power on the good right engine, she kicked in more right rudder. Both of these acts would keep the torque from flipping her over, but it would also reduce her ability to climb. The left engine caught again. She adjusted the mixture and power controls. Her eyes swept the gauges. She was losing airspeed and altitude.

The left engine faltered again. More black smoke spewed from the exhaust. Suddenly the right wing began to come up. The left engine was dead. Instinctively, Evelyn kicked in more right rudder and turned the wheel right to trim up. The wings leveled, but with the nose in a climbing attitude and decreasing airspeed, she had only seconds to make decisions. Now the gear, exerting a tremendous amount of drag on the airfoil surfaces, needed to come up. And that dead, windmilling propeller needed to be feathered.

With her left hand, Evelyn reached down and pulled the landing gear lever up. Continuing the arc, she closed the throttle, returned the mixture control lever to OFF, and then shut down the left engine fuel pump. Reaching down between her knees, she flipped a switch to feather the left engine prop.

Seconds had gone by, seconds she did not have. One of three choices had to be made immediately. In an instant, she rejected two of the three. She could turn to the right "downhill" into the good engine.

But that would put her over Harrisburg. The image of a P-38 crashing into houses, spreading death with gasoline fires and jagged metal pieces, was the first rejection. What about the Susquehanna, ahead and to the right? An excellent swimmer, she could release the top hatch, roll down both windows, then ditch it in the river. But would the impact leave her unconscious, strapped in her seat as the plane sank? Reject option two. Suddenly, there it was; Beacon Hill, dead ahead. The torque of the good right engine had caused the plane to go left. For Evelyn, only one choice remained, to the left "uphill" where there were only a few farmhouses. She had to gain enough altitude to fly over or go around Beacon Hill, somehow conserving enough power to make it back to the airport.

Yet, Evelyn knew a cardinal rule of flying twin-engine aircraft was never to turn into a dead engine. In fact, the operating manual had stated it clearly: "Do not make turns into the dead engine unless trim and speed have been established."[4] But circumstances did not allow her this choice.

She started a shallow, climbing bank to the left, knowing that any turn would cause a loss of airspeed. Keeping the towers on top of Beacon Hill in her view, she pushed the right throttle forward and eased up a bit on the right rudder. The crippled P-38 yawed, and skidded to the left. Watchmen on duty at the Radio Range Station watched her plane go by, barely missing the tops of the 150-foot towers.[5]

Evelyn knew she was going down. Yesterday, coming in on the flight from Columbus, Ohio, she had seen a field, a clear spot, just this side of a wooded ravine. She would put it down there. This young woman had set her biplane down in many a pasture while barnstorming in Nebraska. But the P-38 was no biplane. It weighed tons, and was barely flying.

A few feet above the partially-thawed ground, Evelyn pulled back sharply on the control wheel. The plane shuddered as the nose tried to come up. With no more lift, the P-38 stalled, hanging in the air for a brief moment. "The descending aircraft struck a cluster of trees with the left wing tip and hit the ground in a flat position...."[6] With an incredible thud, the P-38 skidded broadside a distance of about ten feet. Inside the cockpit, the second hand on the clock stopped moving. The time was 10:30 a.m.

There was no sound. No birds greeted each other. No squirrels darted here and there. No movement from the cockpit. The Plexiglas canopy was lying upside down a few feet ahead of the right prop. In the bright morning sun, the wind blew a little wisp of smoke away from the left engine.

"Profound Silence,"
April 3, 1944   Beacon Hill
New Cumberland, Pennsylvania

Married In Haste

The twentieth of October was a beautiful fall morning. Almost silently, an occasional wisp of wind moved the yellow leaves of cottonwood trees growing beside the clear-flowing waters of the Musselshell River. Toward the north, up a long, long, gentle slope, lay the town of Melstone, Montana. A ranching, railroad town, Melstone was "a happy, prosperous incorporated little city"[1] in 1919.

Inside a private maternity home, there was no silence. Babies were crying in some rooms, and from one came the occasional moans of a twenty-seven-year-old woman who was experiencing the pains of a first childbirth. As Elsie Haeske Crouse lay there, waiting for the next contraction, perhaps she reflected on the circumstances which brought her to this small farming community in central Montana.

Seventeen months earlier, she had looked forward to returning to New Leipzig, North Dakota, the residence of her older sister, Minnie, and her husband, Walter Harke. There she would help out

Elsie Adelia Haeske, Evelyn's birth mother, circa 1910

in Walter's mercantile and care for a baby niece born later in November. The May 9, 1918, edition of the *New Leipzig Sentinel* had even reported Elsie's return:

> Miss Elsie Haeske of Fall Creek, Wisconsin, arrived in the city last Friday, and is assisting with the work at the W. E. Harke General Store. Miss Haeske is well acquainted with the people in this part of the state and her many friends will be pleased to renew old acquaintanceship.[2]

Elsie was used to working. The unexpected death of Gustave Haeske, when she was only eighteen months old, left a fatherless household of eight children. Around age twelve, she began baby-sitting the younger children in the neighborhood. Later, in mid-teens, she worked in the telephone office and then waited tables at the residential Kneer House owned by her uncle.[3] Members of German-American families took care of each other in times of need.

That summer of 1918 in New Leipzig, Elsie made a new acquaintance. Orla Edward Crouse came from his home in Miles City, Montana, to work as a carpenter for Henry Bellman, manager of the New Leipzig Equity Exchange. Later, Orla signed on as a drayman with City Dray and Transfer Line.[4] Picking up freight from the local depots of the Northern Pacific and the Chicago, Milwaukee, and St. Paul Railways, he had as one of his deliveries the Harke General Store. Each day Orla found an excuse to stop by the counter and visit with the pretty, dark-haired Elsie. During one of their conversations, he asked her to go to a dance held after the opera house performance. Elsie loved to dance. The good times lasted through summer and the clear, crisp days of fall. The snow came, then melted. By spring, whatever their feelings for each other, the relationship had evolved into a responsibility neither one was able or willing to assume. The May 15, 1919, front page headline read: "Married In Haste But All Is Well." The *Sentinel* article followed:

> Orla Krause, one of the faithful and trusted of the City Dray and Transfer Line, resigned his position last Wednesday and the following morning with his intended, Miss Elsie Haeske, boarded the train and being interviewed by the reporter, "whereto" was told to her home in Wisconsin, and

her companion was to accompany the lady as far as Mandan [North Dakota] to see there would be no mistake in getting the right train. And there you are. Here comes a telephone message from Carson [North Dakota] in the early forenoon that Miles [Orla] and Elsie had stopped off at that point and secured the necessary preliminaries and were joined in the bonds of holy wedlock....

The groom is an estimable young man, ...an industrious worker, and while here has made many friends....

The bride, an accomplished young lady...is known by everyone in this community.... Her amiable disposition and sociability have won for her many friends that wish this happy couple a happy and prosperous journey through life.... They will make their home for the present at Miles City, where the groom formerly resided.[5]

On May 8, 1919, Orla and Elsie exchanged wedding vows in front of Ben Mooney, Judge of the County Court. The bride was twenty-seven years old and four months pregnant; the groom was twenty-one. Being pregnant and unmarried in 1919 was a disgrace. Minnie Harke made several intercessions on behalf of her sister. One of these was to get the couple to elope. Another was to convince Sheridan Crouse, Orla's father and a highly respected physician who practiced in Melstone, to accept Elsie in his home at Miles City. There she would work as a housekeeper until the baby was born.

For some time the relationship between Dr. Crouse and his son had been strained. Perhaps Orla hadn't felt he belonged in this family. His own mother had died when he was only two months old; and, until his father remarried two years later, he had lived with his paternal grandparents. By 1919, Dr. Crouse and his second wife had two daughters of their own, each of whom showed exceptional abilities in their study of music and the arts. Orla just didn't seem to fit in, and the hard-working dawn-to-dusk doctor considered his son irresponsible.

There is little reason to believe Orla stayed with Elsie in Miles City, or made the 112-mile train ride to Melstone when it was time for the baby to be born. Orla was simply not ready for the responsibilities of marriage or fatherhood. The marriage ended in divorce.[6]

As soon as Elsie was well enough to travel, she returned to Miles City carrying her infant daughter. Now there were more decisions to be made. Elsie had an eighth grade education and no career skills which would allow her to work and at the same time care for her baby. Seeking support from her family was out of the question. Elsie's mother died, never knowing about the birth of her granddaughter.

Furthermore, Elsie could not stay indefinitely with the Crouses. What was she to do? Sheridan Crouse had an idea. As company physician for the Chicago, Milwaukee, and St. Paul Railway, he knew of a couple who desperately wanted a family. John and Mary Sharp had been married since 1905 and were unable to have children. Perhaps an adoption could be arranged.

Employed by the C M and St. Paul line for several years, John Sharp was the telegraph operator at the Kinsey, Montana, depot. He and Mary were also social friends of the Crouses, often visiting in the doctor's Miles City home at 209 N. Stacy. They knew Elsie and liked her, sympathizing with the realities she was forced to confront. At some point, someone suggested adoption. The moment of silence which followed must have seemed like an eternity to all. But the step was taken. Within the promises and arrangements made, an atmosphere of respect and sensitivity prevailed. Genevie, the baby's middle name given to her by Elsie, would be retained, in an alternate spelling, in the child's adoptive name. On December 22, 1919, Lois Genevie Crouse became Evelyn Genevieve Sharp, the legal daughter of John E. and Mary K. Sharp.[7] In later years, Elsie Crouse would be reintroduced to Evelyn as " Aunt Elsie."

Evelyn's first home was at Kinsey, Montana, forty-five miles northeast of Miles City. John and Mary operated an end-of-the-line boarding house, a nearby pool and dance hall, plus a country store. A favorite attraction to young and old shoppers was the flat-bottomed jars filled with assorted stick candies. Mildred Arvidson still remembers the ones with the "white insides and the sweet chocolate outsides."[8] Young Dan Haughian, a boy of twelve years, made many trips by team from his home at Little Sheep Mt. down to the rail line at Kinsey. Driving twelve miles one way, he loaded a wagon with hay and other grain for stock at the ranch. Because of the distance, Dan ate at

Sharps and stayed at the boarding house overnight. He remembers John as being "a nice, friendly person."[9]

On one particular evening after a dance, a fire burned Sharp's store and adjoining buildings to the ground. John's dreams of his Kinsey Kountry Klub went up in flames. He was one of the first three directors of the Klub, buying in at $5 per share. Now that his shares lay in ashes, he once again moved on. Taking Mary and nearly two-year-old Evelyn, he relocated in Billings, where Masonic Lodge 113, A.F. & A.M. listed his occupation as grocer.

"Me at about a year and a half old." 1921, Montana

I Want To Drive An Airplane

By 1924, the Sharps were living in Nebraska. The *Hastings City Directory* listed Mary K. Sharp as the owner of a grocery store at 233 West High, two blocks west of the Union Pacific Railroad tracks. The Kimball County Security Company had sold the large Buswell Addition lot to John E. Sharp for $3000, and he immediately transferred it to Mary for the sum of $1. This legal maneuver was not unusual when trying to protect investments from bankruptcy proceedings. A large, two-story wooden frame structure became the residence for the Sharp family and several young women who attended either the high school or Hastings College. The tree-shaded, second-floor porch, which allowed cooling summer breezes to flow through, was a favorite respite for the women who had come from the country or small towns in the surrounding area. Large glass windows on the first floor identified the Sharp's grocery operation

"Evelyn At The Controls," three years old, Hastings, Nebraska, 1922

at the front of the house, while the back part served as living and sleeping quarters for John, Mary, and Evelyn.

In 1926, Evelyn made a friend; her name was Thelma. With matching Buster Brown haircuts and complexions browned by the warm, Nebraska sun, they could be seen walking, sometimes hand-in-hand, to the near-by Longfellow Elementary School. Later, under the shade of mature ash trees, the little girls played house. Evelyn, with her dressed-up stuffed toy dog, and Thelma, with Evelyn's porcelain head doll, could spend hours in their world of grown-up pretend.

Evelyn and Thelma, Hastings, Nebraska, 1926

For Evelyn, however, circumstances beyond her control catapulted her from that world of make-believe into one of reality. Edna Osgood Reiber, a high school roomer, remembers being awakened in the middle of the night during one of Evelyn's asthmatic attacks. Edna lay there, listening to the uncontrollable wheezing coming from the room below. It seemed an eternity before the doctor arrived and miraculously returned quiet to the night once more. Undoubtedly a most terrifying experience for everyone, the attack was to be followed by recurring bouts into the adult years of Evelyn's life.

The early to middle 1920s brought forth the era of the flying barnstormer. Pilots, with their daredevil theatrics, flying World War I Curtiss Jennies and German Fokkers caught the attention of a little brown-eyed girl who lived atop the highest hill in Hastings. She firmly declared, "I want to drive an airplane."[1] Never mind a father's admonition with respect to her asthma. Even at this young age, Evelyn Sharp was alert and determined.

On March 31, 1928, John Sharp moved himself, his wife, and daughter to a Sandhills ranch 112 miles north-northwest of Hastings.

Evelyn enrolled in the third grade at Dry Cedar Country School, a large, two-classroom, wooden frame building sitting on the dividing line between Wheeler and Garfield counties.

On May 17, 1928, *The Ericson Journal* reported news from the Dry Cedar School.

> Mrs. Ray Cudaback took her school children on a hike Tuesday afternoon, then brought them back by way of her home and treated them to fruit salad and cake. They all report a fine time and their teacher a real pal and entertainer. They are all so sorry that school is nearly out so they can have no more hikes and flower pickings.[2]

That spring the Sharps planted potatoes, melons, sweet corn, cabbage, and other crops of home-grown produce in the sandy soil east of the house. John mended pasture fences, sorely in need of repair, and he bought machinery for the planting and harvesting of hay. Milk cows, steers, heifers, pure-bred Buff Orpington chickens, ducks, mares, and a saddle pony completed the menagerie of their new Sandhills homestead.

Summer came, and so too the typical drought-producing winds of the Sandhills. In stark contrast to a yard of wind-blown sand, the stately, wooden windmill, symbol of life in this area, continued to pump its life-giving sustenance to the carefully tended garden. The results of that care were evidenced in the produce delivered by John Sharp and eight-year-old Evelyn. Loading a lumber wagon pulled by a nine-year-old 2,650 pound team of black mares, they drove five and one-half miles to Ericson, Nebraska, established themselves in farmer's market fashion, and enjoyed the fruits of their labors.[3]

A new teacher had been hired when Evelyn returned to country school on September 3, 1928. Having arrived on the passenger train just a few days before, Miss Ruth Cutler from nearby Wolbach, Nebraska, soon established the routines of the day. Classes for the younger children were held in the east room, while the older seventh and eight graders had their subjects taught in the smaller west room. Water from nearby Little Dry Cedar Creek was carried in a large tin pail by the older children; each child brought his/her own cup. Bread and butter sandwiches, a piece of fruit, or maybe a piece of Mom's chocolate cake were packed in gallon-size syrup buckets.

A pot-bellied stove was the source of heat. Willows, cut from the creek banks by the boys who did not take school seriously, were stacked chest-high alongside the lumps of coal in a basement room. With signs of an early winter, perhaps Miss Cutler found increased incidents of day dreaming. Not so with Evelyn. Two classmates recall her being very good in school, or as they put it, "pretty smart."[4]

In those days, walking was the usual way for most kids to get to school. But this year, much to Evelyn's delight, it would be different. *The Ericson Journal* reported: "Eveline Sharp thinks it is great fun to ride a pony to school."[5] Never mind the animal was of such a size that it necessitated her mounting from a fence or the thick, wooden rails on the schoolhouse steps. One day her splendid transportation even gave her an excuse to play hooky. On Thursday, October 27, 1929, "Eveline Sharp missed school because her horse got more green corn than he could digest!"[6]

Maxine Severns, two years younger than Evelyn, lived directly north of the Sharp ranch. She recalls the fun at those country school recesses where everyone played games together because of the small number of students. Pump, Pump, Pullaway and Annie, Annie, Over were great favorites.[7] But the times were many when young arms could not muster the strength to get the balls over the barn, and the horses neighed as if in gentle disapproval.

There was no playground equipment provided at Dry Cedar School so the children created their own. One day several students brought some wood scraps and nails from home. When they finally fashioned a basketball hoop on the end of the barn, a whirlwind, typical of that region, promptly blew through and took the backboard with it. Not easily discouraged, the young carpenters retrieved the broken pieces and constructed the backboard once again.

Dale and Robert Philbrick, who lived two ranches to the north, remember Evelyn with fondness. She was a "happy little girl and pleasant to be around."[8] Often after school, especially when the weather was nice, Evelyn chose to lead her pony and walk with Dale and Robert to the entrance of their property. As they waved good-by, she maneuvered the animal close to the fence and with no hesitation, leaped from its top rail onto the pony's back to continue the trip home by herself.

Dale and Robert also recall the excitement of the annual Christmas program and the pride felt when their father felled a cedar tree tall enough to touch the schoolhouse ceiling. The children strung popcorn and cut colored circles from construction paper for tree decorations. They reenacted the timeless Nativity Scene, sang familiar carols, and practiced their lines for plays. Many of those who could memorize easily had several parts in different plays. But the most excitement revolved around the name drawing for the gift exchange. Near the end of the evening, a white-bearded man dressed in a coonskin coat stuffed with feather pillows, burst through the cloakroom door. As he pulled the sweet, juicy oranges and polished red apples from an old burlap feed sack, the more knowing children whispered to their friends, "That's not Santa. That's Robert and Dale's dad." And amidst all the gaiety, perhaps some parents remembered similar Christmases and wondered what the future would hold for their children.

It was extremely cold the first part of the new year. *The Ericson Journal* reported "children who have to ride to school are having some very disagreeable weather to contend with."[9] In fact, during the last week of March, Evelyn boarded with her teacher at Mrs. Will Ainsworth's, a residence close to the school.[10] In April, ranchers discovered hundreds of pounds of frozen potatoes in their cellars; never before had such losses occurred.

Whether it was the freeze or something else, John Sharp held a clean-up sale on December 12, 1929. The handbill indicated he had disposed of his ranch and wanted to sell his personal property, which included an inventory of cattle, horses, chickens, ducks, field machinery, hay equipment, and trucks. Unlike the preceding year, "The South Side Items," a column in *The Ericson Journal*, had made no mention of the Sharp family that summer and fall. One can surmise that weather and economic conditions, coupled with recent costs to start up the ranch, had taken its toll. The newspaper reported Mr. Sharp was pleased with prices the sale offerings brought. Soon after March 20, he would locate in Ord, some twenty miles to the southwest, "helping farmers keep their tools in order."[11]

Cinders and Double-dip Cones

*C*oming from a country school, it must have been a bit overwhelming for ten-year-old Evelyn Sharp to walk into that large South School classroom in late March. Miss Lucille Witter, Evelyn's fifth grade teacher taught in one end of the room, while the sixth grade occupied the other. Only the traditional subjects of reading, spelling, geography, numbers, and language were marked that semester. Evelyn earned B's. Mary Sharp probably didn't realize the Ord School System would be responsible for the remainder of her daughter's public school education. Since her marriage to John at the young age of sixteen, they had lived in three states and occupied more than double that number of residences. John always had another idea. Mary seemingly went along.

On April 3, 1930, the following ad appeared in *The Ord Quiz:*

*"Me on Ray Cook's car.
Ord , Nebraska, 1930, Age 11"*

Expert Lawn Mower sharpening and repairs. Will make them cut like new. Give us a trial. Guaranteed Work. We Pickup and deliver. Electri-Keen sharpened which is same method used by leading lawnmower manufacturers. Phone 372. Sharp, the Sharpener. 1617 O.[1]

Mary also had different work. Under "new and permanent management of Mary K. Sharp," the Ord Laundry had reopened with "new and experienced help." [2]

That fall, school began on September 4. Evelyn's class moved to the north end of the large combination classroom where Marguerite Stark assumed dual roles as principal and departmental sixth grade teacher. Not long after, a "deal was closed by which J.E. Sharp became the owner of the Bluebird Confectionery. He is putting in a lunch counter, and will serve lunches in addition to his soda fountain, candy, and tobacco business."[3]

In October, the Ord businessmen began their first of many promotions, showing appreciation to the neighboring communities and rural residents in the North Loup Valley. As in Hastings, people in this simple farming community were fascinated with aviation and its continuing technological development. An aerial rodeo featuring a Ford Tri-motor, a fifteen-passenger airliner from Rapid Air Lines (Rapid City, South Dakota), and a tiny two-cylinder Aeronca, billed as the smallest plane that would really fly, were the main attractions. There was no admission fee to Ed Zikmund's pasture-airport, five miles northwest of Ord, and rides costing a penny a pound were offered to enthusiastic spectators. But how much did each person weigh? A scale would provide the answer, yet could cost the barnstormer money. Those on the hefty side probably wouldn't want their weight advertised. A prudent decision was made with "passengers deciding the charge."[4]

Within a week after the air show, another aviation project was in its developing stages. This time, however, it was in the hearts, minds, and hands of Mrs. Stark's sixth graders and the fifth graders taught by Miss Witter. With paper, scissors, and paste, Evelyn and her classmates transformed a large sandbox table into a 1930's airport. They designed and built aeroplanes, reports indicating some of the homemade creations showed real talent. Evelyn earned membership on the Sixth Grade Honor Roll that semester with nine B's and an A in spelling.[5]

In the summer of 1931, Evelyn Sharp and Norma Mae Snell were very good friends. Both girls lived downtown above the businesses of their respective parents. As they sat on the curb beside M Street, the eleven-year-olds whiled away many an afternoon removing silver foil from the insides of empty cigarette packages retrieved from the gutter. They had been told the foil could be redeemed for money. Upon reflection, Norma Mae Snell Kaufman thinks it was probably a way of keeping two young girls out of mischief.

The unusually severe winter of '31-'32, with its intense, sustained cold, was the crowning blow to the residents of north central and northeast Nebraska. The summer had brought swarms of grasshoppers so massive they obscured the light of the sun, and the drought-producing winds had nearly denuded the precious soil. The Ord Quiz reported "Stock Is Dying, People Starving In Drought Area." There was "not so much as a spear of grass raised."[6] An appeal went out for the donation of cash, flour, feed, baled hay, or alfalfa. The Northern Nebraska Drought Relief Project, spearheaded by the Noll Seed Company in Ord, assumed the responsibility of collection and distribution. Rail cars were provided free of charge by the Burlington Railroad. This project was to be the beginning of a series of collective efforts organized by the community of Ord to help those in time of need. The Ord Quiz newspaper, established in 1884, would play a major part in defining this successful role. Not only would it supply the informational background for a particular need or cause, but it would provide direction and organizational support through its editorials and articles. One of the oldest newspapers in Nebraska, The Ord Quiz was truly the bulwark of a community at its best.

With the winter nearly behind, it was time to focus attention on spring's arrival. In March, The Ord Quiz proposed an official flower contest. Residents voted for their favorite flower, and a plan for every school child to acquire free seedlings was announced through the school. Love of flowers, fondness for the wholesome hobby of gardening, and a respect and interest for neighbors' lawns were goals of the project. Residents, encouraged to keep all spare slips and turn them into a central location, selected the petunia as the official flower in Ord for 1932. There was hardly a residence or a business that did not choose to participate.

In the meantime, John Sharp was working on another business venture, leasing the old Ravenna Creamery building. It had stood idle for four years, but more than $300 of repaired machinery turned it into an operation capable of producing one hundred gallons of ice cream per day. He advertised both vanilla and fancy flavors, in bulk and brick form, with shipping available to the nearby towns of Scotia, Elyria, and Burwell. *The Ord Quiz* applauded the external refurbishing of an abandoned building, as well as an employer of several men throughout the summer.[7]

The Home Ice Cream Factory also provided work for Evelyn. From the back of a homemade, horse-drawn, two-wheeled cart, she drove up and down the streets of Ord selling ice cream cones. Chalky, her large, light-colored work horse, and Perp, a tiny black and white dog, waited patiently as she scooped frozen dessert from the thirty-six inch tall metal cans. Once in a while, some of Evelyn's friends were allowed to ride, but Virginia Klein Cruce remembers Evelyn "had to be all business" when she was selling her nickel, double-dip, throat-cooling ice cream cones.[8]

"Double-dips For A Nickel." Chalky, Perp and Evelyn, 1932, Ord, Nebraska

When a day's work was done, Evelyn removed Chalky's harness, pulled the straw flowered hat over his ears and untied several silver bells from around his neck. Then, with four of her friends, she climbed onto Chalky, all fitting nicely into his long, sway back. They headed for the North Loup River where, amid splashing and laughter, Chalky stood patiently while the girls gave him a bath. Never was a horse in such poor physical condition treated with so much love and kindness.

In August of 1932, *The Ord Quiz* reported, "Evelyn Sharp fell while riding horseback and landed in a bed of cinders. Dr. Kirby McGrew was called and bandaged the bruised and injured places. No bones were broken and Evelyn was not laid up for long. The doctor has now removed the bandages and claims she was a lucky girl."[9] In a few years, Evelyn found herself in a similar predicament. This time she begged Jim Ollis for a ride on his pony. As she took off at a high lope, he yelled for her to keep a tight rein. The horse and rider approached an intersection; it was Evelyn's intent to turn left, but Beauty was of a different mind. She was hungry and her barn was to the right. Beauty turned, and Evelyn flew off. Jim Ollis prefers to remember that as Evelyn's first solo.[10]

Data supporting what the people of the community already felt began to surface in the weekly newspaper. By September of 1932, the Valley County Courthouse records showed forty-nine farm foreclosures compared with a total of twenty-nine in 1931. Eggs were eight cents a dozen, and wheat, corn, and oats were thirty-eight, thirty-six, and twenty-eight cents a bushel, respectively. It was no surprise to read that the farmers in the Valley were burning corn instead of coal that winter.

A local optometrist, a man whose name would become synonymous with the promotion and development of Ord, ran the following advertisement:

NOTICE

In the past year nearly every child that has come to me for attention has been a severe case. It is evident that perhaps on account of present conditions there are many bad cases that are being put off....If you have a child whom you think has a very noticeable case of eye trouble and the lack of money is interfering, I will take care of them at your price. ...if you cannot pay, and will be satisfied with a frame a little out of date, I will fit them free of charge. ...offer is made only for children of grade schoolage, in Valley and Garfield counties, and for two months.

Dr. Glen D. Auble[11]

In that third year of the Great Depression, H. C. Leggett, owner and editor of *The Ord Quiz,* also realized accommodations had to be made regarding the price of his newspaper. He issued a special subscription price, whereby 963 people read the paper for $1 that next year. The regular price was $2.

There were other signs of hope and evidence that people were committed to helping each other survive the difficult days of the Depression. The Chamber of Commerce selected Dr. Auble to head a Christmas decoration committee. Elaborate arrangements of lights adorned the Courthouse columns and each of the city's street light standards at the four corners of the square wore boughs of fresh evergreen and red ribbon streamers. Colored panes of cellophane inserted inside the glass globes cast a warm and cheerful glow on the faces of those who strolled by.

The Ord Rotarians sponsored a project to build a public skating pond. The school donated lots on the north side and the city graded an eighty-by-two-hundred-foot-long rink, donated water, erected light poles, and furnished electricity. It was truly a community project. All residents of the area were welcome, and it was a particularly happy place for the social gatherings of Evelyn and her seventh grade friends. A game of Crack the Whip would often be followed by cocoa and cookies at the nearby home of a Campfire Girl.

In its Christmas message, *The Ord Quiz* congratulated the people of the North Loup Valley for standing up to Old Man Depression and taking it on the chin. "One good thing about such Tough Times, is that we have reverted to a lot of simple home pleasures once known but of late years well forgotten. We are finding pleasure once more in our own home circles, and in the good, but simple things of life. 'And to you and yours we wish the Merriest Old Fashioned Merry Christmas!'"[12]

On February 23, 1933, the newspaper headline reported the feasibility of constructing a system of dams and canals on the North Loup River. Projecting a drop of eight feet-per-mile, preliminary findings concluded that the river would support a hydroelectric irrigation project serving 100,000 acres of farmland. The initial steps included a survey at a cost of $3,750, but if the results were negative, or the federal Reconstruction Finance Loan fell through, no monies would be returned. *The Ord Quiz* foresaw the town's reaction and its editorials encouraged Ordites to look at this issue from the perspective of the farmer. In essence, the City Fathers knew the well-being of the business community was in direct correlation to the prosperity of her country neighbors; sometimes they just needed a reminder. After years of drought and dust-bowl conditions, enthusiasm for a dependable water source began to build. The Burlington Railway offered support in transportation costs. To many, the power-irrigation project was a beginning for the end of the Depression.

That spring, operating capital was tight. In an *Ord Quiz* ad, John Sharp advertised for a "partner with some capital to buy produce and mfg. ice cream. No get rich quick deal, but a good place for money to earn money. Can see principle every 10 days. Must be ready by March 1st. Inquire shortly. Home Ice Cream Company. Ord, NE."[13]

The Ord Public School District was operating $10,000 in the red. During normal times, the tax payment would be 90-95% of the total amount assessed, but this year it was only 50%. Teachers were not given contracts in the spring so that, if needed, additional cuts could be made. Because of the financial constraints, the Superintendent went before the School Board and asked to have his salary reduced.

Nationally, Franklin D. Roosevelt closed all banks without notice from March 8 to March 16, 1933, but it was nearly business-as-usual in Ord. The merchants issued their own scrip which the banks promised to back when they were allowed to reopen. Spearheaded by information and a sense of direction from *The Ord Quiz*, the people once again adjusted and made the best of this disruption in their lives.

Six weeks later on a beautiful Easter Sunday, Evelyn and four of her eighth grade classmates joined the Ord Methodist Episcopal Church.[14] A sixty-three-by-eighty-five foot tile-roofed structure of pressed brick and stone, the library-style church with its youth-centered activities became an important part of her life. In earlier years, Evelyn and several of her confirmation class had been introduced as Sunbeams in a Children's Day Cantata. Dressed in yellow with gold crowns and wands, the girls gave a "short drill" and sang "It's Just Like God, the Father." Near the end of the program, the church was darkened with the exception of a lighted cross in the chancel. Evelyn and a choir of forty children closed the service singing "I Think When I Read that Sweet Song of Old."[15]

Messages From The Community

*I*n the fall of 1933, Evelyn registered as a freshman in the Ord Public School's four-year high school. Required courses included English, algebra, domestic science, and gym. Related science, domestic art, and glee club were her choices of electives. A complete set of her semester related science class notes showed a perceptive interest in, and understanding of, the mechanical workings of a clutch, differential, and universal joints.[1]

A favorite after-school activity was the Girls' Athletic Association (GAA). Held every Tuesday and Thursday from four to six p.m., the organized activities, under direct supervision of an instructor, were soccer, speedball, volleyball, basketball, baseball, and other sports of a competitive nature. The unorganized activities, with no school supervision, included hiking, roller skating, bicycling, ice skating, golf, and tennis. Letters were earned by accumulating a total of 225 points during the year, 175 points coming from supervised competitive games and the remaining 50 from unorganized activities. A tom-boy by 1930's standards, Evelyn excelled in the world of athletics. Only she and Irene Whiting, her best high school girlfriend, were awarded Girls' Athletic Association letters their freshman year.

In the fall of her ninth grade year, amid the flickering light of two starry-eyed jack-o-lanterns, Evelyn and members of her Campfire Girls Troop told ghost stories at their annual Halloween Party. Fortunetelling, bobbing for apples, and screams of blindfolded initiates, stumbling across ditches, through darkened alleyways, and down "imaginary stairs"[2] at the Glen Auble home created a camaraderie which extended into adult years.

Special projects at school also built friendships. In November of 1933, Mary Sharp, and other mothers of the freshman domestic science class received invitations for breakfast. The balanced menu included fruit and cereal, a combination meat and egg dish, toast, and a drink. In freshly-laundered, newly-pressed aprons, the girls served breakfast, then anxiously awaited their mothers' much-needed approval.

Just before Christmas in 1933, an unfavorable report on the status of the North Loup Project arrived. Based on population and unemployment, Nebraska had already received an excess of appropriated funds. But such news did not discourage the townspeople. It was the holiday season. Four fifteen-foot fir trees from nearby Jones Canyon were cut, loaded into wagons, and brought into the Town Square. Crisscrossed strings of brightly colored lights and shiny tinsel ornaments connected the evergreens to each side of the Courthouse.

That same month, the Ord Chamber of Commerce decided to apply for Civil Works Administration (CWA) funds to build a federal airport. Their plan called for leasing some pastureland northwest of Ord. They agreed to pay C. J. Mortensen, a local banker, twelve-dollars-per-month rent and move Western Public Service Company's high-tension line located at the west end of the proposed airfield. The $5,000 project would furnish labor to men who were eligible for CWA funds. Actual work began in March.

In February of 1934, the Ord School Activity Fund found itself short of money. The twenty-five cent per semester stamp book, which could be used as admission to all school-related activities and athletic events, did not create the solvency expected. The book's purpose was to underwrite the philosophy of "all paying a little and so bringing the benefit to EVERYONE, not just a privileged few."[3] For the first time in the school's history, a lack of funds forced the proposal of an all-school, money-making carnival. To generate publicity for the fundraiser, the Ord High School Band led a parade of happy-faced clowns, bicycles and coaster wagons decorated with streamers, simple cardboard floats, and a menagerie of favorite pets. Its length extended four city blocks, winding around the Courthouse Square. At five-thirty, members of the home ec class and the Junior Girls' Reserve served "business men's" and "school mam's" lunches and 'common hot dogs.'[4] Normal Training girls, who could become teachers upon graduation from high school, provided free baby-sitting. Twenty-five different attractions, including one-act plays, slide shows, musical performances, and a Queen of the Carnival Coronation Ceremony, offered something for everyone. The efforts of all participating netted a sum of $175, and a sense of school-community spirit as well.

It might be inferred that those feelings of pride were still in evidence when local citizens of the community observed students, in midday, digging dandelions from the front lawn of the school. They didn't realize it was another of Superintendent Millard D. Bell's bribes: no study hall for those who chose to remove yellow flowers. The students "cooperated nobly"[5] and within a day or two, the lawn was once again green.

A subject that continued to receive much press that summer was the issue of alcohol and its control. In 1932, the nation repealed the Prohibition Amendment. In April of 1933, the Nebraska Legislature passed its Beer Bill. Now in 1934, the application for a beer license at John's New Cafe in Ord lay on the appropriate desk in Lincoln, awaiting one of the first official approvals from the Liquor Commission. That application was granted.

Everyone, however, was not as enthusiastic as John Sharp about the return of legal consumption. *The Ord Quiz* reminded its readers of the times before Prohibition when women could not safely walk the east side of the square, that being the area designated by city council for drinking establishments. Sunday morning services and evening temperance meetings at the Ord Methodist Episcopal Church spoke to the evils of drink. The church preached the negative effects of any kind of alcohol consumption.

Being an active member of the Methodist Epworth League, a young adult fellowship group, Evelyn must have given some thought to the mixed messages she was receiving from home and church. On August 9, 1934, the issue became further complicated when the newspaper reported, "Liquor Law Violators Plead Guilty, Fined. A search of the premises Friday morning resulted in no find, but a buy the day before had been made by a state man. John Sharp pleaded guilty and was fined $100 plus $19 in costs."[6] He had been caught "bootlegging" whiskey.

John would never be granted a Nebraska liquor license again. From now on, Mary applied as manager of the establishments and was approved for the on-off sale licenses. He turned his attention to the remodeling and construction of a "roadhouse" operation at the southeast corner of town. Perhaps the new investment and his liquor violation fine led to a decision that he could no longer afford to keep Chalky. An ad in *The Ord Quiz* read:

> For Sale. One white pony. Just the pony for kiddies to ride to school. J.E. Sharp, Ord Cafe.[7]

If not in saleable condition, Chalky would be a prime candidate for the glue factory. Fortunately, Richard Burrows, Evelyn's high school classmate from a nearby country school district, was looking for affordable transportation to the city schools. John and Richard agreed upon a price, and Chalky moved west to wide open spaces. Richard liked Evelyn and promised her riding privileges.

When classes commenced that fall in 1934, Ord Public High School had again retained its North Central Accreditation status. With an enrollment of 256 students, the school offered courses of instruction in agriculture, business training, college preparatory, dramatics and speech, homemaking, manual arts, music, and teacher training. Opportunities for extracurricular activities were available in athletics, band and orchestra, Future Farmers of American, Girls' Athletic Association, boys' and girls' glee clubs, Girl Reserves, Hi-Y, pep club, cheerleading, and theatrical productions. Competitions were scheduled that year in academics, agriculture, athletics, business and commercial, dramatics, and music. In his weekly *Ord Quiz* column, entitled "Back Forty," Jesse A. Kovanda, sponsor of Evelyn's sophomore class, reported, "Ord teachers are specialists in their lines of teaching and thoroughly experienced. They keep up-to-date by attending summer school voluntarily. Ord school buildings are new, modern, safe, and sanitary. The high school is completely fireproof." [8]

Combination locks were issued to the students for the first time that year, their ten cent deposit to be refunded the next spring. But perhaps the most exciting announcement was that, once again, students would have a high school yearbook. Budget constraints and the economic depression so pervasive within the community had resulted in its being discontinued for several years. Under the able leadership of Miss Bernice Slote (a first-year faculty member who would later become a distinguished English professor at the University of Nebraska), Ord businessmen and *The Ord Quiz* pooled their resources and expertise. Each week the full-page copy of the school newspaper, written and edited by the *Oracle* newspaper staff, would be published in *The Ord Quiz*. The *Chanticleer* yearbook staff would be responsible for pictures and special issues. Each edition of the *Oracle* was dedicated to a business person who had helped to underwrite the cost. Probably to no one's surprise, the first issue was dedicated to Dr. Glen Auble, a successful optometrist who "has the interests of Ord High School at heart." The copy beneath his picture read:

> Those who know Dr. Auble know that under his quiet exterior is concealed the ability to do plenty of hard work, and that he never shirks any task which will end in betterment to Ord, whether it be for our schools, our musical life, our Chamber of Commerce, or something in his own line of business. If you are not acquainted with him, step into his store some day soon. He will be glad to meet you, whether you come with favors or hard work.[9]

At the end of the school year, *The Ord Quiz* agreed to bind the *Oracle* newspapers in a black, twenty-two-by-fifteen-and-one-quarter inch leather-like folder, selling them "at a very low cost."[10] The yearbook project was an example of a business community and a school in partnership.

In late September of 1934, the Loup Valley Activity Association accepted Ord's Girls' Athletic Association invitation to host the Fall Play Day. Each of the ten affiliated schools could send up to fifteen girls. Miss Viola Crouch, sponsor of Ord's GAA, and several of the girls helped to organize the program. A welcome was given; a baritone solo, two selections by the Reserve Girls' Glee Club, and a flute duet completed the introductory activities. The afternoon was divided into equal time periods so that each girl could participate in a game of kittenball, basketball, soccer, and speedball. In the 1930s, the emphases in Nebraska girls' athletics were cooperation, sportsmanship, fun, and friendship. Any kind of competition with a goal toward winning was frowned upon. Team members were selected from different schools so no two girls from the same school could be on the same side. For athletes like Evelyn and her best friend, Irene Whiting, these rules neither curbed nor broke their competitive spirit. They played to win.

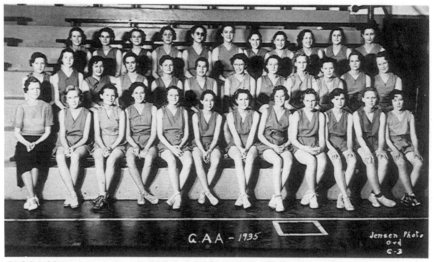

Girls' Athletic Association, Ord High School, 1935. Evelyn is 4th from the left in the first row.

After the games, the girls assembled in the school auditorium with the rest of the Ord student body to hear an address by Nebraska Senator George W. Norris. Touring the state to promote interest in his proposal for a one-house legislature, he spoke of the founding of our government and schools of that day. At the end of his speech, students consumed bushel baskets of red apples and over three hundred donuts prepared by Evelyn's sophomore home economics class. Later that evening, after a community dinner at the Methodist Episcopal Church, the high school band escorted Senator Norris back to the school for a meeting with his voting constituents. With a logic understood by most penny-pinching Depression residents, the senator would eventually see his unicameral (one-house) legislature bill become Nebraska law.

In early November of 1934, there was much excitement centered around the huge boxes which had been delivered to the Ord High School band room. The local American Legion Fidelity Post No. 38, knowing the school district had no money for new uniforms, had assumed responsibility for a fund-raising drive. Professors from the University of Nebraska, their students, and their families had presented a musical program in the summer, but another fund-raiser was necessary. This time, Dean Duncan, high school vocal and instrumental music instructor, and his American Legion Male Chorus took the stage. It was clear from newspaper headlines that top billing had been taken by the Minstrel Show, rather than by a selection of old Negro spirituals. "'Warblin Sam,' 'Gumwad Johnson,' 'Apricot,' 'Puffball,' and 'Mushmouth' bring forth many laughs and much applause."[11] Interestingly enough, not one "Letter to the Editor" with respect to equity appeared in the next week's *Ord Quiz*. One has to remember, however, or at least understand that even Nebraska's most famous and respected black cowboy was referred to as "Nigger Amos Harris" in his front page obituary.[12] Certainly that would not be accepted today.

A sense of pride and tradition was exhibited by the ninety-five members of the Ord High School Band as they were presented to the community on Armistice Day, November 11, 1934. In their brilliant new red-and-white uniforms, the band marched smartly behind the American Legion Color Guard onto the grounds of the Courthouse Square. A contingent of ex-servicemen, the high school color guard, and the student body fell in behind. After the eleven o'clock whistle blew, a time-honored tradition symbolizing the end of World War I, a short prayer was offered. Band director Dean Duncan signaled for his band to rise, and those in the audience also rose, helping young children place the correct hand over their hearts. With the sun shining brightly on a crisp fall morning, the community joined the band in singing "The Star-Spangled Banner." Patriotism and honor for those who had died in the service of their country were messages Evelyn heard and saw practiced early in life.

A photo session was held on the Courthouse steps immediately following the ceremonies. The picture, later published in the January 1935, issue of *The Legionnaire* magazine, brought national recognition to the local Post for its money-raising efforts. Many band members and their mothers looking at that picture in later years probably also recalled the wash-day drudgery of ripping and restitching each red stripe to a pants leg.[13] "Colorfastness" in fabric was not an option in 1934.

That Christmas, John Sharp, other business people, and several service organizations made a collective effort to see that the "known poor" of Ord had enough to eat on Christmas Day. Their children would be remembered with some small token from Santa, and so that no one would be cold, coats and mittens were collected. "Twenty-six dressed dolls, toys, candy, peanuts, and trimmed Christmas trees were reflective of a great deal of charity work, done quietly by friends or neighbors, showing a genuine desire to help others in true Christ-like manner, without credit."[14]

Evelyn witnessed evidence of a depressed economy in her youth, perhaps overhearing conversations between her father and his customers at John's Cafe. The 1934 economic conditions forced a flurry of farm mortgage activity at the Valley County Courthouse. County Clerk records noted 283 filings valued at $904,926 in 1934 compared to 124 at $347,213 in 1933. Many of these were foreclosures, though some were a second chance at refinancing through the government's Farm and Rural Development Act. Extreme heat with little rain had again left too many crops in the field and too little money for the banker. Adding to the disgust, frustration, and impatience of many, somewhere in Washington, DC, the money for the North Loup Hydroelectric and Irrigation Project was on hold.

But 1935 was not without hope and plans for the future. Grant and loan applications to the federal government were written for a modern township library and new post office building. An innovative "talkie" machine with three amplifiers for low, intermediate, and high notes replaced the previous single range sound system at the Ord Theatre. At a cost of $750, *The Ord Quiz* opened its own photoengraving plant, the first weekly newspaper in Nebraska to do so. And high school band members and community musicians played summer band concerts each Wednesday evening on the steps of the Valley County Courthouse. It was reassuring to Dean Duncan, also the city band director, that instrument mouthpieces would not take a three-month vacation.

Spirit was especially high for Evelyn and a group of sophomore girls the third week in January of 1935. The present senior class had held the annual soccer tournament trophy since their freshman year. Forward Evelyn Sharp and her GAA classmates thought it time for the three-year tradition to be "shattered."[15] Led by Irene Whiting, "elected captain because they think she will do her best to help them win," an inspired sophomore soccer team defeated the freshmen, then the seniors, and finally the juniors. But victory did not come easily. The first game was a "flip of the coin from the start to the finish."[16] Although ahead by four points at the half, the sophomores got themselves into a tie by the end of the second half. In a two-minute overtime, guards Virginia Clark, Norma Mae Snell, Lorraine Kusek, Marjorie Coe, Ruth Haas, Josephine Romans, and Dorothy Auble pulled their defense together and kept the freshmen from scoring. Final score: sophomores 16, freshmen 14. In the second game, they led the seniors at half by a margin of five. The score was 12-7. The two teams fought to a standoff in the second half of play, neither team "being hardly able to score on the other's defense."[17] Forwards Sharp, Whiting, Wilma Krikac, Virginia Weekes, and Virginia Klein did not fold. Inspired by each other's enthusiasm, they broke from the huddle with a renewed confidence. The senior girls were experienced and outweighed their opponents by several pounds, but sophomore athletic prowess and determination won out. Final score was sophomores 13, seniors 9. The tournament championship was at stake in the third game. Exhilaration as well as exhaustion began to take their toll. Though four points behind at the half, the sophomores proved to be unbeatable. Scoring 14 points in the second half, they held the juniors to 2. The final scoreboard read sophomores 21, juniors 13. Evelyn and her teammates knew they were the best class at Ord Senior High; they felt a sense of pride some would never forget.

The last week in January, the *Oracle* school newspaper ran a special edition confirming the feelings of the sophomores. "One of the most active classes in school, members take part and excel in every school activity as well as ranking close to the top in scholarship rating."[18] You could find their well-attended parties in the high school auditorium where games of Ping-Pong, indoor baseball, and the card game of Rook seemed to be popular entertainment. An evening at the movies culminated with cheerleader Virginia Weekes leading class yells from the motion picture stage. Walking home, several sophomores were already making plans to defend their trophy. Class spirit and a sense of cohesiveness were high.

Taken Out In Trade

_I_t soon became apparent to Evelyn and others in the North Loup
Valley that Jack Jefford had brought his flying school to Ord. All
over town, people reported sounds of airplane engines soon after
the sun rose. In partnership with his brother at Jefford's Aviation Services in Broken Bow, Jack offered flight instruction twice a week at Ord.
His credentials read well: 2,400 hours of flying time, holder of a transport license, and nine years of flying with no crashes for either him or
his 261 students. A Curtiss Robin, Eaglerock Flyabout, and a four-passenger Stinson-Detroiter cabinship made up an impressive fleet of
dual-controlled training aircraft.

A room and boarder at John's Cafe (1634 M Street), Jack Jefford
found an eager audience at the end of the day for his hangar flying
stories. Evelyn was no exception. One evening, she overheard her father and Jefford discussing his past-due room and board bill. Flight instruction payments had not kept up with expenses, and not wanting to
shut down the operation at Ord, Jack Jefford offered John Sharp a
deal. Will he take flying lessons for his daughter out in trade? She held
her breath.

On Monday, February 4, 1935, Evelyn recorded the following on
a sheet of white tablet paper: "Learned to fly while in the air. I was up
one-half hour. Pilot's name is Jack Jefford. Plane was a 3 cylinder Flyabout. Holds only 2 people. License number: NC14428."[1] It was two

weeks before she flew again, but Evelyn would continue to keep journals, entitled "Flying Lessons," until her solo flight thirteen months later. With no way of knowing the profound effect flying would have on her life, Evelyn did realize her world would never look or feel quite the same way again.

In the meantime, preparation was being made for the Loup Valley, District 4, Fifth Music Festival in Ord, an opportunity for critique before the district music contest. Evelyn anticipated performing with the Girls' Glee Club and the Ord Chanticleer High School Band. The evening after the all-day competition, a capacity-filled auditorium heard the massed Boys' and Girls' Glee Clubs sing "Love's Old Sweet Song" and "America the Beautiful." "The Ord Band, however, was the favorite of the Ord organizations and was asked to repeat its performance with several numbers." A special feature was the Nebraska Wesleyan A Cappella Male Chorus from Lincoln, Nebraska. "Seldom has an Ord audience been privileged to attend such an enjoyable and complete musical program."[2]

On March 21, 1935, *The Ord Quiz* reported, "Thousands of tons of Nebraska dirt are on the move and damage to farm lands is estimated in the millions of dollars."[3] Extending from the horizon to thousands of feet above, a massive wall of black cloud approached from the north. A tornado had been feared. Blinding dust obscured street lights only a few feet away, and sixty-mile-per-hour winds stalled car engines. The writer concluded that darkness came an hour earlier.

Winds blowing the rich, black, loess soil of Nebraska to states south shifted direction in early May. Now tons of reddish-yellow dust from the soil of farmlands in Kansas and Oklahoma were borne northward. Several Ord businessmen, instead of sweeping or shoveling their sidewalks, decided to temporarily save back muscle and put their mathematical skills to work. With careful calculations showing one-seventh pound of dust for every square foot of sidewalk, they estimated 1,227,022 tons had been left in the county.[4]

As if these conditions were not troublesome enough, a devastating rain and hailstorm hit the Valley the following month. In some places, the ice pellets stood ten feet high. Bridges and fences were washed out and away, chickens and livestock pounded to death, and the North Loup River, unable to be contained, expanded its banks a mile to the east. Nature and its destructive forces were a frequent topic of conversation at John's Cafe.

Anxious for summer to arrive, Evelyn and her friend, Irene Whiting, were hard at work in their sophomore sewing class. The teacher had approved their required stitches on paper, and the girls had had no difficulty in selecting a fashionable sun-backed dress pattern. They could hardly wait to wear their matching green and white creations. After all, their "sister" dresses of wine-colored wool, white-collared and cuffed, had been the object of many a conversation the previous fall.

By May 17, 1935, Evelyn had flown six hours in three different aircraft—the Flyabout, Curtiss Robin, and five-place Stinson. She recorded on her white tablet paper two different instructors, Jefford and an unnamed pilot from Wayne, Nebraska. Her training included takeoffs and landings, figure eights, stalls, tailspins, and turns. In a February 28 journal she noted, "the first four landings were good, but in the last two I bounced. Jack said it was o.k. though." One entry recorded her being twenty-five minutes late to school. This must have been of some concern to Evelyn because after another noon-hour lesson, she wrote, "This time I was not late for school."[5]

Perp and Evelyn (nicknamed "Tarzan"), December 1935, Ord, Nebraska

Her father and Perp, a black and white dog of Heinz 57 variety, sometimes rode along for her flying lesson. John was a very large man and because of his weight Evelyn was not able to land the plane on those days. She had not been taught short field landings, which meant setting the plane down as close to the approach end of the runway as possible. There were no mechanical brakes on the aircraft, only a skid under the tail section which eventually dragged the plane to a stop. Evelyn's journals indicated a choice of runways for practicing. One day her best landing was in the corn field. On another, it was the frozen North Loup River.

For Evelyn, flying was fun and she often, in her own simple way, described it as lovely. She even enjoyed the time spent in the air while other Jefford students were being instructed. Perhaps flying afforded her the same kind of peace which Amelia Earhart so eloquently referred to in her poem, "Courage."[6]

But there was another side to flying of which Evelyn was mindful. She recorded an instructor-generated stall with its loss of lift and resulting tailspin as interesting. A more common response from someone her age might be one ranging between scary and great fun. But Evelyn had a respect for the airplane, knowing that the pilot who walked away from a landing had chosen to act rather than react. Jack Jefford was a masterful teacher.

The Junior-Senior Banquet held on May 15, 1935, signaled an end to Evelyn's second year at Ord High School. Since tradition dictated the sophomore class provide entertainment, Evelyn, Irene Whiting, and Virginia Clark volunteered to do a "clever rope dance."[7] In keeping with the western motif, they dressed in high-topped boots, brown riding skirts, white shirts, and colorful, orange bandanna handkerchiefs. Fifty-seven years later when asked about the dance, Irene Whiting, with a twinkle in her eye and half-smile replies, "Well, you can bet it wasn't fancy."[8]

Recognition Night was a time set aside at the end of the school year for awarding official high school letters. For the second consecutive year, Evelyn was presented a letter recognizing her superior achievement in the Girls' Athletic Association. She and Irene had been the only two girls to receive the letters their freshman year. When the *Oracle* school newspaper ran a light-hearted column, "Where You Find One You'll Find The Other,"[9] it was no surprise to find the names of Irene Whiting and Evelyn Sharp. They were inseparable.

Evelyn's next flying lesson was not written in her journal until early fall of 1935. Perhaps the crash of Jefford's Flyabout in May was at least part of the problem. A pilot, who was having his Curtiss Robin refabriced at Jefford's Aviation Services in Broken Bow, borrowed the Flyabout for a quick trip home. He was killed soon after takeoff from Lamar, Colorado, when a wing broke off the fuselage. Harold Montee, Omaha inspector for the US Department of Commerce Aeronautical Bureau, identified a defective cold weld in the plane's construction as the cause of the accident. In her journal, Evelyn made a special note about the last time she flew NC14428, and her scrapbook included an article about the accident. It described the plane fluttering down like a leaf before it eventually nosed into the ground. Certainly Evelyn must have realized that, instead of Terry Hatchett, she could have been at those controls.

Evelyn and aviation appeared to have their own public relations director in Irma Ellis Leggett, an associate editor of *The Ord Quiz*, who wrote an entertaining weekly column called "Something DIFFER-ENT." "Airplane travel is getting safer by the minute. Pilots undertake a course of training more complete than an auto driver. I'm tired of hearing about its danger. I'm all for airplane travel. As soon as there's any prospect of getting to use the knowledge, I am going to learn to pilot a plane, so there. Now you know about that—

"Ord has a bunch of air-minded students. Young Miss Evelyn Sharp is said to be a natural born pilot, who took 'aholt' just like that. She is the daughter of Mr. and Mrs. John Sharp, aged 14 or 15."[10]

With school out, summer activities centered around the North Loup River, swimming near Anderson's Island, and Campfire Girls' outings at Mortensen's Cabin. The Hugo Players, a most popular group of thespians in central Nebraska, would be performing in Ord for the nineteenth consecutive year. New plays and able actors were promised. Valley County residents looked forward to this chautauqua, as well as the rains which the troupe traditionally seemed to bring. John's New Cafe at 125 N. 15th was one of several merchants where tickets could be purchased for a dime.

In August, the Schell Brothers Four-Ring Circus came to Ord. A "mammoth menagerie" including African jungle tigers, bears, and ponies was advertised in *The Ord Quiz*. With admission prices of ten cents for children and a quarter for adults, it was billed as the greatest circus bargain ever offered. Although the following week's paper reported only one elephant, three lions, a bear, and a few ponies, the undeniably misled community seemed to enjoy the performance.

With only a few days left in August, *The Ord Quiz* advertisements reflected the beginning of another school year. Supplies at the McLean and Sorensen Drug Company were featured at the following prices: pencils, three for five cents; fountain pens, fifty cents; twelve-inch wooden rulers, four cents; erasers, four cents; eight water-color paint box and brush, thirty-five cents; and five hundred sheets of best grade paper, thirty-two cents. A special enticement was a free school pencil given with every purchase of ten cents or more. On September 5, 1935, three hundred students walked through the doors of Ord High School. Seventy registered as juniors.

Evelyn had received little flying training since early summer. Needing money, her instructor had left the Sandhills to "fly weather" for the US Government in Tulsa, Oklahoma. Although Evelyn did write four flight entries in her journals the first week of September, the instructor(s) and plane(s) were unnamed. The next entry recorded a lesson in a Travel Air at Grand Island. The instructor was Stover Deats. Her last three entries of half-hour lessons were very brief: no dates, names, or aircraft designations. Undoubtedly disappointed, Evelyn would wait for Jack Jefford's return.

Within two weeks of opening, the Ord Public Schools were dismissed for the Valley County Fair. The depressed economic conditions in the early 30s had forced the Fair Board to discontinue the event for three consecutive years, but 1935 found the community promising support. A man always ready for a new business venture, John Sharp and Evelyn set up a corn-popping machine near the very popular fast-car races. The winning race car used one bank of a V-8 Hispano-Suiza airplane motor, reportedly having cylinders so big "you could stick your head in 'em."[11] Popcorn sales were good, and the 1935 Valley County Fair was a financial success.

A Natural

*B*y January 7 of 1936, Jack Jefford had returned from flying weather for the government to the Sandhills of Nebraska. Evelyn was eager to fly. On the twenty-ninth of that month, she took a forty-five minute lesson in his new, yellow, Aeronca C-3. Better known as the "Flying Bathtub" because of its distended body shape, it had a two-cylinder opposed 36-hp engine which consumed four gallons of

"A Frozen Runway" — North Loup River, Ord, Nebraska, January 1936

gas per hour. Jack Jefford offered dual instruction at $7 and solo for $6. NC15291 landed and took off five times on the frozen North Loup River that day, with the final touchdown in a nearby field. The student pilot was encouraged. "Almost ready to solo,"[1] Evelyn wrote. Though her assessment was somewhat premature, a pilot can identify with the confidence a competent flight instructor can impart to a student. Jack Jefford was one of the best; his later flying as a bush pilot in Alaska, and as a Civil Aeronautics Authority (CAA) inspector for that region, would become legendary.

As dawn filtered along the edges of the old cloth shade hanging at her tiny bedroom window, Evelyn was vaguely aware of the sounds and aromas coming from her mother's kitchen below. She lay there for a bit, enjoying the last few moments of the warmth in her bed. Then she remembered it was Wednesday. Jumping out of bed, she hurried across the cold floor to pull the shade aside. The sky was cloudless, bright and blue. It would be a beautiful day for flying.

Sometimes it was hard to pay proper attention to school matters on flying days, and Evelyn was sure the hands on the wall clocks moved more slowly. She forced herself to concentrate, however, keeping an eye on the sky. It remained clear with unlimited visibility.

On the white tablet pages of her flight journal, Evelyn recorded:

Lesson 25

March 4, 1936

25 minutes. Made 5 landings and Take-offs. Then soloed. Was up about 5 minutes. Made good solo landing. I now have 13 hours flying.

On the fifth landing, Jack Jefford had instructed Evelyn to come to a complete stop. Thinking the request strange, she wondered if this were the day, the day she would fly by herself.

Evelyn, I'm going to let you solo. Go ahead, she's all yours.

Gosh! Is my heart pounding! The moment I've been waiting for for over a year! I sort of hesitate a moment and then I make up my mind—I jam down the throttle and head down the runway.[2]

She held the stick forward to bring the tail up to flying position. Then, pulling it back slowly to increase the angle of attack, Evelyn felt the weight leave the wheels. She was flying.

"Gee. I'll never forget the moment I took off! What a thrill! After taking off, I circle and zoom the field several times." Remembering to clear the engine every fifteen seconds or so until both cylinders hit, "I settle down for a perfect, three-point landing. Jack grabs my hand and there I am—my first flight done completely successful."[3]

The next day, The Ord Quiz reported Jack Jefford's appearance at the weekly city council meeting. He asked them to investigate the leasing of a field closer to Ord; the one used presently was on the Gregory farm, six miles to the north. He reported Ordites were learning to fly, and it was likely several planes would be purchased.

The following week, the first of several solo parties was held at John's Town Tavern, John Sharp's latest business venture on the outskirts of Ord. The recently-chartered eighteen-member Ord Aviation Club was celebrating the solo flights made by three of their own; Evelyn Sharp, C. B. Gudmundsen, and Ed Parkos. Seventy-five guests included two Lincolnites—Nebraska Aeronautics Commission chairman, Charles Doyle, and Ray Bebee of Sidles Airways Corporation—several pilots from the Hastings, St. Paul, Callaway, and Burwell areas, instructor Jack Jefford, and a number of local people. Cronk's Orchestra played music for dancing, and LaVern Duemey set up a display of several airplane models he had made as a hobby. The paper reported most guests preferred to spend the evening discussing aviation and its recent developments.[4] Not really a surprise to those who have been in the presence of pilots.

John Sharp was proud of his new business and the compliments he received. His two-year dream of building a showplace operation, which would include a ballroom, supper club, town tavern, cabins, and a filling station, was finally coming together. And Evelyn, "the apple of his eye," was the center of attention. That night the world must have looked pretty good to John Sharp.

Another person who felt Evelyn pretty special was Irma Leggett, an aviation enthusiast who penned "Something's DIFFERENT" for The Ord Quiz. "Evelyn Sharp, 16 year old Ord aviatrix has been receiv-

"Six Pilots And A Proud Pop," pictured from left to right: Jack Jefford, Howard Jones, Elwin Dunlap, Evelyn, John Sharp, Ed Parkos, Carl Nicholson, Mortensen Field, 1936

ing statewide recognition of her ambition and ability to fly. Whether she is the youngest Nebraska miss to fly a plane alone is not known or whether she is the youngest in the United States. But her friends and admirers are making extravagant claims, leastways. And there is no doubt she deserves praise for her courage and ambition. Especially in these days, when everyone but this writer thinks flying is a good way to commit suicide, and practically a sure way, too."[5]

The public was interested in the reactions of those who knew, loved, and cared for Evelyn:

> Mr. and Mrs. Sharp express no undue concern over the "flightiness" of their daughter. Perhaps it's because she is, in spite of her skyward tendencies, a very serious-minded and reliable young lady. She does schoolwork far above average and takes a prominent part in many school activities. Her outside interests include Campfire Girls, dancing, horseback riding, tennis, hiking, and hunting.

She is really a "natural" according to her flight instructor.... Few among the hundreds of students he has taught have had the "touch" that enabled them to learn to pilot a plane as quickly as Evelyn. Before making her solo flight, she had thirteen hours of flying time gained at irregular intervals over a period of thirteen months. She has flown in several different kinds of ships, a Stinson, two OX-5 Robins, Travelair, Fairchild, Flyabout, and an Aeronca.

And as she continues to use that sky as a playground, the eyes o' Ordites are on her, watching, waiting, and admiring; knowing that here is a little girl who really is going places. Ambitious and determined, she sets her goal to be the youngest girl transport pilot in the United States.[6]

Stories and pictures of the pretty young pilot began to appear in newspapers and magazines throughout the United States. Wire services picked up the story over teletype, and photographers, lugging cameras and tripods, tried to capture the spirit and nature of this sixteen-year-old girl. Because of the widespread publicity, Evelyn received letters from admirers in Ohio, Illinois, Kentucky, and a dozen other states, congratulating her, asking favors, requesting answers, enclosing snapshots, and quoting poetry. "It is rumored that she may even have received a few proposals of marriage, but Evelyn won't say. Her interest is reserved for flying."[7]

One admirer, from a small Nebraska town further west, read of her achievement and penned the following:

Here is to Evelyn Sharp:

Nebraska, the center of these United States,
Is gaining in favor at tremendous rates,
As Freemen led the Homesteaders out our way,
You are leading our people in the air today.
For millions of years the land and the air,
Have been unnoticed in nobody's care,
People like you, with courage and skill
Put those things at our mercy and will.
The air is the place for travel and speed,

It spans all the nations of different creed;
It hovers above oceans, rivers, and land,
Its conquering is the greatest achievement of man.
So here is greetings from an admiring friend,
To the youngest aviator in this wonderful land,
Your opportunities are unlimited,
But remember in accord,
Your passengers are your folks, your state,
And your Ord.
—Edward Nielsen, Cozad, Neb., March 23, 1936.[8]

Another admirer sent her an inch-and-a-half turtle with a brightly blue painted shell. She christened it Aeronca, after the aircraft in which she had flown solo. A new dog, another Heinz 57 variety, dutifully responded to his name of Contact, the warning each pilot yells before cranking the propeller. She seemed to enjoy attaching aviation terminology to the animals she loved.

Evelyn was in love with flying, its art and its skill. There was nothing else quite like the freedom and control she felt while in flight. But she tried to keep her school/community responsibilities and her flying in perspective. Two more solo parties were held at John's Town Tavern before the end of spring. A total of ten students now flew off the newly acquired C. J. Mortensen property three miles north of town. The Ord High School Band and Girls' Glee Club continued their practices for the State Class B Music Contest, while the Ord business-men were busy raising money to send the ninety-member group to Kearney, Nebraska. In their favor, a gas war had lowered the price of fuel to 19.1 cents.

The thirty-two member Girls' Glee Club, in their brand new red, white satin-trimmed robes, sang two selections at State Music Contest that spring, "The Lilacs Are In Bloom" by Tyson-Treharne and "The Call of the Morning" by A. J. Silver. The judges were impressed, awarding them a superior rating. No one could tell the faculty wives, who had stitched bolts of red material, or Dean Duncan and Superin-tendent Bell, who had tied threads and pressed garments only a few days before, that their efforts had been in vain.

Soon after the music competition, Dean Duncan and his band

who had earned second place at State Music Contest, were on the streets of Ord practicing parade drills. Tradition dictated the band would lead the Memorial Day Parade to the cemetery and play for the services. In conjunction with this holiday to honor all veterans, Evelyn and her Campfire Girl friends helped the American Legion Auxiliary with its traditional poppy sales. The girls made $95.40, the proceeds going for local welfare work. As Irma Leggett wrote, Ord needs to "take good care of our own."[9]

On June 3, 1936, Evelyn and her flight instructor Jack Jefford flew to Lincoln, Nebraska, in his Aeronca C-3. An aviation chart pasted in her scrapbook was marked off in ten-mile increments, showing the route of the flight. Above the map, Evelyn noted: "My first cross country…where I secured my Amateur License."[10] Having logged twenty-six hours, the minimum number was twenty-five, Evelyn was granted her amateur license by Harold Montee, Aero-Inspector. This license allowed her to fly farther away from the airport.

That summer, she continued to practice takeoffs and landings, stalls, loops, and other flight maneuvers required for a private pilot license. The little yellow Aeronca became a familiar sight in and around the one-quarter mile landing strip adjacent to the beautiful blue North Loup River. A fellow student pilot once described the field as a peat bed where one had to "navigate" the clumps of grass. Sharp seemed "to be a natural," he says, "a seat-of-the pants flyer."[11]

Put It Out, Private Pilot, Perfect Evening

*D*ubbed The Rainmaker by local farmers, Harry Hugo and his entourage of stage players pulled into Ord on June 29, 1936. As predicted by every amateur weather forecaster in Valley County, a terrific gale and rainstorm swept out of the northwest. The show tent, pitched on the Haldeman lots south of the Bohemian Hall, blew down, tearing badly in several places. A large elm tree in front of Don's Battery Station toppled over and landed atop Sophie McBeth's beauty parlor across the street. Trees in the Courthouse Square, at the park, and around many residences, were broken off. Because of a rapid temperature drop, it was feared hail had fallen west of Ord. But such was not the case; the corn had been saved for the grasshoppers.

By the first part of July, the government poison allotted for grasshopper control had been depleted. It was suggested you make your own; the recipe appeared in *The Ord Quiz*:

6 pounds white arsenic
100 pounds wheat bran
3 ounces amyl acetate
10 gallons water

Mix dry ingredients first; mix wet ingredients next; Combine, using a spade or wooden paddle to mix. Bare hands and forearms should be coated with cup or axle grease to keep poison out of pores or skin abrasions.[1]

"A flight of grasshoppers numbering in the billions passed over Ord late Monday afternoon and evening."[2] Their attraction to the arc lights at the softball field nearly caused the game to be called off. The long-legged creatures with their incessant shrill chirping were a spectacle Evelyn and her teammates had never seen. Some of the young children were frightened by the deafening noise. Everyone was relieved when the main flight, borne by a stiff north-northeast wind, did not descend.

But grasshoppers were not the only phenomenon which would cloud the skies for Evelyn and her family. A front page headline in the July 2, 1936, *Ord Quiz* read: "Three Are Fined For Intoxication."[3] On Thursday afternoon, three people, all at different places, had been arrested for drunkenness. By Friday afternoon, John Sharp had pled guilty, and after paying his $10-and-costs fine, was released from city jail. His dream of a supper club with dancing and live entertainment slowly began to fall apart. The first disappointment was a denial for a beer license at John's Town Tavern. Though no official reason was given, the newspaper reminded its readers of his arrest during Prohibition. His next request for a dance hall license was also denied. This time the city council made reference to an unofficial vote at a previously held regular election; voters had made it clear they wanted no beer or dance hall licenses issued outside the central business district. They wanted to keep police costs and enforcement problems at a minimum. For John Sharp, it was another financial failure and eventually another move for his family.

Undoubtedly disappointed and probably embarrassed, Evelyn continued to create a life for herself. In early August, sounds of "Hey you, get off my foot!... Who's got my pillow?"[4] disturbed the gentle quietness of the area around the Mortensen summer cabin. Ord's fifteen Campfire Girls were trying to organize camp cots, bedding material of every shape and size, brilliantly colored bathing suits, toothbrushes, firewood, and Kodak cameras for a week's worth of roughing it.

Up at six o'clock in the morning, the girls made their beds, survived a chilly dip in the nearby North Loup River, and devoured a steaming hot breakfast of bacon and eggs. Cholesterol was not a health issue in 1936.

Cooking, nature study, sign language, leather handicraft, basketry, and reading offered several options for recreation the rest of the day. Each one of these, when completed with a certain degree of skill, could lead to degrees of rank in the Campfire Girls' Club. Evelyn earned honors in nature study and swimming by the end of the week. But there was another part of camplife that Evelyn particularly enjoyed; she loved planning the initiation ceremonies. Irene Auble Abernethy remembers her welcoming into the organization quite vividly:

> Knowing that every good Campfire Girl needed to practice the art and skill of fire building, the members directed the initiates to build the largest fire ever.[5]

In a manner so prescribed in the manual, the girls carefully selected and cut the driest of wood. Painstakingly, they stacked the different thicknesses in the cabin fireplace and struck a match to the shavings. The initiates waited, but there was no praise. There was no response. Finally, one of the members from somewhere in the back began to chant, "Put it out! Put it out! Put it out!" Others soon picked up the song. The initiates looked at each other in disbelief. On their hands and knees, the fire builders crawled out the back door of Mortensen's Cabin and over to where Evelyn was manning the handle of an old-fashioned pump. Lying on her back, each initiate stared, wide-eyed into a spigot which had never before looked quite so big. Sometimes Evelyn brought the handle down with ease, allowing a trickle of water to fall into an initiate's mouth, while at other times, she pushed it more forcefully, causing the girl to get drenched. No matter what amount of water stayed in the mouth, each initiate crawled back to the fireplace and spit on the now-blazing fire. The task, of course, proved impossible, but the older Campfire Girls, some doubled over in laughter, had had their fun.

Working for *The Quiz*, LaVerne Lakin, a classmate of Evelyn's, reported camp life from a more serious perspective. "After a week of character-building companionship with each other, the girls returned to their everyday duties more determined than ever to fulfill and uphold their club oath: To seek beauty, give service, pursue knowledge, be trustworthy, hold on to health, glorify work, and to be happy."[6] As the Campfire Girls said their good-byes at the end of the week, they wished each other Wo He Lo (Work, Health, Love), feeling a kinship with what Lakin had reported.

Later that month, after four years of "hoping and praying," the United States Congress approved the North Loup Hydroelectric and Irrigation Project. Whistles shrieked, bells clanged, and fire sirens blew from 10:30 a.m. until well after noon. "Men and women went wild with joy" in small towns across the North Loup and Middle Loup Valleys. Dean Duncan made arrangements for an impromptu band concert on the steps of the Courthouse, and a pavement dance that night attracted young and old alike. "It was the largest evening crowd present in Ord for many years."[7]

Spirits were also high for the seventy-five members of Evelyn's senior class as they registered for their last year of high school. A picture of their 1936 Sport Championship Banner, which they had won after defeating the other classes in a variety of athletic contests, appeared in *The Ord Quiz*. They were quoted as saying, "Yes sir, we're the 'tops' in Ord High School. What! You don't believe it? Say, just take a look at this banner."[8] Evelyn, captain of this year's senior soccer team, and starting classmates, Irene Whiting, Virginia Klein, Wilma Krikac, Josephine Romans, Virginia Clark, and Ruth Haas were determined to keep the class spirit trophy. Irene Whiting had no difficulty in recalling the contest. "We played hard, but darn it, we got beat,"[9] she says matter-of-factly.

New airplanes and dare-devil pilots brought thrill-seekers in the Loup Valley out to Mortensen Field. The Inman Brothers Flying Circus, with its fifty-cent rides, barnstormed off the peat bog in a fourteen-passenger Ford Tri-Motor, a twelve-passenger Tri-Motor Stinson, and a six-passenger Stinson. But the highlight of the day was a 4,000-foot parachute jump. No doubt some people remembered back to an earlier time when a local prankster, Mike Perlinski, created hype for another air show. As spectators watched from the other side of the river, they gasped in horror when Mike's chute failed to open. It was not until some time later they learned a dummy had duped them.[10]

In early October of 1936, a countywide celebration was held for the groundbreaking of the North Loup Project. Expectations might be characterized as being a bit high: "Ord welcomes the North Loup Valley and the whole world." The Methodist Church prepared a supper of a hot roast beef sandwich, mashed potatoes, cabbage slaw, coffee, and pumpkin pie, nominal cost being two bits for adults and fifteen cents for children. For entertainment, Jack Jefford promised to "shoot the works" in The Jeep, a nickname for his yellow Aeronca C-3. The paper reported death-defying stunts of upside-down flying, Immelman turns, barrel rolls, loop-the-loops, and falling leaf. Concluding with a sideslip that brought his plane almost to the ground before flattening out and gliding to safety, it was "A great exhibition by a great aviator!"[11]

Evelyn and flight instructor Jack Jefford, November 1936, Ord, Nebraska

In November, American Education Week provided an opportunity for students to shadow someone in a career of their choice. The Ord Business and Professional Women's Club, of which Evelyn would later become an honorary member, suggested that graduating seniors spend a week in the real world of work. "What schools do is sound in principle, but weak in practice since they can't afford to buy equipment for vocational training."[12] Evelyn chose aviation as her career, with Jack Jefford her supervisor. Classmates Lester Pearson and Stella Geneski were placed at Sharp's Cafe.

That school-community partnership made it possible for seven-teen-year-old Evelyn to fly to Grand Island on Monday, November 9. Having acquired the fifty hours of solo flight time, she now had to put her plane through a certain number of maneuvers in a manner satis-factory to Harold Montee, the government aviation inspector. Her fi-nal flight test was to demonstrate entry into and exit from a series of four tailspins. "Evelyn zoomed over the field, headed into the sky, and turned eight tailspins, coming out of them perfectly. Those who saw Miss Sharp qualify say it was a thrilling sight to see her handle the

plane in spite of the fact there was a stiff wind from the north."[13] When interviewed, Evelyn said she thought the government test was easy to pass. With a private flying li-cense in her possession, she was now legally considered airworthy to fly any class of single motor airplane.

The license also made it legal for Evelyn to fly passen-gers for pleasure; she honored her mother with the first ride. Mary Sharp had not been as enthusiastic about her daugh-ter's flying as was John. In fact, Evelyn's initial flying ex-periences had been kept a se-cret from Mary. But in an in-terview some years later, Mary told a reporter she enjoyed flying to Grand Island to do her shopping. It was faster.[14] On November 13, 1936, Evelyn logged a one hour flight in Aeronca NC15291. In her log-book, under remarks, she recorded her passengers as "Mother, Daddy, 3 friends."

"A Private Pilot," November 1936, Ord, Nebraska

As the holiday season approached, several of Evelyn's classmates organized invitational dances. She was a good dancer and popular with the boys. LaVern Duemey, a classmate whose hobby was model airplane building, thought his dance steps needed some polish. He felt comfortable in asking Evelyn for help; she quickly agreed. LaVern hoped she would be more successful with this instruction than with the one last summer. Evelyn had wanted to practice her life-saving technique and had pulled LaVern under water several times while trying to "save" him.[15]

Some of the Christmas parties were held in homes while the larger ones needed the Masonic or Bohemian Halls. The hosts, usually three or four girls, rented the hall, cleaned it before and after, and made arrangements for decorations, music, and the usual refreshments of fruit punch and vanilla wafers. One of the parties, hosted by Lillian Kusek, Armona Achen, and Dorothy Auble, included thirty couples from the Ord, Burwell, and St. Paul areas. An amplification system, on loan from the Auble Brothers Music Store, played the popular records of the day: "I Only Have Eyes For You," "Red Sails In The Sunset," and "Happy Days Are Here Again." LaVern Duemey, who sometimes was a member of a live orchestra at these dances, found himself that night on the dance floor. When Evelyn and her partner whirled by, she and LaVern cast knowing winks at each other. He decided she was much better at dancing than "life-saving."

As the young people left the hall that evening, their attention was drawn to the Courthouse Square. One hundred Christmas trees, five-foot tall and decorated, had been placed along curbs

"Shall We Dance?" Evelyn, LaVern Duemey and Scottie, November 1936

in the business district. An illumined old Santa with reindeer and sleigh stood atop the Courthouse. Perhaps some of the broken toys the Campfire Girls had repaired for Ord's poorer children were wrapped and in that sleigh. As hundreds of brightly-colored lights canopied the area from the dome to the four corners of the Square, several couples, holding hands, stopped to look. Evelyn was not the only one who thought it was a magical ending to a perfect evening.

Don't Forget Me, "Amelia E."

Sometime after the first of the year, Evelyn received an invitation from Belle Hetzel. The Omaha South High School aviation teacher was interested in organizing an area chapter of the Ninety-Nines Club — an eight-year-old organization of licensed women pilots who took pride in listing Amelia Earhart as their first president. In 1947 and 1948, Belle Hetzel would serve in that same capacity. Over lunch in the Gold Room of Omaha's prestigious Fontenelle Hotel, five Nebraska women pilots discussed the blizzard-like conditions and the eight-below-zero temperature raging outside. Each pilot had left her "flying wings" in the hangar. Evelyn and her father, who came along to see "what the group was like,"[1] thumbed a ride with a local Ord truck driver in order to make the two-hundred-mile trip. The group met John's expectations and on January 30, 1937, Evelyn became a charter member of the Missouri Valley Chapter of the Ninety-Nines Club. At that time, there were only 444 licensed women pilots in the United States. In Nebraska there were eight, and Evelyn Sharp, with sixty-two hours flying time, was the youngest.

The coming of spring meant extra practices and performances for the district music contest in Albion. That year, all 101 music students, either as a group or as individuals, earned fourteen superior ratings. A month later at the state level, the Girls' Glee Club earned a superior, while the band came home with an excellent rating. Second overall in that competition, Ord High School needed only one more point to tie for first place. Irma Leggett acknowledged their efforts in her weekly column:

> Ord musicians have a sense of achievement and reward for faithful hours of practice, working toward a certain goal is worthwhile and day after day practice brings results.[2]

When the seniors in the Girls' Athletic Association decided they wanted the April Play Day to be different, there was some hesitation in asking Ord Superintendent C. C. Thompson for permission. Would he remember a couple of years earlier when, as principal of Arcadia High School, he had caught Evelyn Sharp, Wilma Krikac, and several others "ya-hooting" some boys through his open windows in study hall? The girls, who had been dismissed early so they could go straight home and prepare the evening meal for a home economics requirement, had instead piled into Wilma's car and driven south to Arcadia.[3] If Mr. Thompson remembered the incident, he evidently appreciated their spirit. The girls' request for an extended Play Day was granted.

In late March of 1937, the Ord High School Thespian Club received word their application for membership in National Thespians had been accepted. Only six other schools in Nebraska belonged to the organization. Ellen Servine, a first year dramatics teacher, had come to Ord with much enthusiasm and many ideas, one of them being a dramatics club. "The aims are to sponsor, not control, all dramatic activities in Ord High School, provide an incentive for more interest in dramatic work, and increase abilities of all club members."[4] Evelyn, Dorothy Auble, LaVern Duemey, Barbara Ann Dale, Armona Beth Achen, LaVerne Lakin, Leonard Sobon, and Irene Whiting formed the nucleus of Thespians, presenting several plays during the probationary period. "The big project of the year… was the presentation of a complete three-act play, "Spooky Tavern."…It was a huge success with the largest crowd ever to turn out for a home talent play…."[5]

Ellen Servine, also serving as president of the Business and Professional Women's Club, used her dramatic talents to instruct the public. A recent state law revision made it legal for women to serve on juries, but individual counties still had final say in the matter. Hoping to show the competencies of women jurors, Miss Servine staged two identical mock trials, one with male jurors and one with female. Ord attorneys served as defender, prosecutor, and judge. When the jurors were polled, the verdict was the same. The women's vote was unanimous; the men rendered one that was 9-3. A large audience attended the test trial, the women in the community showing most interest.

Their senior year, Evelyn and Irene dated two boys from Burwell, Nebraska. During spring break, the two girls grew restless; they were bored. What could they do to entice their boyfriends away from work? Ideas of entrapment came quickly. Enlisting the help of a very good friend, they talked Jack Janssen into making a phone call to a Burwell filling station. When Ray Hahn, Irene's boyfriend, answered, he heard Jack frantically tell him the two girls "had gone flying and crashed into a fence."[6] He was to get Willy Shafer, Evelyn's boyfriend, and come quickly to Irene's home.

As Jack put the phone down, the giggling began. Where shall we hide? What will we say? Within seconds, however, they began to sense the reality of what they had done. Knowing from

"Boyfriend And Girlfriend," Wilson (Willy) Shafer and Evelyn, Ord, Nebraska, circa 1937

which direction the boys would come, the three young conspirators stood behind the floor-length curtains at Irene's front room windows, peering through openings in the lacy material. They waited anxiously for the sight of Ray's familiar Model A truck. Within minutes, a vehicle in front of a roiling cloud of dust appeared in the distance. But it was not the truck they were expecting. It was a black, Model A Ford

Coupe, the Hahn family car. Upset that his girlfriend might be dead, Ray had called his parents and they insisted on coming. It was Irene who answered the frantic knocking at the front door. Amid the "Are you all right?", "We thought you crashed!", and "What happened?", Evelyn and Irene hemmed and hawed, looked down sheepishly, and admitted the truth. Admonishing lectures and proper apologies followed. On this day, the three pranksters had not only ended their boredom but learned a lesson about crying "wolf."

Yet pranks can be a two-way street. On another day, when Evelyn and Irene again missed the attention of their boyfriends, they borrowed horses for a trip to Burwell. Riding along the railroad bed offered smooth ground with virtually no traffic. Besides, the pretty girls had fun waving to the honking cars and trucks on nearby Highway 11. There was also an element of adventure when crossing bridge trestles with no side protection. On their way back to Ord, the girls suddenly realized a Model A truck had pulled alongside. Recognizing each other, they all yelled and waved, until the truck picked up speed, leaving the girls far behind. Evelyn and Irene looked quizzically at each other, knowing Ray and Willy were up to something, which more than likely was no good. When the girls turned the corner, giving them a clear view of Irene's house, they could not believe their eyes. There, hanging in Irene's bedroom window for "the whole world to see," was a pair of her panties. When asked some years later if he had any recollection of this shameful behavior, Willy Shafer smiled sheepishly with a look of "Yeah, I remember."[7] His wife, Velma, rolled her eyes toward the ceiling with a sigh indicating that after fifty-some years of marriage there were no surprises.

Apparently Irma Leggett didn't need to remind Willy and Ray that spring had arrived. In her column, she wrote, "The tulips are popping through and the grass is greening."[8] Readers needed to get their chickens corralled so they didn't eat the garden seed. Gutzon Borglum reported work on Mt. Rushmore was resuming after winter suspension. Abe and Teddy were the next to be blasted.

On May 15, 1937, a special goodwill train, sponsored by the Omaha Chamber of Commerce, pulled into the Ord Burlington Railroad Depot. On hand to welcome it was the Ord High School March-

ing Band. As soon as the concert was over, Evelyn "reluctantly de-
clined an invitation to inspect the new train," having to hurry home to
help her mother who was suffering from a broken ankle. However,
Evelyn did tell a reporter she remembered her last trip on a train only
vaguely. It was "a short ride in Nebraska with Mother to see Daddy.
Then a telegraph operator, he was temporarily transferred to another
office. After commencement this next week, she hopes to come to
Omaha and ride the Zephyr. If she does, she will bring her two year-
old Scottie, a constant companion." The *Omaha World Herald* article
concluded:

> To keep fit, Miss Sharp has never taken so much as a puff of
> tobacco nor a sip of beer. She drinks milk instead of coffee,
> tries to get eight hours of sleep nightly. She weighs 114
> pounds and is 5′ 4″. Aviators who have seen her in the air
> declare she has excellent possibilities of someday becoming
> one of America's best women fliers.[9]

A press release for "Growing Pains," the senior class play, featured a picture of Evelyn's dog. "An animal of purest Scottie

*"Growing Pains" Senior Class Play, May 1937. (Evelyn on stairs, in front row,
second from top)*

blood...He has been going through his part faithfully during the last two weeks of practice and is anxiously awaiting his first stage performance." The play, with a cast of twenty-five seniors, seven of whom were Thespians, depicted the "joys and sorrows of awkward age. The McIntyres see their boy and girl tossed in the cataracts of adolescence and can help little further than give directions from a distance, advice which carefree youth, of course, always reject. Many things happen to all, but the end is bright and promising."[10]

The following week, *The Ord Quiz* reported "much credit must be given to Scottie Sharp for his efforts in portraying 'Rascal,' the much-sought-after Scottie dog in the play."[11] This article was only a forerunner to the press coverage and media attention which would eventually follow her dog. Even in her own playbook, Evelyn underlined Scottie's name, rather than her own.

Less than a week later, on May 20, 1937, Evelyn and her classmates entered the high school and found the entire building "transformed into a modern ocean liner." It was the evening of the Junior-Senior Banquet. Class colors of blue and white were predominant in the nautical decorations, favors, name places, and uniforms of the junior class "stewards." "Gorgeous baskets of flowers were used in profusion for the dedication of the 'Whithernow', a steamer which had pulled into O.H.S. Harbor." The menu, prepared by the ladies of Evelyn's Methodist Episcopal Church, included Neptune's Fruit, Pilots' Waves, Ice-Bergs [sic], Portholes, Sailor's Delight, Search Lights, Anchors, Lighthouse, Barometer, and Life Savers. Dinner music and speeches, given by class members trying to express their feelings, also reflected the nautical theme: Launching, Ship Ahoy!, Bon Voyage, High Tide, Sailing, Breakers, and Dropping Anchor. As the seniors and their guests prepared to disembark the ship, the "Anchorette" orchestra, dressed in blue and white sailor uniforms, struck up "Anchors, Aweigh." Spontaneously, several seniors broke into song.[12]

On the following Tuesday, after much pleading with administration, the senior class was dismissed early for its picnic at 3:00 p.m. With the impetuous optimism of youth, the students piled into cars and headed for Mortensen's pasture, never noticing the fast-moving cold front coming in from the west. In a matter of minutes, the skies opened up and torrents of pelting rain turned the country dirt roads into a slick skating rink. Drivers lost control. Cars ended up in ditches. As the students, covered with mud and soaked to the bone, returned to the school for their picnic, Superintendent Thompson and Principal Stoddard greeted each one with a knowing smile.

Dorothy Auble had been selected to read the Senior Will at Class Night, a lighthearted, less formal activity. As a good friend of Evelyn's, Dorothy tried hard to keep some composure as she read Evelyn's wishes. "Evelyn and Irene hereby will Raymond and Wilson to Lydia Blaha and Alice Cronk."[13] Cheers of applause rose from the seniors; the girls were members of the junior class. Willy was also included in The Class Prophecy for Evelyn. "Evelyn Sharp has become our really famous senior by flying from Ord to Wilson Shafer's home in Burwell in nothing flat. Ain't love grand?"[14] A year ago, Willy's good friend had penned similar feelings in Evelyn's memory book:

> Ashes to ashes,
> Dust to dust.
> If it weren't for you,
> His lips would rust!
>
> Your friend,
> Raymond Hahn[15]

Because of expense, the Ord *Chanticleer* yearbook for 1936 and 1937 graduates had been combined. Evelyn's class was featured as juniors. Every picture in her yearbook for both junior and senior classes had a signature, many of them including a handwritten message:

Dearest Evelyn,

Someday I'll be reading in headlines about you. You will be successful with your ability to find and give the best.

> Love,
> Barbara

To the high flyer, I wish no falls.

> Sincerely yours,
> E. Servine

Don't forget me! "Amelia E."

Joy Auble

May you put Amelia to shame! Good-Bye, Honey—

Laverne L. Hansen

Longer messages were written on the inside covers:

Dear Tarzan, Tailspin, & etc.,

I shall always remember you as my best friend. And all the fun we had together. Don't forget the times we went swimming and the hill that David & you & Bob & I parked on. And the night we had Jack's car and went eighty-five miles an hour in. And when you become the World's best pilot, don't forget "your pal."

With Love,
Irene Whiting
(Beans)

"Good Looking Horse." Evelyn and best friend, Irene Whiting June 1936

Dear Evelyn,

I shall always remember you as a true friend & full of fun. I think I shall never forget our good times together when at M.O.D.R.T. Club, and on hikes. Thanks for teaching me how to drive your old jalopy at the racetrack.

With Love,
Virginia Clark[16]

A small, white invitation, very simple in design, requested John and Mary Sharp's presence at commencement exercises on May 28, 1937. Neither of them had graduated from high school. With the first strains of the "Pomp and Circumstance" processional, Evelyn and her classmates, dressed in red gowns and white mortar boards, marched into the auditorium. These were moments of pride and excitement for all parents, but also ones of quiet reflection. Two months earlier, a tragic car accident between Burwell and Ord had claimed the lives of two senior boys, Harold Haskell and Harold Melia. Both popular athletes and "clean, fine, hard-working lads," they were respected and missed by the people in this community.[17]

Graduated as best girl athlete, Ord High School, May 1937

James E. Lawrence, editor of *The Lincoln Star* newspaper, admonished the graduates at commencement to keep faith in Nebraska. "...better times are ahead for everyone," he said. "The North Loup Project [offers] 'unlimited opportunities.'"[18] Perhaps Evelyn wondered that night what it could offer her. She would not have long to wait for an answer.

1937 Chanticleer Graduates; Evelyn, 4th row down, 3rd from left

City Fathers Buy A Cub

*I*n the summer of 1937, Evelyn Sharp "takes to the water instead of the air."[1] The local Red Cross Chapter, feeling a responsibility to offer free swimming instruction to Valley County residents, asked Evelyn to head their program. With no pool in the county, the children had to swim in the North Loup River; and, though the waist-high water was relatively unchanging, the channel shifted often, occasionally making a deep and dangerous hole. "...parents are most interested in their children becoming proficient swimmers and [learning] to be careful in the water," *The Ord Quiz* reported.[2]

At Red Cross expense, Evelyn enrolled at the First Aid and Water Safety School in Colorado Springs, Colorado, on June 28, 1937. She learned to administer artificial res-

"A 'Picture' For A Friend,"
photographic design by LaVerne Lakin, circa 1937

piration and became skilled in other methods of water safety. At the conclusion of the six-day class, she received a card indicating satisfactory completion of the Standard Course of Instruction in First Aid to the Injured.

Upon returning to Ord, this seventeen-year-old woman initiated her summer swimming program. On the banks of Anderson's Island, a public park and recreation area given to the city in 1915 by William A. Anderson, Evelyn met with her classes. There she explained the twofold purposes of the program: to learn the "art of swimming"[3] and teach safety in the water.

At first the swimming lessons were held in the North Loup River near the west end of the steel, three-span bridge. But it soon became apparent that the current was too swift for the younger children, so they moved to a gravel pit area straight east of M Street. An area of safe water was fenced off, and students ranging in ages from four through twelve were expected to stay inside the lines. Two classes were held each afternoon, three times a week. Starting with the basics of breathing, a student could move through various levels of skill competencies. Evelyn worked toward qualifying as many as possible for the Junior Life-Saving Certificate; the more able students enjoyed "riding the current" as they practiced their strokes. She even instructed adults in their own private class. Her efforts and expertise brought forth recognition from the local newspaper: "The school is progressing nicely under the tutelage of Evelyn Sharp, who is proving herself an expert teacher."[4] She taught 125 students to swim that summer.

With her swimming responsibilities behind her, Evelyn joined twenty-six of her Methodist Episcopal Church friends at their annual retreat in Long Pine, Nebraska. Members of the Epworth League youth group, they swam, played games, hiked the trails in heavily forested hills, and canoed in waters formed by the gently flowing Long Pine Creek. In a picture postcard written to "Mom," Evelyn described her one-room cabin living accommodations with seven girls, and in one to "Pop," a hike to the top of a very high Chicago and Northwest Railroad bridge trestle.[5] She neglected, however, to tell either parent of her dancing plans. Charlie Zangger remembers. "Some of us sneaked

"Conversation At Camp," Evelyn and friend, Long Pine, Nebraska, August 1935

out for the dance at Long Pine after 'Lights Out,' but none of us made it. Our sponsors were too smart."[6]

Articles and pictures in several Nebraska newspapers that summer featured Evelyn, not only for Ord's successful swim program, but also for her goal to obtain a transport license. "To be the youngest girl transport pilot in the United States. That's the aim of Miss Evelyn Sharp."[7] A transport or commercial license required a minimum of two hundred hours.

But once again Evelyn's flying had come to a stop. Between November 13, 1936, and June 14, 1937, she logged only three entries, one of which was just ten minutes in length. Jack Jefford, now managing the Hastings Airport, had closed his operation at Broken Bow and moved south. Not long thereafter, his yellow Aeronca slipped into a dive from a vertical bank and spun into the ground. Chris Hald, a student pilot, was killed, and the damage to NC15291 which had impacted the ground at a sixty-degree angle, was extensive. The wings had been crumpled, the fuselage was twisted, and the engine had been driven back into the cockpit.[8]

Another plane, which Evelyn had flown earlier, was consumed by fire. The sequence of events leading to this disaster was reminiscent of a Laurel and Hardy movie. Two men from Burwell, neither having ever touched the controls of an airplane, decided to fly Ed Kull's Aeronca to Sargent one afternoon. Flipping a coin to determine pilot in command, the winner climbed into the pilot's seat while the other prepared to hand-crank the prop. After several tries, the pilot got the switches flipped correctly and soon the engine started. The copilot climbed aboard and they began to taxi the tail-dragger across the open field. With confidence building, the pilot gave it more throttle, causing loss of directional control. A farmer who owned the field adjacent to the airport was burning his fence row, packed thick with tumbleweeds. The wing tip snagged a part of the fence and was pulled into the flaming brush. The fabric ignited, the pilots abandoned ship, and the Aeronca was reduced to its skeletal remains.[9]

Jack Jefford returned to Ord for a two-day visit on June 14, 1937. Taking advantage of his Taylor Cub, Evelyn practiced landings and flew five more passengers, recording their names in her special register. As she logged the one hour and forty minutes of flying time, Evelyn mentally calculated the hundred and forty hours needed for a transport license.[10] She must have sighed and closed the book.

John Sharp, knowing he could not afford to buy his daughter a plane, shared these feelings one night with his good friend. Wencel Misko suggested John talk to one of the Auble brothers who had a reputation for helping others.[11] Dr. Glen Auble, "a man who never shirks any task that will end in betterment for Ord,"[12] felt the idea had promise. Evelyn had already proven her promotional attraction. If he could get Ord businessmen to come up with a down payment, here would be an opportunity to help a young woman achieve a goal and, at the same time, bring some much-needed publicity to Ord and the North Loup Project. Dr. Auble was "amazed at how Ord cut loose and raised a very substantial payment."[13] Their decision to help Evelyn would create a new focus during Depression Times and with it would come an increased pride in this Valley County community.

It was very warm and quite humid on the evening of August 17, 1937. Hoping to get a breath of fresh air, Evelyn had gone outside to sit on the steps. Her room above the kitchen was stifling. She heard the phone ring; Jack Jefford was on the other end. If she could be in Hastings by eight o'clock the next morning, he would fly her to Omaha to pick up the new plane. "Then pandemonium broke loose! No girl was ever wilder with excitement than Evelyn!"[14] The new Taylor Cub NC19532, flown in from Pennsylvania the day before, was waiting on the ramp when Evelyn touched down. Pleased, but matter-of-fact about the silver, two-seated aircraft, she wanted to fly it by herself before her father and she started back. Taxiing about the field for a few minutes, she checked the rudder, elevator, and aileron controls. They seemed fine. After a brief run-up where engine gauges and instruments checked-out, she turned the plane onto the runway. Evelyn pushed the throttle forward. Remembering takeoff procedures, she allowed the tail to come up before increasing the angle of attack. In a matter of seconds, she was airborne. Mindful of the critical nature with this aspect of flight, she allowed herself only a few moments of exhilaration. At last she was flying her very own plane. Perhaps her dreams really would come true. In 1937, seven women in Nebraska were aircraft owner-operators, and at seventeen, Evelyn was the youngest.

John Sharp watched proudly amidst a small group of curious onlookers as his daughter practiced a few takeoffs and landings. When an *Omaha World-Herald* reporter asked him his feelings, he responded. "She is quite a girl. Never gets excited. Got her career cut out for her, now she has this plane. Doesn't care much about school or housework. Just interested in flying."[15]

While Evelyn and John were flying back to Ord late that afternoon, convection currents were causing typical Midwestern thunderheads to build in the west. When they ran into a "heavy, twisting wind," Evelyn set the plane down in a harvested wheat field. As the storm blew through, she told her father she thought they could make it to Grand Island before dark. They took off, only to run into a heavy rainstorm near Aurora. Having to land again in another muddy stubble field, they spent the night in the airplane. Evelyn later recalled, "This was a most restless night...across the road was a cemetery and every time the lightning flashed, it gave the place a weird aspect. Every time the rain stopped, the mosquitoes began biting."[16] Her father's description read a bit differently:

> Mr. John Sharp didn't get much sleep that night, his daughter wanted to talk airplanes.[17] "Upon the early arrival of daybreak...I was still asleep...," Evelyn arose and wiped all the moisture from the plane.
>
> "Let's get the motor warmed up and sail to Hastings!" announced Evelyn, waking me out of a perfectly sound sleep.
>
> "Sail is right," I muttered to myself, "in this mud and water. I was surprised, the plane took off easily."[18]

The flight to Hastings was beautiful, the air after the rainstorm as smooth as glass. John had an opportunity at breakfast that morning to congratulate Jack Jefford on his technique in training pilots.

Jefford replied, "To make a successful flier, you must have a reasonable young duck that will mind its master—old ducks sometimes know too much—it is useless to waste time on them. Evelyn has been both sincere and willing in her flying and she has done just as she was told to do and nothing else until she gained self-confidence."[19]

On that flight, John realized how easily and precisely the airplane responded to Evelyn's touch of the controls. Convinced that women could pilot aircraft as well as men, he perhaps thought about the unlimited opportunities which awaited the women fliers of the future. He and Mary would do whatever they could to help their daughter get her transport license.

After returning to Ord, one of Evelyn's first promotional activities was the beauty pageant at the Valley County Fair. Sponsored by the Business and Professional Women's Club, it was to be staged in a "strictly clean and high class manner."[20] There would be no bathing suit competition and evening dresses were eventually barred, the Fair Board feeling some of the contestants might not be able to afford them. Seventy pretty girls, including Evelyn, competed for the title of Miss Valley County and an all-expense paid trip to the State Fair in Lincoln.

Evelyn did not win. Perhaps she had
on that old plaid skirt, the one Willy
Shafer, her Burwell boyfriend, always
remembered her wearing when they
were with each other. There was little
money for "good" clothes in Depression Times.

An aerial photograph of the
large Diversion Dam, in the North
Loup Project southeast of Ord, appeared in the August 25 issue of *The
Ord Quiz*. The readers found it fascinating to see the workings of their
community from above. This would
be the first of several "sky-foto [sic]"
promotions featuring classmate La-
Verne Lakin as photographer, and
Evelyn Sharp as his pilot.

"Reflections By A Lily Pool,"
Ord, Nebraska, circa 1937

In the same edition, there was a picture of Evelyn standing next
to her new Taylor Cub. Beside her were several members of the Ord
Falcon Model Airplane Club, most of them being old high school
friends. An open tournament of model airplane flying had been held
on the field where she hangared her plane. Adolph Sevenker, a friend
of her father's, had some time ago fashioned a wind sock from a six-
teen-inch loop of Number Nine wire. Charlie Zangger, the young man
who had been part of the group that had tried to sneak into Long Pine
to the dance, took note of that wind sock when it was time for his turn
to compete. He and one hundred other people enjoyed that lovely afternoon at Mortensen Field. The next year, Evelyn would be asked to
judge a model airplane building contest in Grand Island, a promotion
for the movie premiere of "Men With Wings," the first aviation picture
made in Technicolor.

By the first of September 1937, Evelyn needed only eighty-eight
more hours to complete the flying requirements for a transport license.
That week she made several flights to Hastings, and also trips to Dan-
nebrog, Comstock, and Grand Island. She had climbed to an altitude

of 7,000 feet and practiced spirals and 360s. Since she had taken delivery of her plane about two weeks earlier, Evelyn had spent forty-two hours in the air, taking up over eighty passengers.[21] Who were these people who would take their first plane ride with a seventeen-year-old woman? They were doctors, lawyers, and bankers from the business community, classmates, teachers, and principals from the high school, friends of friends of friends, and the farmers in the Valley who would ride when it was too wet to be in the fields. For example, #4 in her register was Miss Viola Crouch, sponsor of the Girls' Athletic Association; #15 was James Hurst, a racing pilot in his own right; #39 was Scottie Sharp, her dog whom she sometimes counted as a passenger; #83 was Dr. Lee Nay, a local osteopath; and #102 was Pud Garnick, a 1934 Ord graduate. They were her admirers from all walks of life, responding with enthusiasm and support.

Milo Bresley, a classmate always eager to fly with Evelyn, lived on the "wrong side" of the North Loup River. When able to get away from chores on the family farm, he hiked to the river's widest part,

James Hurst's Ford V-8 Arrow Sportstar, 1938

waded across, and climbed the sloping bank to the quarter-mile run-way on the other side. In those early flights, Evelyn inspired Milo to become a student pilot, and later he logged over ten thousand hours for all three branches of the United States Armed Services. Some fifty-five years later, still remembering her with fondness, Milo turns the pages of a scrapbook containing newspaper clippings and pictures he took of her.[22] With an interest in photography, Milo captured some of the earliest moments of this young woman and her love for flying.

A Lost Cub

"*E*velyn Sharp Will Be First To Land On New Arrasmith Field,"[1] the headline read on a front page story of the September 15, 1937, *Ord Quiz*. A few days before, after receiving a letter from the Grand Island Chamber of Commerce requesting her to advise them as to when she could come, Evelyn "at once informed them that she would come anytime that suited their convenience."[2]

The following Monday, on September 20, Evelyn and LaVerne Lakin, who had been promoted to news editor for the Ord newspaper, flew over fields of harvested wheat and still-maturing green corn on their way to Grand Island. They hit several air pockets as the morning sun began to warm the surface of the earth. When Evelyn noticed LaVerne's pale complexion, she laughed, gunning the engine to regain lost altitude. LaVerne tried to focus his attention on the expert manner in which she piloted the plane. "Flying with Evelyn is a real thrill—no kidding. She checked each wire, gauge, and strut before departure. Most girls and boys of Evelyn's age would undoubtedly get the 'big head' if they had even the smallest percentage of the publicity thrown on them that is given Evelyn. Not this young lady. She is a business-like 17 year old girl who's in the game of aviation for all its worth. Friends? She has hundreds of them, ranging in age from six to eighty-six."[3]

As they approached Arrasmith Field about eleven o'clock, the wind and blowing dust reduced visibility, making the aircraft more difficult to control. Evelyn circled the field, losing some altitude. And then, after one more circle, she brought the plane around again, setting it gently onto the runway. Dressed in light beige boot pants with high leather boots, brown suede jacket, and a white leather flying cap, Evelyn stepped down from the cockpit. Included in a large gathering to

"First To Fly In," Arrasmith Field, Grand Island, Nebraska, September 20, 1937

greet her were her father, representatives of the Grand Island Junior Chamber of Commerce and Rotary Club, and several Ord businessmen. The guest of honor at a Rotary Club luncheon that noon, she was "the most popular girl in Grand Island...when she gained the distinction of being the first lady"[4]...on the new $400,000 Arrasmith Field.

The latter part of that week, Evelyn flew to several Nebraska towns to distribute air bills promoting the Arrasmith Dedication and Air Show. Behind the cabin on both sides of her Taylor Cub fuselage, a two-line dark blue inscription read:

"The Ord"
"Evelyn Sharp, Nation's Youngest Aviatrix, P.L. No. 34711"

She handed out postcards which pictured herself, the plane, and some with her dog, Scottie. Many of these autographed cards were put in special boxes and drawers, remaining there still today for a grand-child to see.

"Sideslipping her flashing silver plane out of the heavens into a beautiful three-point landing at the Ord Airport,"[5] Evelyn was soon to record her two-hundredth hour. With a wind from the northwest, she had cut power on the downwind leg, flew a short base, and quickly banked the airplane onto final approach. "Alighting from the plane to receive a hearty handshake from her father, her first words were: 'Boy, if I can only pass that exam.'"[6] Having just accomplished the first step toward a transport license, she was already thinking about the next. A headline in *The Ord Quiz* two days earlier read, "Evelyn's Air Tutor Will Fly In Alaska."[7] The paper reported he had left at once for Alaska where he would fly transports between Juneau and Nome. Under Jefford's supervision, Evelyn had planned to get hands-on experience with a variety of planes and engines at his maintenance shops in Hastings. She needed his tutelage to pass the transport license exam. Now she would have to find someone else.

On Saturday, the twenty-eighth of September, Evelyn returned to Grand Island for the Arrasmith Airport Dedication. Making her head-quarters at the exclusive Wolbach and Company, a central Nebraska department store on the corner of Third and Pine, she autographed postcards and handed out special "Miss Evelyn Sharp" ribbons. An added promotion was a drawing sponsored by Skyrider shoes. The

"Flying High With Wolbachs...central Nebraska's largest department store,"
marketing promotion, Grand Island, Nebraska, September 1937

winner would receive a toy Taylor Cub, just like the one Evelyn was flying when she had officially opened the new airport.

Later that day from his office in Dayton, Ohio, Orville Wright of Wright Brothers' fame, pressed a golden telegraph key, sending a message to officials in Grand Island. Members of the American Legion Post 53 fired a ten-gun salute, and the dedication festivities were under way. "Ordites report that one of the general questions to be heard admidst the crowd at the airport was, 'Where is Evelyn Sharp and her plane?'"[8] Surrounded by autograph seekers, she signed official programs, saying hello to old friends and welcoming new ones into her circle of admirers.

That evening, "...men and women without an airship—took Arrasmith Field for their own...."[9] Some 2,300 people, paying admission of $1.50 a couple, danced to Little Jack Little's ballroom music until the wee hours of the morning. At least 700 people, unable to get in the large Arrasmith hangar, danced on the tarmac outside. The audience was cosmopolitan, including executive heads of business firms as well as those who drew weekly paychecks. Attire ranged from "formal evening gowns to street dresses, and from business suits to the popular 'soup-and-fish,'"[10] a style of clothing named from the variety and abundance of food served at formal dinners. As the men and women danced, chatted, and laughed with each other, it was an evening they would long remember. For Evelyn, it was even more special. That afternoon, her silver and blue plane had been hoisted by block and tackle to the inside top of the hangar. There, it would "fly," glistening in revolving white light. One can only imagine the thoughts and dreams of its seventeen-year-old pilot as she danced below later that night.

In October of 1937, *The Ord Quiz* and the City Light Depot sponsored a two-day cooking school. They wanted Evelyn to model, but she had very few clothes appropriate for such a public appearance. Wencel Misko, John Sharp's good friend, asked his daughter-in-law if she had anything Evelyn could wear. Mae Lee Misko, now a mother of two, thought of her college-day outfits packed away upstairs and came to the conclusion they would never fit again, anyway.

Evelyn enjoyed the mornings spent with Mae Lee while her

"Fashions Befitting The Thirties,"
Ord, Nebraska, circa 1937

young boys were asleep in their rooms below. "She seemed happy as a lark"[11] as they climbed the winding stairs to the attic. Carefully untying each suit box, Evelyn marveled at how beautiful the clothes were. She had never seen so many swimsuits, play clothes, dresses, and elegant formals. Preening before the full length mirror, perhaps Evelyn saw herself as others did. Olive complexioned with dark-brown eyes and lashes, she was a very pretty and pleasant-looking young woman.

Knowing that "youngest in the nation" records do not last forever, Evelyn turned her attention toward preparation for the transport license exam. She must pass flight tests as well as written tests on meteorology, navigation, airplane engines, and airplane construction. With her interest in sports and healthful living, the least of her worries was the physical exam. Kenneth Holmes, who had taken over Jefford's duties at Hastings, coached her on a few of the more technical flying maneuvers she was required to perform for the government inspectors. On the twenty-sixth of October, he and Evelyn flew to Lincoln for the long-awaited tests.

"Evelyn 'Flunks' Transport Exam, Will Try Again in Three Months" headlined the November 3, 1937, edition of *The Ord Quiz*. When confronted in Lincoln, "Evelyn told them [reporters] point blank that she had 'flunked' the written examination....'I didn't have enough instruction, I guess. But, I'll get more.' Evelyn is no quitter—she still has high hopes of becoming the youngest transport girl pilot in the United States."[12]

Evelyn must have appreciated the concluding paragraphs in the front page article:

> Experienced airmen who hoped that Evelyn would pass the tests said that they weren't surprised when she failed. Even the "old timers" in the field of aviation confess that the government test for a transport license is a "plenty tough" examination.

> Can you answer this one? Give 5 reasons why a motor might backfire through the carburetor and tell why with explanation. That is an example of the 40 test questions which Ord's young aviatrix was to answer.[13]

Several papers in Nebraska carried the story of her failure to pass the exam. She did not paste a single one in her scrapbook.

Evelyn flew only three more times before the end of the year. Under "remarks" for the first flight, she recorded, "just scouting around." The last two indicated she practiced landings, takeoffs, 180s, and 360s. Since Evelyn flunked the transport exam, her plans for earning a living through aviation, that was taking passengers for hire, were on hold. It also meant she would not be able to repay Ord businessmen nor keep up payments on her new Taylor Cub.

On December 3, 1937, Evelyn was initiated into the Mizpah Chapter 56, Order of Eastern Star in Ord. Her father, a member of the Masons since 1905, had, along with her mother, been members of Montana's Custer Chapter 25, Order of Eastern Star, in 1919. For a Christmas project in 1937, Evelyn helped other members of her Eastern Star chapter collect canned goods in large wooden barrels. The poor in Valley County had not been forgotten.

Three days before Christmas, a picture of Evelyn in a "Yule Tide Greeting Card" was published in *The Ord Quiz*. The inscription read: "My Christmas present has already been received in the form of the fine support you have given me in my flying career. Merry Christmas, Evelyn Sharp."[14]

With very best wishes
for a Merry Christmas
and a Happy New Year

"Christmas Greetings From Evelyn And Scottie," Ord, Nebraska, December 1937

In January of 1938, John Sharp "became unable to meet the payments on the airplane" and he "voluntarily gave up all interest in"[15] the silver J-2 Taylor Cub. But Evelyn did not give up. Adequate ground school instruction to obtain her transport license was not available in the area, so she made inquiries about a course offered at the Lincoln Airplane and Flying School in the capital city. It was just what she was looking for, but it cost money neither she nor her parents had. Once again, under the competent leadership of Dr. Glen Auble, the people in the community rallied to her side.

On the evening of Thursday, January 20, 1938, a benefit dance was held in the Ord Dance Hall. Under the direction of Dr. Auble, a fourteen-piece band made up of several 1937 graduates and other local musicians played popular favorites of the era. Couples on their first dates, newlyweds, and those whose marriages had been strengthened by tough times of the Depression danced to "The Very Thought of You," "It's Only a Paper Moon," "Pennies From Heaven," and "I've

Told Every Little Star."[16] A well-known Ord Thespian Quartet made up of Leonard Sobon, LaVern Duemey, LaVerne Lakin, and Jack Janssen presented a very popular stage show. These classmates of Evelyn's donated their time and talent, as well as the Auble Brothers Jewelry Store giving a diamond ring for a door prize. As the people from Ord and the surrounding communities of Burwell, Sargent, Arcadia, and North Loup entered the hall, Evelyn greeted each one while pinning a small souvenir airplane made of metal on their lapels. With a warm smile she thanked each of them for coming. Some offered words of encouragement and support, while others, not knowing what to say, merely nodded and returned the smile.

A Stairway To The Stars

*U*sing the proceeds amounting to nearly a hundred dollars, Evelyn "started a course at the Lincoln School of Aviation Monday morning."[1] She would make her home with Herman and Winifred Mattley, the owners of a beautifully landscaped, two-story frame home on the corner of 31st and Kleckner Court. Their twenty-year-old daughter Chelys, a good friend of Evelyn's, was a cousin to Harold Haskell, one of the senior boys who had been killed in a car accident just before graduation. Evelyn and Chelys, both sports-minded, looked forward to reminiscing about earlier times, such as when they initiated the swimming season too early one March. Emerging from the icy waters of the still partially-frozen North Loup River, their bodies were numbed by the cold. They ran to their car parked on Anderson's Island seeking comfort in its relative warmth. As feeling began to return to their extremities, they sensed pain in the bottoms of their feet. Looking down, the two swimmers were horrified. Their soles were covered with sandburs. Gritting their teeth and moaning with each pull, the two girls extracted them gingerly, one by one.

Ground school classes started early at the Lincoln Airplane and Flying School; it was not long, however, before Evelyn found some "fly-boys" interested in picking her up. So as not to disturb the rest of the household with a ringing alarm, she devised a silent wake-up call. Before going to bed, Evelyn tied a fifteen-foot length of cord carefully around her big toe, dropping the other end out their bedroom window. Lying down, she made sure the string was not hung up on something below. In the morning, when it was still dark outside, the "fly-boys" coasted up to the house. Crawling out of the car, one of the young men stumbled around the west side of the house. He gave a firm yank on the dangling cord. Standing there, he did not wait long until he felt a similar tug from the other end. It was only minutes until the front door opened and Evelyn came bounding out. The invention worked—the Mattley household was still sound asleep.[2]

In a March 28, 1938, letter written from Kleckner Court, Evelyn told Auntie Pat Lobenstein she had learned to loop and snap roll.

> It sure is fun. I study meteorology, navigation, engines, airplane construction, rules and regulations, and theory of flight. It sure is hard.

> The weather has been perfect. It has even rained a couple of times. Gee, the trees are almost out and everything. The robin red breast bob all around. Thanks a lot for the pin money. I used it on a pair of stockings.

> I've got to go horseback riding at Pioneer Park, swim at the YMCA, and play tennis at Muni Court. The girl I stay with and I do exercises all the time. We sure have fun. Her folks are sure nice to me.[3]

Evelyn wrote many other letters while in Lincoln that winter and spring of 1938. Some of those included ones addressed to Richard Severson, her boyfriend attending Peru State College in southeast Nebraska.

Jan. 24, 1938

Dear Sevie,

> I got your letter today when I came home from school. …First I made several drawings of a plane and then took a landing gear apart. Next we took a tail of a plane apart, and put it together again. …Wowie! It seems funny. I was the only girl in about 75 boys.…

Gee, I wish you could call me every morning and wake me up. It makes me feel so good. I dreamed about you last night. The heck of it is I can't remember what I dreamed. ...if I wanted you to remain a hermit. No,...I want you to get out and enjoy yourself and don't sit around and study too much. Please go out and get acquainted with the gals.... I'm not afraid you'll get drunk because that's your own business. If you really want to you will but perhaps you won't want to, I hope. When you write me, tell me what all you do and all about your friends. I'll tell you all about my new acquaintances and what I do. I won't hold anything back. That will be more fun writing to you that way. Oh, yes, I'll adopt your way of pitching woo. Do you mind?

Please write as soon as you get this letter and I'll answer as soon as I get yours.... Oh, yes, last night we went down to the radio station KFAB and listened and also visited Jack Hitchcock.... Please write soon.

> Love (I mean it),
> Evelyn

Jan. 30, 1938

Dear Sevie,

...How are you and the fems coming along? I've been enjoying myself here. I went to a dance with Jack Hitchcock, you know the banker's son last Wed. ...Bump Ford came over to Mattley's and helped me study. He is one of the school's best students. Friday night Chel and Rollie and Dick Leash and I went out to Kings' Ballroom to the dance....and Saturday evening Chel and I saw Lincoln High beat Central in basketball. ...In school Al Ku and I have done in one week what it usually takes the boys two weeks to do. ...We have covered a vertical fin, timed valves, lined fuselages, lined tails, etc. and we are now making a rib for a wing. ...I am going to keep mine. It sure will be a masterpiece.

...I have your picture right by Scotties by my bed. You aren't jealous of Scottie are you? Gee, Sevie, I really miss you and, of course, Scottie. I think I have news for you. I'm not sure. We are trying to arrange to come down next Sunday or the Sunday after that. Don't pin too much on it though. I'll write....

> Love,
> Evelyn

Feb. 13, 1938

Dear Sevie,

How did you get home? No trouble I hope. Why didn't you call me up this morning. I waited at Mattley's until 12:20. ...I sure enjoyed being with you. It really must have affected me because I couldn't sleep much that night. ...Well, I'll close because words fail me. Don't let the bed bugs bite.

> Love,
> Evelyn

Feb. 16, 1938

Dear Sevie,

How's Peee rooo coming along? Are the dames still as numerous as fleas on a dog and the boys few and far between.

That OX-5 motor and I have been struggling along together. It better run when I get through if it wants to keep from the junk man.

Sevie, you take things too much to heart. Of course I want to keep going with you if you still want to. The answer to your question is "No. I don't think we should break up" Savvy? Or do I have to knock it into you. Why do you want your ring? ...Gee thanks for the Valentine. Mother sent me a box of homemade candy....

> Love,
> Evelyn

March 1, 1938

Dear Sevie,

...Boy, hasn't the weather been swell? I went horseback riding yesterday, beg pardon, I mean Sunday. Jack Fennemore and I went. You know, he's from Utah and he can really "ride em, cowboy!"

The past two nights, Monday and Tuesday(today), I have stayed home and studied, as you would say "like hell." Beg pardon, the first part of the evening last night, Monday, I went to the coliseum to a swimming meet. Texas vs. Nebraska. ...I'm supposed to go out and take some time tomorrow but from the looks of the weather, maybe I won't. ...Well, I must sign off.

Love,
Evelyn[4]

Evelyn continued writing to Richard through 1938. Postmarks on the envelopes included Lincoln, Ord, and Chicago. In all her letters, she wrote the word "love" above her signature. And though she meant it, she was beginning to realize that her feelings could tie her down.

At eighteen, like her girlfriends, Evelyn had hopes and dreams; but unlike them, she had a perspective they could not have had. She was on her way "up," made possible by her flying skills, her age, community support, and the fact she was a woman. She understood that other high school girls who had graduated could look forward to college only if their fathers could afford it, or if they could obtain some kind of scholarship. So if she didn't graduate from Lincoln Airplane and Flying School, what could she do? The answer was obvious—return to Ord, knowing she had disappointed her family, her friends, but more importantly, herself. Perhaps she could find a job at one of the local stores, but more than likely, she would marry a home-town boy, and raise a family in Ord or somewhere close by.

But this was not for Evelyn. She would use her skills, age, and gender to chart a course for her future. At home, in her community, and at school she had been encouraged and pushed to "be all you can be." Sure, she wanted those same things her girlfriends did: security, home, family, and love. In Richard Severson she had a boyfriend she loved and wouldn't have hurt for the world. But she did, as one of the four roads leading out of Ord eventually took her away from the comfort and security of that wonderful, small farming town. Unlike Dorothy and Toto, whose "yellow brick road" took them back to Kansas and Aunt Em, Evelyn's road was a stairway to the stars leading her away from Richard, away from Nebraska, and toward a fateful meeting with Aunt Elsie.

The first week in April, Evelyn received two telegrams — one asking her to make a personal appearance on the Grand Island Capitol Theater stage for the premiere showing of a new movie. All expenses would be paid. The other wire was from Dr. W. W. Arrasmith, a State of Nebraska Aeronautics Commissioner for whom the new Grand Island airport had been named. He wanted her to submit "pilot and ship data"[5] with respect to eligibility for the nationwide celebration of the Twentieth Anniversary Commemorative Air Mail Flight. Evelyn said yes to both.

When she arrived at the Capitol Theater on April 23, 1938, another telegram was waiting for her: "JUST LEARNED OF YOUR PERSONAL APPEARANCE AT OPENING OF 'TEST PILOT' CAPITOL THEATER. WE THINK IT IS SWELL GESTURE ON YOUR PART. THANKS. HAPPY LANDINGS.

CLARK GABLE AND MYRNA LOY"[6]

Evelyn shared this telegram with the movie audiences in Grand Island as well as her invitation to take part in the upcoming air mail flight. Theater management reported sell-out crowds at every showing that weekend, believing "almost as many came to see Evelyn on stage as to see the famous movie stars on the screen."[7] A popular attraction, she would make several stage appearances at aviation movie premieres within the next year.

Evelyn returned to Lincoln the next day to continue her schooling, but also needing to figure out some way to get a plane for the air mail flight. "Something will turn up,"[8] she later told a reporter. Andy

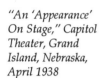

"An 'Appearance' On Stage," Capitol Theater, Grand Island, Nebraska, April 1938

Risser, a barnstorming pilot from Norfolk, Nebraska, eventually loaned her his Taylor J-2 Cub.

Chelys Mattley, the friend with whom Evelyn stayed, often accompanied her out to the Lincoln Municipal Airfield, watching her practice the required maneuvers for her transport license. The only woman in the flying school, Evelyn had once again earned the respect of male pilots. Chelys remembers one of their comments: "She's a flier who can land on a dime."[9]

Friday, the thirteenth of May, did not prove unlucky for eighteen-year-old Evelyn. At a banquet given in her honor at the Cornhusker Hotel, she was presented a transport license by Charles S. Doyle, secretary of the Nebraska State Aeronautics Commission. Hosting the event was Miss Delpha Taylor, another Ordite, who was secretary to Supreme Court Justice Bayard H. Payne. Evelyn now held the distinction of being the "only commercial licensed flier of her sex in the state at the present time."[10] Chelys beamed with a pride reserved for a very special friend.

When Evelyn returned to Ord, plans for an extended three-day air mail celebration spearheaded by the Chamber of Commerce were well under way. Dean Duncan and the Ord High School Marching Band were rehearsing for a concert to be given on the west steps of the Courthouse, and the Parker-Watts Circus was in town for afternoon and evening performances. Arriving by train from Grand Island, the

"Can Land On A Dime," Lincoln Airplane and Flying School, May 1938

circus cars full of exotic, pacing animals had been shunted to a side
track of the Union Pacific Railroad and unloaded. Rounds of applause
welcomed the circus performers high atop their magnificent African
elephants at the noon parade around the Courthouse Square. Signs in
the store windows read: "Stock up for the summer." Ord merchants
were offering "bargains in food, clothing, and in almost everything
people use."[11] For advertisement purposes, *The Ord Quiz* published
one day early.

The morning of May 19, 1938, dawned with an unusually heavy
fog along the North Loup River. As Evelyn flew the first leg of the air
mail flight, north from Grand Island's Arrasmith Field, she saw the
bank of clouds hanging low on the horizon. Looking for holes she
could "punch," Evelyn circled the area where she thought Mortensen
Field should be. She saw nothing. With a solid layer below, no visual
reference to the ground, and no way of knowing how long it would be
covered, Evelyn made a decision to get some more fuel. Executing a
180-degree turn, she banked her plane to the east, landing at North

Loup about ten minutes later. In her second attempt to find the airstrip, she found an opening where the morning sun had burned off part of the fog bank. Maneuvering the little orange-colored monoplane through a fluffy tunnel of white cotton, she spotted Mortensen Field and landed the Taylor Cub safely.

Photos of this historic day commemorating air mail flight, showed Evelyn stepping from the plane in boots and breeches, wearing a jacket of the type worn by air mail pilots and a colorful bandanna tied over her brown hair. A pistol was strapped to her right hip. She was greeted by an assemblage of postal employees, representatives from the Chamber of Commerce, the Legion Post, the Loup Valley Agricultural Society, the County Superintendent of Schools, friends, and relatives. A special presentation of a gold locket was made by Viola Crouch, a former and much-admired Girls' Athletic Association sponsor, who was now president of the Business and Professional Women's Club. Evelyn had been made an honorary member of the organization the previous year.

Mail clerk Roy Severson gave Evelyn several air mail letters to be addressed personally, and the cameras of Nebraska Press photographers and the Loup Valley Camera Club snapped and clicked. From the

"Me on Air Mail Day waiting for ship to be gassed," Mortensen Field, Ord, Nebraska, May 19, 1938

postmaster's car, with a United States flag draped across its top, Alfred L. Hill retrieved the thirty-three-pound locked pouch of six-cent-stamped air mail letters. The American Legion had sponsored special red, white, and blue envelopes bearing a cachet with a picture of Evelyn and a map of the Central Nebraska Air Mail Week Route in and out of Grand Island. Pertinent demographic and geographic data about the Loup Valley had been organized on an insert and more information about its hometown pilot and the first air mail pick-up at Ord was inside. The Ord Chamber of Commerce encouraged everyone to buy several cachet envelopes since one of the purposes of the flight was to help determine additional air mail routes. The government was interested in knowing which other towns could be added to air mail deliveries.

With the presentations and press obligations met, Evelyn was anxious to fly. She was already late because of weather, and there was

"Flying The Mail,"
Mortensen Field,
Ord, Nebraska,
Evelyn and Alfred
L. Hill, postmaster,
May 19, 1938

a twenty-two mile flight to pick up mail in Greeley before trying to make connections with the United Airlines plane in Grand Island. Strapping herself in, she checked the wind sock. It was hanging limp, part of the reason for the slow dispersal of fog that morning. Clearing the trees at the far end of the runway, she touched the mail pouch and smiled. Inside were three special letters she was sending. One was to Spencer Tracy, a movie star in "Test Pilot." Acknowledging its receipt in a letter dated May 23, 1938, Tracy thanked her for her good wishes and said he would put the cachet envelope in his son's stamp collection.[12] Another letter was to Chelys Mattley and her parents.

                                                    May 19, 1938

Thank you for everything you did for me.

                             Sincerely,
                             Evelyn Sharp

Fifty-four years later, Chelys recalls, "She was always grateful for whatever anyone did for her."[13] The third letter was to Richard Severson, her boyfriend at Peru State College:

Dear Sevie ,

Here's a cover (air mail) to remember me by.

                             Love,
                             Evelyn[14]

By one-thirty in the afternoon, Evelyn had returned to the Ord Airport with a leather bag of letters from Grand Island, some of them having been mailed just that morning in towns one hundred miles away. This time the skies were a brilliant blue; a crowd of three hundred people watched her land, cheering and yelling when the plane touched down. Acknowledging their welcome with a smile and a wave, she picked up a second pouch of mail and threw it in. Then, walking around to the front, Evelyn laid the ends of her fingers on both hands across the right blade of the propeller. With her feet shoulder-width apart, she pulled down sharply. The magneto fired. The engine had caught. In the crowd, tears came to the eyes of Wencel Misko who had lent support to his good friend, John Sharp, when he was trying to find a plane for his daughter. Overcome with emotion and not wanting other people see him cry, Wencel moved to the back of the well-wishers.[15] The first and only woman to qualify for this air mail assignment in Nebraska, Evelyn flew sixty pounds of mail, numbering some 2,500 letters, from this North Loup Valley community by the end of the day.

Off Again, On Again, Gone Again

*M*ail addressed only to Evelyn Sharp, Ord, Nebraska, began piling up at the small, local post office. *The Ord Quiz* reported her receiving about 150 letters from practically every state in the nation. Evelyn was especially proud of two letters — one from Eleanor Roosevelt, a good friend of Amelia Earhart, and the other from Nebraska's governor, R. L. Cochran. "But," the paper added, "she thinks just as much of the ones she has received from more humble admirers."[1] Someone sent her a copy of *Airpost Journal*, a stamp collector's magazine. Inside, a picture and an article highlighted her day-long air mail pilot adventure.

The following Monday evening, on May 23, 1938, Evelyn was honored at an Ord Rotary Club dinner. In a tribute to their hometown aviatrix, James P. Misko, vice-president of the First National Bank, summarized her short flying career and then focused his text on a recent conversation:

> About two months ago, when I was in Lincoln, I was invited to visit the school (Lincoln Flying School, Inc.), which I did. I met Mr. Bowers, the superintendent of the school, and when he learned I was from Ord, he asked me if I knew Evelyn. I told him I was happy to say that I did. He said, "I'll have her come to the office. I think she is working in the engine room,

today, and if she is she won't be very presentable but she is a dynamo in intellect, courage, and skill." Then I inquired how she is getting along and as to her chances of making the grade. Instead of giving me a direct answer as I expected he said, "Well, we have had several young women as students here in the past and I am sorry to say they didn't all come up to our expectations, (then my heart dropped down in my shoes, but it soon came up again when he said) but Miss Sharp is a different type of girl. She entered the school with the expectation of making good. She is a brilliant student, hard work[ing], attends strictly to business. Her manners of conduct command respect of everyone. She is the pride of the school." I said to myself "Such compliment[s] and such endorsement of character would make heaven smile and her parents and friends weep from joy."[2]

When the applause subsided, Mr. Misko than directed his comments to Evelyn:

To attain any degree of success in the art of aviation, it requires physical fitness, good habits of like [life], courage, endurance, hard work, and perseverance, and Evelyn, though in your teens yet [you] have all of these qualities I just mentioned. We are proud of you and wish you well, and no matter what fame you may achieve, we plead with you to retain your priceless, sweet, kind, and loving disposition.[3]

With these concluding remarks, the Rotarians, many of whom had contributed to the Taylor Cub down payment, stood and applauded. Evelyn responded by telling them that "Ord always will be her home and that she hopes to bring fame to this city by her achievement in aviation, which she will make her life's work."[4] There was another round of applause, and as Mary Sharp, seated at the head table, observed the feelings of this community, she must have wondered what life held for her only child.

The demand for public appearances increased, but Evelyn needed an airplane. Telling promoters she would fly if arrangements for a plane could be made, she carried passengers the first week in June at Norfolk and Columbus, Nebraska, and Yankton, South Dakota, just across the Missouri River. She recorded flying NC17525, the plane flown in the air mail flight, and a new one, another Cub, she was just trying out.

Evelyn returned to Ord with no plane and decided to teach swimming again. With the construction of dams and spillways underway for the North Loup Project, parents were more anxious than ever for their children to have swimming and water safety skills. It was rumored that many youngsters played below the Ord Dam, a most dangerous place.

By July 29, Evelyn and Arden Clark, a 1938 graduate of Ord High School, had been hired by the local Red Cross to teach three junior, two senior, and one adult class. But questions about swimming weren't the only ones asked by some of the younger students in the "biggest ever"[5] beginning class. They wanted to know about those marks on their teachers' backs. Enamored by tans, she and Arden had taped adhesive in the shape of their own initials on the upper part of each other's shoulders.[6] With a solemn expression, Evelyn told the younger children it was so they could tell their teachers apart. They looked up at her quizzically, some cocking their heads to one side. But when Evelyn smiled, their wide-eyed, tiny faces broke into grins.

Evelyn also organized a two-week life-saving class, teaching the methods of rescue and resuscitation used in lifeguard work. By the end of the summer, "178 Loup Valley adults and children knew how to swim better."[7] And parents felt more secure.

On July 27, 1938, *The Ord Quiz* reported John and Evelyn in Grand Island.[8] No explanation was given. But in the same issue, they were reported seen a few days later selling airplane rides in Greeley, raising money "to pay for a plane."[9] Stover Deats, owner of Deats Aviation Service in Grand Island, had a 1930 OX-5 Curtiss Robin he was willing to sell. One of Evelyn's instructors back in 1935, Stover no doubt had recently seen her picture in William Ferguson's "This Curious World."[10] A nationwide, cartoon feature, it highlighted her attainment of a commercial license at the age of eighteen. Wanting to help a former student, Stover Deats must have offered John Sharp a deal.

According to US Department of Commerce records, the bill of

sale for NC551N was dated and signed on August 11, 1938. Deats held the lien until August 23 by which time Evelyn had borrowed five hundred dollars to pay it off. On September 1, John transferred the title to Evelyn, who assumed ownership of a 90-hp, three-place, high-wing monoplane. The tachometer read 672.55 hours.

That afternoon, Evelyn flew her new Curtiss Robin into Diller, Nebraska, for the community's two-day, forty-second annual picnic. A handbill, circulated some days before, advertised "sky-rides" for a dollar. "Buy now—avoid the Rush,"[11] it warned. *The Diller Record* reported, "The little lady of the sky made quite a hit with the Diller folks. They showed much confidence in her ability to manipulate her plane and bring them back to earth safe and sound.[12] Off again—On again—Gone again."[13] Evelyn took up twenty passengers on August 11, 1938, and fifty-four the next day, just a beginning to the thousands who would eventually ride with her in the next two years.

Because of publicity received on the air mail flight nearly three months earlier, Evelyn was asked to ride "the side of 'Lindy' Wiemers red, white, and blue decorated 'letter' car."[14] She stood on the running board as the car followed the Pony Express and RFD (Rural Free Delivery), two other entries representing the Post Office in the seventy-five unit parade. Later that evening, Evelyn was "presented to the audience from the grandstand where she made a short address concerning aviation."[15]

Other activities at the Diller Picnic were representative of the twelve county fairs she would take in by September 29, 1938. They included afternoon band concerts, played under the cool shade of mature trees at the city park, and evenings of dancing, provided by popular radio orchestras such as Vern Wilson at KMMJ. A highly publicized attraction was Texas Jack and Lone Star Rose. Advertised as a trick rope and whip cracking specialist, the Original Texas Jack "whips his wife with a twenty foot blacksnake, and she likes it."[16] A three o'clock baseball game between Diller and neighboring communities provided an opportunity to show town loyalty, and a water fight between the Diller and Odell Fire Departments gave everyone who was in the vicinity of the wriggling, often unmanageable, black hoses a chance to cool off.

On August 20 and 21, 1938, the dates of the Bassett Rock County Fair, promotional advertisements included Evelyn's credentials:

> She has been flying for over three years, has about three hundred hours, and has carried over three hundred passengers.[17]

The Rock County Leader reported, "Miss Sharp is of pleasing personality, interested in outdoor sports, and is completely taken up with aviation which she plans as a career. In spite of the windy weather, she was kept busy here,"[18] flying sixty-three people on August 21.

In September, Evelyn took in several two-day county fairs. After a long, hot day of giving rides to people at the Platte County Fair in Lindsay, she flew up to Newman Grove "to try out our new swimming pool. A small, comely brunette, it could be seen flying was not her only accomplishment.... Although Miss Sharp tried out all the diving boards, she showed a little reluctance about diving from the top board. Maybe she can't stand high altitude.

"...Miss Sharp has won many honors in her field and has many admirers, she is very congenial and appears to be remarkedly level-headed, for which she is also to be admired."[19]

Evelyn told the reporter that even though her plane was old, it was still good, not having any "casualties yet."[20] From Lindsay, she flew to the Antelope County Fair in Neligh, back to Ord for three days of barnstorming, and on to Albion, Grand Island, North Loup, and Bassett. On September 22 and 23, she took in the two-day Cherry County Fair in Valentine, staying an extra four days because interest in sky-riding was high. She finished the month with appearances at Ord, Grand Island, and St. Paul.

On Wednesday, October 19, 1938, after two days of giving rides at the Holt County Fair in O'Neil and an additional five days thereafter, Evelyn penned a reply to a letter from a new friend in Kansas City. She had been corresponding since September with Glenn Buffington, a young man interested in aviation personalities because of a seventh grade English writing project some years earlier. Evelyn told him he could keep the full-page Rotogravure section from the September 18, 1938, edition of the *World-Herald*. Entitled "All Around Girl," it pictured her in hunting costume with her dog, Scottie, swimming at Anderson's Island, playing saxophone in summer band concerts, hitting tennis balls at the local court, and stitching her own clothes at a sewing machine. Working on the OX-5 engine, she was characterized as a grease monkey, wearing a one-piece white jumpsuit with red shoulder lapels and a white-starred bandanna kerchief tied over her hair. Another shot showed her hand-propping the wooden Fahlin propeller on the old Curtiss Robin. Today, that same propeller, serial number 3104, hangs above a display of Evelyn Sharp memorabilia in Dave Williams' fixed-base operation at the Ord airport.

In her letter to Glenn Buffington, Evelyn continued, "Made some good money, but it has gone for payments on the Robin. I still owe about $300 and cold weather is setting in. I have been ill for the past two days with asthma and I'm so weak that my writing doesn't look so good. I've had asthma ever since I was two. I would like to advertise the World's Fair, but my parents are not financially able to help and I don't know where to get backing or contracts. Am trying my best to get a flying job before winter sets in and I'll certainly hope I'll succeed."[21]

On October 31, 1938, Evelyn and her father flew into Fullerton, Nebraska, where the people of St. Peter's Church were celebrating the twenty-fifth anniversary of its founding. In an Ord High School "O" letter sweater, borrowed from one of the boys because girls were restricted from wearing them, Evelyn posed with several members of the Roman Catholic clergy and R. L. Cochran, the governor of Nebraska. She recorded another forty-four passengers in her register that day.

Six weeks later, on December 19, 1938, Evelyn wrote Glenn, telling him about a bill for new tires and a recent overhaul on the Curtiss Robin, costing $155. "No, I'm not planning any hop, no money to hop on—ha! ...I owe close to $400 now. Perhaps spring will bring flying jobs or even Santa Claus might slip one in my stocking."[22] With a common interest in flying and a growing respect for the friendship of one another, Evelyn and Glenn would share an ongoing correspondence for several years.

Elevators, Tires, & Rods

On Thursday, January 5, 1939, Evelyn and John Sharp flew to Broken Bow, Nebraska. It was from this airport in 1935 that Jack Jefford and his brother, Bill, had expanded their aviation services to Ord and other communities in north-central Nebraska. As Evelyn neared the landing strip north of town, remembrances of earlier flights with her former instructor in his four-passenger Stinson-Detroiter crossed her mind. In four months, she received a letter from Jefford stamped:

> Emergency Air Mail Flight
> Route N. 78185
> St. Lawrence Island to Nome[1]

Beneath was Jefford's signature as the pilot, his brother, Bill R. Jefford as copilot, and Ila M. Dougherty as postmaster. Later that year she read of his heroic rescue efforts when a small airliner on its 600-mile Nome-Fairbanks run was forced down by a broken oil line. On board was Bill Jefford's wife and their fifteen-month-old son. Dog teams scoured the ground while Jefford and his brother searched by air. "Jack sighted the stranded party...after flying into the teeth of a roaring Arctic storm. Unable to land because of rough terrain, he dropped food and warm sleeping bags in parachutes."[2] In her scrapbook, Evelyn pasted several articles recounting events which would make Jack Jefford's name a legend in bush country flying.

As Evelyn turned downwind at Broken Bow, perhaps wondering what it would be like to fly in the Alaskan bush, she imagined it had to be cooler than the nearly treeless Sandhills of Nebraska. She "hopped" twenty-seven more people on her first day at Broken Bow, but the second day was a "bad one,"[3] only three people showing up. The Curtiss Robin flew home early.

Looking forward to the weekend, Evelyn rose early on Saturday, the seventh of January. Although there were plans for a two-day stint of sky-riding in Kearney, she was more excited about spending some time at Kearney State Teachers College where her Lincoln friend, Chelys Mattley, was enrolled as a freshman. With limited opportunity to be around people her own age, Evelyn loved the good fellowship and gregariousness of the students on this small college campus. They welcomed her, too, many in awe of the panoramic view afforded them from the back seat of the old Curtiss Robin.

Evelyn told a college newspaper reporter she would like "to do advertising some day perhaps in the way of good will tours for a gas or an oil company.... I get plenty of fan mail, and I try to answer every letter I can. Most of them contain questions about flying although some write for my picture. One girl even asked for one of my buttons."[4] On a more personal note, she disclosed her preference for the nickname, Sharpie, rather than the more formal Miss Sharp or Evelyn. That name would identify her, especially in aviation circles, for the rest of her life.

One night in Case Hall Dormitory on the Kearney campus, Evelyn and Chelys reminisced about their trouble-making days when Chelys visited Ord. Most people in 1937 drove to the out-of-town high school football games, but not these two. They flew an airplane.

As a silver-winged tail-dragger approached the city limits of a small community where the game was to be played, Evelyn turned to make eye contact with her copilot. Chelys nodded and grinned, giving her seat belt a slight tug. Pushing the control stick forward, Evelyn put the Taylor Cub into a gentle dive. As the plane picked up speed, the sound of the propeller biting early evening air caused the heads of those in the stadium to turn skyward. "Nearly everyone recognized Evelyn Sharp's plane"[5] as she buzzed the full length of the field. Pulling the stick back, Evelyn brought the silver Cub around for a landing in a nearby open field. By that time ground transportation was on its way; sedans, pickups, and even coupes converged on the landing site. Oh, to be young, pretty, and a pilot.

Usually football games were finished well before dark, but on that particular night, the contest ran late. As Evelyn and Chelys approached Mortensen Field at Ord, light was still being reflected from the North Loup River, but the nearby grass field blended into the darkness below. With limited forward visibility, the girls stuck their heads out the windows, trying to judge their distance to the ground. After a couple of hard bounces on the main landing gear, the tail skid made contact, dragging the airplane to a stop. Evelyn vowed that was a situation she would never let happen again.

On February 4, 1939, Evelyn celebrated a flying anniversary with a small group of well-wishers; it had been four years since she had taken her first lesson in the Eaglerock Flyabout. Using the yellow elevator of her Curtiss Robin for a table, Evelyn cut a double-layer chocolate cake with four candles atop while chatting with an *Ord Quiz* reporter. She told him she had landed in thirty-one different towns, her barnstorming tours numbered twenty-three, and she had carried over one thousand persons since August 1 of last year. "She says that stunt flying is much more fascinating than safe flying. But," she added, "if you once get started stunt flying, you can't stop. And then, you're very likely to get your neck broken."[6] Spectators quickly became bored and expected the pilots to perform more dangerous and life-threatening stunts. Perhaps Evelyn remembered a Sunday afternoon air show in Grand Island when she was stunting in a small Taylor cabin ship. The craft, a little more than a powered glider, was difficult to handle in high winds, "but in Miss Sharp's expert hands was put through its paces in faultless style."[7] Some spectators evidently saw it a bit differently. They became impatient with the long delays between her stunts and laid on their car horns.

Still looking for a way to market her aviation skills in the business world, Evelyn and her mother drove out of Ord at four o'clock, the morning of March 1. Their destination was Fort Worth, Texas, where the Southwest Aviation Conference was playing host to many famous fliers and well-known aviation executives.

Conference registrants included Blanche Noyes, a speed racing personality who now served as a government air-marking supervisor and pilot for the Civil Aeronautics Board; Jimmy Doolittle and Roscoe Turner, speed pilots and holders of many international records; Jimmie Kolp, who had recently won a trophy at a spot-landing contest in Dayton, Ohio; and Jacqueline Cochran, winner of the famed 1938 Bendix Air Race Trophy. Jean La Rene Foote, a pioneer female commercial pilot, W. G. Skelly, oil executive and aircraft manufacturer, Al Williams, former Navy test pilot and now manager of the Gulf Oil Corporation aviation department, and Clinton Hester, administrator of Civil Aeronautics Authority were also in attendance.

Holding one of the miniature gas model planes used for a banquet decoration, Evelyn was the only delegate to rate front page photo coverage in the *Fort Worth Star-Telegram*.[8] She also received recognition in an article entitled, "Hen Party Is Held, By Those Who Flew The Coop." The "hens" referred to were members of the Ninety-Nines Club attending the conference. Instead of "Spring clothes, the up hairdo, or the servant problem, these women talk of hammerhead stalls, overcast fogs, and instrument boards. They're a tough group to glamorize because each presents herself as a normal woman who uses red fingernail polish, plays bridge, or makes her own clothes." The article reported Evelyn as making "every stitch she wears," but she was also characterized as the "baby flier,"[9] who, at nineteen, was one of thirty-four women in the United States holding licenses to pilot passengers for hire.

There were meetings and speeches, demonstrations and exhibits, and more meetings and speeches. On occasion, Evelyn slipped away and went joy-riding, but not in a car or even an airplane. This woman from a small town in Nebraska enjoyed riding the elevators in the prestigious Hotel Texas. In some respects, it gave her feelings similar to flight.

And then it was over. In the excitement of those speeches, exhibits, and interviews, one day had blended into another. For Evelyn, the conference had ended too quickly, yet it had focused her dream more firmly than ever to find her future in aviation. As they left the Hotel Texas, some of the women drove to the airport and flew their own planes homeward. Not so with Evelyn and Mary. Bad weather in Nebraska had forced them to drive. Now they pointed their car northward for the seven-hundred-mile trip home across Texas, Oklahoma, and Kansas. It was not an uneventful journey. Five times they stopped beside the road to fix flat tires. Those were mere inconveniences, quite manageable for a young woman who could refabric tail sections or wings, time valves, and replace rocker arms. In a moment, the jack was under the car and the wheel removed. The tire casing was pried loose on one side with tire irons, the tube inspected and patched. Then the tire pump was brought forth, the tire inflated, and the wheel bolted back on the car. It took about an hour. Of course, there were other solutions in those days when neighborliness and courtesy were not dead. Any number of "Galahads" traveling the road would have been more than happy to rescue two damsels in distress. Such was the case when connecting rods broke, not once, but twice. Even Evelyn had to await a tow into the next town for repairs. In addition, a leaky head gasket filled the crankcase with water. On these occasions, Evelyn and her mother cursed the "weather gods" which had forced them to leave the Curtiss Robin in Ord.

Evelyn continued to receive and accept requests for public appearances. Before leaving for Fort Worth, she had been an "extra on the stage" for the new movie, "Tail Spin," featuring Alice Faye, Constance Bennett, and Nancy Kelly.[10] A film glamorizing the lives of America's female racing pilots, it had premiered at the Liberty Theater in Loup City on February 20. Three weeks later, Evelyn spoke to the aviation committee of the Junior Chamber of Commerce in Lincoln. While in the city, she contacted the Lincoln Airplane and Flying School for information about getting an instructor's rerating. She learned of a new government program whereby civilians would teach men, and even women, to fly airplanes. Ironically, E. S. Sias, owner of Lincoln Airplane and Flying School, was one of eight veteran flyers called to Washington that May for a hearing on the proposal. Much to Evelyn's pleasure, she also learned the flying school had purchased her silver Taylor Cub on November 4, 1938. Evelyn took it up for twenty minutes on March 18, practicing takeoffs and landings. It must have felt good.

Recognizing the expense of continued maintenance on her Curtiss Robin and its limitation of flying just two passengers, Evelyn launched an effort to secure a different plane. In a letter written to the Stinson Aircraft Division of Aviation Manufacturing, she hoped "some deal might be worked out"[11] whereby she could get one of their new "105" Stinsons. Her letter was referred to the area sales representative, but nothing materialized. She had already lost the Cub because she could not make payments, and now the rep couldn't be convinced that experience, skill, and enthusiasm would make up for financial backing or collateral.

Before Evelyn left Ord for the aviation conference in Fort Worth, Emil Daake, a sign painter and part-time player in a Kearney dance band, heard her interviewed by Grey Sterling at a local radio station. Having seen the words, "Phillips 66," in the sky overhead, he wrote to Evelyn, suggesting she consider "sky-writing" for one of the oil companies. His artistic caricature of Evelyn on several pieces of stationery and outside covers of envelopes caught John Sharp's eye. [12]

The first part of March, Emil Daake came to Ord to discuss his idea of a portable dance floor. Pulled by two trucks, the painted, outside walls would advertise Evelyn as Ord, Nebraska's, Sky-Rider. A scaled drawing designed by John and drawn by Emil was on paper by April 7, 1939. A three-dimensional scale model was built later, but the project went no further, there being no money to finance it. In a letter which Emil Daake wrote to Mr. Sharp and family on March 26, he philosophized. "It's pretty hard as to what to decide, or do these days, it's all a gamble, but the old saying is, To have tried and failed is better, than to not have tried at all, and that is true."

"I am building 'air castles' every day, but one must keep on trying, to reach our goal, keep a stiff upper lip, chin up...."[13]

With payments still due on the Curtiss Robin, Evelyn knew she needed to get an early start on the barnstorming season. Nebraska winter weather did not generate much interest in sky-riding. On April 2, 1939, off a field west of the Loup City Fairgrounds, Evelyn

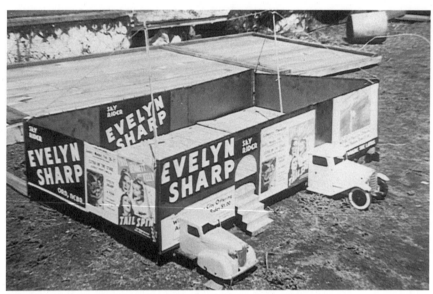

"Another 'Air Castle'?" Emil Daake's portable dance floor, 1939

"hopped" fifty people. A three-day stop in Broken Bow netted one hundred fifty more, and a day in Greeley added an additional thirty-six names to her register. By the end of the month, she had flown in Ord and Spalding, completed a three-day stop in Superior and a six-day stint in Grand Island. On April 30, 1939, Evelyn recorded seventy more names in her register.

Once again, Irma Leggett, associate editor of *The Ord Quiz*, had kind words for Evelyn. "It reminds me Ord gets a lot of dandy publicity through the jaunts of Miss Evelyn Sharp—not only is she a good little flyer, a native daughter of Ord, a corking little swimmer, an all-around girl, but a very attractive miss as well. She has a pleasing personality, and I have never yet seen a picture of her that I thought did Evelyn justice."[14]

Evelyn decided she needed a new picture, but probably not for the reasons Irma expressed. Current handbills and newspaper advertisement featured the Taylor Cub, which she no longer had, and a picture taken of her when a senior in high school. For the new photograph, Evelyn borrowed a boy's Ord High "O" letter sweater with four stripes on the left sleeve. Like her, he too had letters for each of his high school years. With her left hand in the side pocket of her slacks and her right hand on top of the fuselage, the local photographer positioned her beside the inscription on the Curtiss Robin:

"Miss EVELYN SHARP
Nation's Youngest Aviatrix Government Com. License 34711"

She smiled, and Stanley Lumbard snapped the picture. Printed on either a light-green or lemon-yellow colored paper, that photo served as a memento on a tear-away ticket for a ride in her airplane. In 1939, a ride with Evelyn Sharp cost $1. An exception was made for high school girls; they paid seventy-five cents.

"Good For A Sky-Ride, a ticket and token of remembrance," 1938, 1939

Evelyn was not the only one to get her picture in the paper. Her dog, Scottie, was featured as one of Ord's well-known canines whose owner always paid her dog tax on time. Dubbed a "flying fool," he "likes to fly almost as well as his mistress."[15] A constant companion, Scottie's favorite sleeping place was in the plane. In the side-by-side rear passenger seats of the Robin, he lay flat on his back, with all four legs pointing straight up. Evelyn got a kick out of "dumping" the power and watching Scottie float off the seats. Scrambling to regain his equilibrium, he gave Evelyn a dirty look and then promptly returned to his former position. Occasionally, Scottie would open one eye to check on his mistress.[16]

The first of May, Evelyn shared top billing in Ravenna with a $1,000 rooster named Tippy Tin. Raised on a farm near Omaha, Tippy had accidentally discovered a means of keeping chicken eggs clean which resulted in a nationwide recommendation from the chicken industry. If you put a pan of calcium in front of each hen's nest, the mineral would adhere to the chicken's feet and be left behind in the nest. Scottie was not impressed with Tippy's credentials, especially when the rooster took his first ride in an airplane and he was left on the ground.

On Friday, May 7, Evelyn, John, and Scottie flew to Goodland, Kansas, for a weekend of sky-riding. In her logbook, under "Remarks," she wrote "First long X-C (cross-country) trip." Sunday evening, appearing on the stage at the Sherman Theater, she was introduced as "the celebrated girl pilot who has brought fame to her home town, Ord, and to her home state, Nebraska. Aviation experts consider her another A. E. [Amelia Earhart] and are grooming her to fill the place in American aviation made vacant by the untimely death of the world-famous aviatrix of Kansas."[17] That was probably news to Evelyn, but she thanked them for their laudatory comments.

The next day, Goodland entertained the celebrated Glenn Cunningham, the world's fastest miler, and Evelyn Sharp, a "schoolgirl aviatrix."[18] She flew an air show on Cunningham Day, and later, in the afternoon, snapped a picture of the runner crossing the race finish line. But the more-favored snapshot included the three of them—herself, Glenn Cunningham, and her best "boyfriend,"[19] Scottie.

The airworthiness certificate issued to the Curtiss Robin, serial number 567, was to expire on May 15, 1939.[20] On her way back from Goodland, she stopped at Deats Aviation on Arrasmith Field to get the aircraft ready for relicensing. Knowing it would take some time, John left Evelyn and Scottie in Grand Island and caught a bus home.

On May 12, 1939, Evelyn wrote to Glenn Buffington, apologizing for not having answered his letter sooner. "You'll think I have been flying with my nose too high. At present I am in Grand Island getting my plane ready for relicensing. I sure hope it goes through. Please excuse this writing, as I'm doing it on my knee at the airport. Don't make any nose-high turns!"[21]

The Curtiss Robin would be relicensed, but not without cost. On May 24, 1939, the following ad appeared in *The Ord Quiz*:

FURNITURE FOR SALE

Owing to my ship needing a new tail, I am offering my apartment furniture for sale to the highest bidder on the lot north of John's New Cafe, Saturday, May 27. 1 pm. 1 3/4 bed, mattress and springs, Jenny Lind Bed, mattress and springs, white dresser, large mirror, large chiffonier (walnut), 2 piece over-stuffed suite, floor lamp, table lamp, 2 rocking chairs, 2 library tables, 2 9X12 congoleum rugs.

EVELYN SHARP[22]

The Grasshopper

*I*n Grand Island, still waiting for the empennage (tail section) repairs to be completed, Evelyn flew with Clarence McIntosh, who had recently purchased a new Aeronca for $2,500 and was accumulating hours to qualify for a private license. She also drew upon her swimming skills and presented a program for Boy Scout Troop 116 at the Grand Island Congregational Church. "An expert swimmer," she demonstrated "several holds and methods of handling drowning persons."[1]

Since the airplane's airworthiness certificate had expired by the time the tail work was finished, Evelyn was issued a one-day-only ferry permit for a June 3 inspection flight to Lincoln. The aircraft logbook she carried summarized the new periodic inspection report:

Fuselage and Empenage—Fuselage OK-Empenage OK and Painted Rudder recovered-New rudder hinge pin.

Top front flipper cables installed

Engine Installation—OK Installed new temperature gauge

Main Plane—Found Spars and Bearings OK

Weld Right gas tank. new aileron cables.

Alignment of Propeller—OK

Remarks—New Wheel bushings installed.

Inspected by—J.J. Macha A&E16087[2]

The old Curtiss Robin, with an engine time of 519.25 hours, a propeller time of 259 hours, and a total aircraft time of 891.40 hours, passed the critical inspection report. Evelyn quietly breathed a sigh of relief.

By June 8, 1939, Evelyn was back in the business of flying. She "hopped" passengers in the Grand Island and Hastings area, then moved west into Holdrege. Newspaper ads in the *Holdrege Daily Citizen* advertised her arrival on June 15: "Has Carried Over 1800 Passengers In Over 500 Hours Of Flying. Miss Sharp Will Carry Passengers Over Holdrege And The Surrounding Countryside."[3]

On June 19, a special greeting committee awaited Evelyn's arrival at the Schmeeckle landing strip northwest of Cozad. Verna Nielsen, the daughter of Edward Nielsen who composed a poem for Evelyn when she soloed in 1936, was celebrating her sixteenth birthday. Wanting to show off her special house guest for the week, Verna had brought eight of her birthday party friends to the airfield. She remembers yet today how disgusted she was when some refused to fly because their parents had said "it was too dangerous."[4] Evelyn's dog, Scottie, proved to be a greater attraction for them.

At the age of eighteen, Edward Nielsen had immigrated, all by himself, from the Danish lowlands to gently rolling plains in the Platte River Valley. A flag-waver, he sometimes exhibited a display of American patriotism that was embarrassing to his children. But, he had a "lot of faith in the young people of this country and did not pass up the opportunity to put those he deemed deserving in his column in the *Dawson County Herald*. He was the only one around Cozad that had the vision to know what a really special person Evelyn Sharp was."[5] One day on their way back from Hastings, Evelyn asked her passenger if he wanted to go above the clouds. Putting into practice his belief in her skills, Edward Nielsen, in his Danish-accented voice shouted forward, "Evelyn, I'll go where you go."[6] Both of them understood how much more those words really meant.

That summer, Edward Nielsen gave his young daughter permission to barnstorm with Evelyn. Verna remembers her as "very busi-

"Not Enough Milk," Evelyn used this picture to show Ray Johnson her rib bone deformities, 1939

ness-like, very feminine, well-coordinated, and unflaunting,"[7] but her most vivid memory is their eating lunch at the local cafes. The very first time away from home, Verna looked forward to drinking chocolate malts and eating candy bars. She can still see Evelyn, sitting beside her on a counter stool, eating her usual tuna fish sandwich and drinking a large glass of milk. Verna did not know that Evelyn bore rib bone deformities from rickets because she lacked milk in her earlier diet.

Cozad received a much-needed two inches of rain on June 20 and 21, 1939, but the skies had cleared by Thursday noon and Evelyn recorded another fifty names in her register that day. David Stevens, a reporter from the *Cozad Local*, climbed aboard the Curtiss Robin on Friday afternoon, but not before he took what would later be a front page photo of Evelyn, hand-propping the wooden propeller. Taking several pictures of the residential and business districts, he also snapped aerial views of the work being done on the Tri-County Irrigation Project southwest of Cozad, an undertaking similar to the one being built in the North Loup Valley. The photos were published in several editions of the paper, with captions such as "Can you find your place?" creating much discussion within the community. The series concluded with "Cozad is a darned good-looking town from the air."[8]

On Sunday, June 25, 1939, Evelyn flew into Lexington, but mechanical problems with the engine would disrupt her plans for just a two-day stop. Frank Beran, a local garage owner "having extensive training in repairmanship,"[9] had the only set of OX-5 valve grinding tools in the state, with the exception of Omaha. Frank had owned several airplanes in the past and once had flown Evelyn's Robin, NC551N. By Thursday, he had ground six of the eight valves on the 90-hp radial engine. She would return in two weeks to have the engine checked and adjusted.

On the short flight to Gothenburg, Evelyn wondered about her recently advertised flights to view the Tri-County Project. The twenty-five-mile tour, giving local residents a chance to see construction of the much-talked-about Kingsley Dam, cost $2 and that was a lot of money for most people in 1939. Unbeknown to Evelyn, a seventeen-year-old farm boy had been at work in the fields, shocking wheat and doing whatever he could to earn money that summer. An uncle in Ord told "wonderful stories" of this young woman pilot, and he was enamored with pictures of her in *The Gothenburg Times.*[10]

As Mearl McNeal waited for the plane to land on a field west of town, he was not sure what to do, much less what to say. Some fifty-three years later, Mearl unabashedly admits, "I was in love with her."[11] When Evelyn stepped out of the plane, his heart missed a beat. She was prettier than he had imagined. Small, maybe five-feet-four in height, she had dark-brown eyes, and her brunette hair was tied under a scarf. He started toward the plane, then hesitated. She saw him, smiled, and motioned for him to come on.

Making sure his seat belt was fastened, she continued to chat in her happy-go-lucky manner. As they taxied through the knee-high pasture grass to the takeoff area, Mearl was glad she left the windows down. The breeze was refreshing. He thought about how hard he had worked to have money for this, but he already knew it was worth it.

After a 360-degree visual check, Evelyn pushed the throttle for-

"Waiting For A Sky-Ride," Gothenburg, Nebraska, June 29, 1939

ward, the plane slowly gathering momentum. Picking up speed, she pushed the stick gently ahead. Suddenly Evelyn began to fidget. With one hand on the stick, she undid the top button of her blouse. Mearl was aghast and tried to look straight ahead. But out of the corner of his eye, he saw her pull back on the stick and with the other hand retrieve a grasshopper from inside her blouse. When they reached altitude, she turned to the side and asked where he would like to go. Mearl doesn't recall his response. He only remembers she was wearing a pretty blue blouse.

On July 3, 1939, Evelyn flew out of Gothenburg and pointed the nose of her plane to the east. She had recorded carrying ninety passengers in the appropriate column of her logbook for the previous day. Writing "good day" under "Remarks," Evelyn had no way of knowing that number would be her personal best for flying the most people in a single day. Adjusting the trim for best-rate-of-climb speed, she and Scottie reached their cruising altitude in a matter of minutes. At 5,600 feet, the air was smooth as glass. It would be a beautiful flight.

The next stop on the tour was Curtis, Nebraska, where the local fire department sponsored their annual Fourth of July celebration. She flew sixty people that afternoon, but decided to leave early the next day for a "plane check-up"[12] in Grand Island. Early airplane engines needed constant tune-ups to keep them running. She recorded "nice trip" in her logbook.

In the next five days, Evelyn flew at Shelton and Burwell before stopping in Lexington for a one-day check and engine adjustment with Frank Beran, her airplane mechanic. She recorded the landing strip at Shelton as "stubble field." Because of the drag, it took more time to get airborne in this kind of field, but it certainly shortened the landing roll when the tail skid made contact with the stubble.

From July 13 through 16, Evelyn was scheduled to fly at Bertrand. H. E. Waters, editor of *The Bertrand Herald*, traded ads and publicity so his teenage daughters could fly. He wrote, "The one and only Evelyn Sharp soloed down out of the western skies on Wednesday afternoon of this week, and after searching about for a short while, lit in the Opitz stubble field just east of Jesse Dyers."[13] Maxine and Twyla Waters were in awe of this woman who was called the "Queen of the Air."[14] They could not imagine what it must be like to fly a plane and have so many people know you. John Sharp, who followed the barnstorming tour in his pick-up, always tried to make arrangements for Evelyn to stay with a family. Years later, Maxine reflects, "He probably thought it would keep her from running around."[15] But this didn't seem to stop Evelyn. As soon as John left, Evelyn headed downtown with Scottie right by her side. "It was late when she came up those stairs that night; she couldn't keep Scottie quiet."[16]

In a few days Evelyn was lying on a cot in the shade of her airplane wing, waiting for some prospective customers at Cambridge. She wrote to Glenn Buffington.

> I have 600 hours now and have carried over 3,500 passengers—am supporting myself and my mother and dad and have one fellow working for me. The last three days have been my worst days. The most I've taken in one day has been $90.

> We have had some tricky weather the last few days. Dust storms and what not but mostly hot weather. If my plane will just hold out it will be o.k. But, if it doesn't I just don't know what I'll do. I'd like to get a job flying and get a

straight salary. This worry of hit or miss gets me. You got to just keep plugging along, I guess. I am planning to start south in the late fall and barnstorm my way into Texas. Send a letter to Ord and it will be forwarded to me.[17]

In mid-summer, Evelyn received a letter from L. E. Tyson, State Airport Engineer for the Nebraska Aeronautics Commission. It planned to more than double the landing facilities within the state, and her barnstorming tours had made her one of the more credible authorities on Nebraska aviation and airport needs. He asked her to recommend future landing facilities "where they are most needed by pilots and where use will be made of them. They must be located where needed for local activity, where they are valuable for emergency fields along lines of air traffic flow, and of value due to their relative location to other airports."[18] She agreed to make recommendations.

From Cambridge, Evelyn flew to McCook on July 20. She spent four days giving "pleasure rides" and doing spot landings. Part of private flying instruction and often an event of competition when pilots are gathered, spot landings require pilots to use judgment and skill in landing an aircraft on a predetermined runway location. Abeam the approach end of the runway, the pilot cuts the airplane's power. From that point on, the pilot must use judgment, based on current effect of wind, temperature, and humidity, to skillfully adjust airplane control surfaces. The object of the contest is to set the plane down on a spot, without use of power. Evelyn was very good in spot-landing contests.

On July 24, 1939, under the auspices of Clinch Flying Service, Evelyn landed at North Platte for a five-day tour. A KGNF radio promotion encouraged everyone to come out to the airport and "satisfy your airmind"[19] by taking a trip over the city. Hoping to increase business, John Clinch also offered flight instruction for $2 per lesson and advertised his skills as an aviation mechanic.

The old Curtiss Robin was running poorly again. On the twenty-fifth, Clinch noted repairs in the engine logbook:

20 hour check on motor, repaired carburetor throttle, 1 new push rod, motor washed, 2 valves ground, 1 new water

hose, 2 new gas hoses, Mag [magneto] checked, Points cleaned, Valves adj. Oil changed. John A. Clinch A&E11888.

In the daily inspection report in the aircraft logbook, Evelyn added, "Stabilizer hinge fitting adj. and oiled. Shocks down [springs broken]. Wheels loose."[20]

Curtiss Robin struts had earned a reputation for breaking. In landing, a too stiff strut collapsed when the weight of the plane settled down upon it, and a too soft strut provided no cushioning. A strut which bottomed out, also broke. In between was nearly impossible to find. John Clinch knew there had to be a better spring, and like most men of his day he took pride in finding ways to fix things. Experimenting with a variety of farm implement springs, John eventually found an aviation use for the seat springs from a John Deere tractor seat. He reflects, "Curtiss Robin struts worked forever after that."[21]

John Clinch showed Evelyn how to fix engine blow-by, a condition which resulted when piston rings were worn or valve ports were pitted. To decrease the escape of engine gases, she reached in through exhaust ports and put compound on the valve seats, working it by hand, back and forth. In other words, she was grinding the valves without taking the cylinder apart. Not acceptable by Federal Aviation Administration standards today, it kept Evelyn and many other pilots flying in 1939.

On Saturday the twenty-ninth of July, Mary came to North Platte to spend a few days with her daughter and renew a friendship with a woman she had not seen in twenty years. Evelyn would come to know this woman as Aunt Elsie; Mary knew her to be Evelyn's birth mother, Elsie Crouse Rick. Widowed only two months before, Aunt Elsie flew several times with her birth daughter that week. In a letter, some three years later, Evelyn would write of the fond memories she had of those times.[22]

In another letter, Evelyn wrote to Glenn Buffington telling him how hard Mary worked. While Evelyn and John were on the barnstorming circuit, Mary was in Ord, running John's New Cafe at 125 N. 15th. Court records showed she had filed several complaints against men who had tried to beat their room and board bills. Most of the time, the men had no money and were sentenced to jail. By the end of

September, they had lost John's New Cafe, and Mary hired on as a cook at Ben's Grill in Ord.

On August 1, 1939, Evelyn landed her Curtiss Robin, sporting newly installed John Deere tractor seat springs, on the Robert Holmes farm, a mile north of Trenton. She had flown in for the Seventeenth Massacre Canyon Pow-Wow, a celebration commemorating the 1873 Native American battle which ultimately broke the strength and spirit of the Pawnee Nation.

Evelyn shared top billing with Jimmie Lynch and his trained crew of "Death Dodgers."[23] Direct from the New York's World Fair, they flirted with death while putting their stock cars through "crashes, spins, upsets, jumps, etc."[24] After the show, Evelyn and her parents wandered the brightly-lighted midway, often stopping for their daughter to give someone an autograph. As the spectacular Thearle-Duffield fireworks display[25] signaled the end to another celebration, perhaps Evelyn thought how nice it was to be a family again.

Flippers O.K., Elevators Aren't

*B*ack out on tour, Evelyn spent four days in Imperial and then returned to Shelton for their Fall Festival. On August 16, 1939, she again wrote to Glenn Buffington.

> Well, I haven't had such good luck lately—motor troubles mostly. [Two more valves had been ground, a new carburetor installed, and new manifold bolts replaced.] I've gone in the hole quite a bit, but guess if I just keep plugging away the best I can, maybe I'll get on top. I'm still trying to get a job and capitalize on my youth, but so far no luck. By gosh, I'd better do it soon or I won't be the youngest! I sure would like to scrape up the dough to go to the Cleveland Air Races, but I have my doubts if it will be possible.[1]

After a tour at Bassett, she returned to Lexington so that Frank Beran could check the engine, repair a leaky radiator, and install new hose connections. Flying to Stapleton where she would "hop" seventy passengers on one day of a three-day tour, she then moved on to Arnold, eventually returning to Lexington for the Dawson County Fair and Rodeo the week of August 27. On September 2, she wrote the following to the Civil Aeronautics Authority in Washington, DC:

> On August 31, 1939, at Lexington, Nebr. I damaged the elevators & the tail of my fuselage on my Curtiss Robin-No.

"Best Friends," Evelyn and Scottie,
Lexington, Nebraska,
August 1939

N.C. 551N. I was taking off of a quarter mile stubble field with 2 passengers. When I taxied to the south end of the field to take off north there was a slight breeze but when I got ready to take off, spectators said the breeze had died down. As I took off I hit a soft spot which slowed me down considerably. I used all my field and there was a small irrigation ditch at the north end. I had to get over it so I lifted over & of course lost a lot of flying speed. I only had enough to cross the ditch. In the next field there were tall weeds varying from 2 to five feet tall. I couldn't nose the plane down to get flying speed because the wheels and prop would have caught & nosed me over so I held it to the top of the weeds & the tail skid drug in the tops of the weeds & pulled me down.

I stopped the motor & got out & the weeds had pulled the elevators right back [Evelyn drew a picture to show this]. The flippers are o.k. yet and also the vertical fin & rudder but the elevators are not. It pulled a few of the bracings out where the leading edge spar goes through the fuselage. That was the only damage. My passengers didn't even know anything was wrong.

I am going to have the work done at Grand Island or Lincoln & I will have new elevators put on. If the field had been clear of weeds I would have made it easily.

I hope this report is satisfactory. No one hurt and only damaged the horizontal tail surfaces.

> Sincerely,
> Evelyn Sharp
> Commercial license No. 34711

I've been flying 4 and one-half years & have 700 hours flying time & this is the first time I've ever damaged a plane.[2]

The "flippers" Evelyn mentioned were the movable parts of the horizontal tail surface which raise or lower the tail in flight. These were not damaged. However, the immovable part of that surface had been torn from the fuselage. It would be some time before NC551N flew again.

"Weeds Rip Elevators," Curtiss Robin 551N, Lexington, Nebraska, August 31, 1939

Evelyn kept her scheduled appearance for the twenty-fourth annual Eustis Corn Days celebration on September 7, 8, and 9. Although her log book recorded no hours flown at that time, one of her passengers, the nine-year-old son of aviation enthusiast Hugo Boerkircher, remembers the day well. It was hot, well over a hundred by noon. As the plane rumbled down the pasture runway, Roger Boerkircher, who was not able to see out over the cockpit instrument panel, wondered "if they would ever get off the ground."[3] (High temperatures make for longer takeoff rolls because the air is less dense.) At the end of the ride, Evelyn handed Roger a picture postcard, the one showing Scottie hanging out the window of the silver Taylor Cub. On the back, Hugo Boerkircher wrote the following:

Roger Boerkircher
First airplane Ride
at age 9, fair
at Eustis,
Sept 7, 1939
By Pilot Evelyn
Sharp from Ord Nebr
age 19, 1939[4]

Another young person, eleven-year-old Patty Baer, would have also remembered that day, flying several times, no doubt free. Evelyn stayed at Patty's home, northwest of the landing strip, just across the road. Urcell Baer Bartruff, Patty's mother, remembers Evelyn being "a very pleasant" young woman who was always up early. In response to what she wanted for breakfast, most often it was something like "What you have is fine." "She didn't eat very much," Urcell recalls.[5] Patty idolized this woman pilot who slept in the small, narrow guest room of the large, two-story frame farmhouse. Even though there was an eight-year difference in ages, Evelyn and Patty would keep a life-long correspondence with each other.

On Sunday, September 24, 1939, a handbill for an air show, sponsored by the Harlan Iowa Aviation Club, advertised Evelyn in "aerial acrobatics"[6] at the Westrope Airport. Perhaps her program included the popular impersonation of a Little Orphan Annie who was about to take her first airplane flight. With hair pulled up into side pigtails, the little girl would run across the open field and crawl into a plane whose propeller was already turning. Several 360-degree turns and an erratic takeoff would convince the crowd the airplane was out of control. Only a few feet above the runway, the wings pitched and rolled, while the spectators, now on their feet, would be yelling and shouting for more.[7]

Again, Evelyn's logbook entries are unclear, but in a letter to Glenn Buffington on October 4, she wrote of her return from the airshow at Harlan and nearby Des Moines. Records showed Evelyn Sharp to be the new owner of another Curtiss Robin, a 1929 OX-5, which had been delivered to Des Moines for sale purposes on August 30. A letter from Clarke Conway, Assistant Chief, Records Division, attested the sale took place on September 27, 1939.[8]

The next entry in her logbook was October 5, "hopping" passengers at Cozad. Evelyn flew over to Gothenburg the following day, front page headlines in *The Gothenburg Times* reporting use of two planes for flights over the countryside and Tri-County Project. The Curtiss Robins, sister ships of "Wrong Way" Corrigan's plane which "mistakenly" crossed the Atlantic, "are licensed and airworthy. She has just returned from Iowa where she spent time stunting with Allen Bros. Airshow."[9] George Kealey, a licensed pilot from the Holdrege area, had probably flown her old Curtiss Robin into Gothenburg. Evelyn was flying her new one, a slate-blue Robin, NC8325.

Later, Evelyn, her father, and George Kealey judged a model airplane contest sponsored by the Harvest Festival Committee of the Chamber of Commerce. Two levels of competition were offered: Class A for six to twelve-year-old boys, and Class B for thirteen to eighteen-year-olds. First prize in each category was $2 cash, second prize was $1 cash, third, seventy-five cents, fourth, fifty cents, and fifth place prize was a twenty-five cent model airplane. Evelyn charged school-age children seventy-five cents to "sky-ride" with her.[10]

Evelyn and George Kealey flew into Kearney on October 9, 1939, for a ten-day tour. Chelys Mattley, her Lincoln friend, was still at Kearney State Teachers College. On one of their flights above town, they took several pictures of the college campus, the swimming pool, rock garden and recreation park, and, of course, the boys' dorm. Although the *Kearney State College Newspaper* reported Evelyn would stay for the fifty-first Homecoming football game and all-school dance,[11] she flew northeast to Ravenna instead.

That three-day barnstorming tour was cut short because of mechanical problems, but not before Irene Schmale and her twenty-year-old daredevil friends took their first airplane ride. With nothing in her life more exciting than a glass of pale 3.2 beer, Irene and her girlfriend, Lyda Walters, decided they would fly with this young woman pictured in *The Ravenna News*. As Evelyn banked her plane in a 360-degree turn over the Schmale farm home, Irene chuckled. She could hear her mother's scolding voice already, but Irene didn't care. Some fifty-two years later, she still recalls the reproachful words of her mother: "What a foolish way to spend a Depression dollar. What if you had crashed?" Irene thought for a moment. Then she looked at her mother. With a slight upward turn at the corners of her mouth, Irene solemnly replied, "I'd be in pieces."[12] Her mother didn't laugh.

The last entry in Evelyn's logbook for NC8325 was on October 19, 1939, at Ravenna. On January 6, 1940, she wrote a letter to the Records Division of the Civil Aeronautics Authority apologizing for not having completed the proper paperwork for the bill of sale. "I have been away for quite sometime and the ship NC8325 has been stored in the hangar at Grand Island. Thank you so much for being patient. I'll answer immediately next time. I wish you a successful New Year."[13]

Within a month, the forms were in order, and Aircraft Registry recorded her as owner. However, the airworthiness certificate would expire on February 1, 1940. It was never renewed.

In Lexington, Frank Beran had installed new cylinders, pistons, and valves, replaced valve springs, wrist pins, rods, and rings, and linebored the new bearings. The engine on NC551N had been completely rebuilt. On October 20, 1939, Evelyn flew it to Grand Island where Stover Deats "signed the work off."[14]

Evelyn wrote Glenn on the eighteenth of November:

I've been in Lincoln since Oct. 31, trying to get some welding done and some of my tail surface recovered—not mine, my plane's—they are so doggone slow!...I'm planning to stay in Grand Island at the Old Airport, so if you ever decide on a cross-country, drop in....As far as I know, my southern winter plans have been cancelled.[15]

Sometime before December 18, Evelyn returned to Grand Island. She left NC551N in Lincoln.[16]

I Wish I Had A Brother

*B*y January, Evelyn realized that her adventurous life as a cow-pasture, barnstorming pilot had probably come to an end. For some time, she had been thinking about the new civilian aviation training program and making inquiries as to getting a flight instructor's rerating. Wanting advice, she wrote Glenn Buffington. Evelyn would express her appreciation for his "swell encouragement"[1] in a letter written later.

The Civilian Pilot Training Program (CPTP) was a unique government venture taking aviation into every corner of the country. Originally planned to stimulate private flying, its benefits soon extended to establishing a reserve of knowledgeable pilots for the armed forces. That was no accident. Many in Washington and, in particular, the Army Air Force thought of "Our armed force of that year (1939) as more fiction than force."[2] Hitler was on the march in Europe, and if the United States were pushed into war, our small number of military pilots would put us at a distinct disadvantage. But too-recent memories of World War I gave rise to a strong feeling of isolationism in America. Thus was born the civilian "Putt-Putt Air Force,"[3] so named because of the low horsepower aircraft. Its originators hoped the requirement of at least one woman in each class would stave off the warmonger cries. Evelyn just hoped there was a place for her in this mass air-training program.

Worries took their toll on Evelyn's health. On January 9, 1940, she suffered an asthmatic attack, the worst in five years. A doctor was summoned several times during the early morning hours to 385 and ½ N. Walnut in Grand Island. He administered four different hypos; Evelyn could not breathe. But by January 16, there were only remnants of an asthmatic cough. A break in the cold weather gave both her and Scottie a chance to get back outdoors to play in the snow together. Rolling, running, and jumping in snow drifts, Scottie chased his mistress when she pelted him with snowballs. The large, blue-black dog often knocked down his 114-pound friend; she thought him "cute."[4]

On January 17, Evelyn shared some very personal feelings with Glenn.

> "You know, I wish I had a brother I could talk to to help me along. You see, I'm an only child & I'm trying to support my mother & my dad & my dad's getting childish & mother has never been around much & don't know much about business. I don't know many people I can talk to & ask advice 'cause they're all so engrossed in their own problems. That's why, if I had an older brother, I could talk to him & perhaps he'd help me to have courage to keep going till I get where I want to. You know, I get so discouraged sometimes I don't know which way to turn. I guess I'm in one of those moods now or I wouldn't be writing this. I don't know why I'm writing it to you of all people. I guess 'cause you write such interesting letters that I feel I can talk to you. You know, I sit & talk to Scottie lots. He seems to understand exactly what I say, but you know, he can't answer. Oh, phooey, did you ever know anyone as goofy as me. Wait till we meet. You'll think I'm the goofiest little brat in the country."[5]

Glenn and Evelyn would never meet, but if they had, he undoubtedly would have thought differently. He has kept every letter she wrote him.

While in Grand Island, Evelyn spent part of her day at the airport. There was some thought of "starting up"[6] the Old Airport, the one two miles southeast of the new Arrasmith Field, but that required investment money, none of which she had or could ever hope to raise.

In the evenings when John was working at the Old Airport Cafe, Evelyn kept busy. She sewed herself a blouse, then added a hood and a straight skirt to match. She studied Tex Rankin's aeronautical manuals for getting a primary instructor rating, "scouted" dances on Saturday nights, and during the week frequented a popular roller skating rink.

The Cave Roller Rink, built beneath a silver, railroad diner car, became a favorite pastime for Evelyn. She soon became acquainted with Ray Johnson, the rink's sixteen-year-old manager, who invited her to his home for dinner. Twenty-year-old Evelyn and Ray's mother, Carrie Johnson, a struggling single parent of two teenage boys, enjoyed the company of each other. Evelyn returned on several occasions to share the traditional Danish dish, Fricadiller, a meatball mixture of hamburger, onions, and crumbled crackers. She enjoyed this family atmosphere; perhaps it reminded her of home and of her own mother who had stayed in Ord to cook at Ben's Grill.

Ray knew how important his job was in helping his mother meet family expenses. He was always at the rink early, making sure he did the best that he could. From the exterior wooden stairs behind the second-floor rear apartment at 210 N. Wheeler, Evelyn could see groups of people already beginning to congregate at The Cave. That night Ray did not see them. His thoughts had returned to the kitchen, still trying to figure out what had happened in there a few minutes before. They had just finished drying the last of the dinner dishes when he saw Evelyn reach up and pull the chain on the old bare light bulb. The next thing he felt was her kiss. Fifty-three years later, Ray still remembers that kiss and his sense of bewilderment.[7]

The Cave was a favorite hang-out for young people in Grand Island. Eventually the line of anxious skaters would extend from the basement skating area, back up the stairs, out the front door, and down the sidewalk. Downstairs, the skate boys, quickly tightened the nuts in the metal clamp skates before the skaters moved onto the floor. In 1940, an evening of skating cost ten cents; very few people owned their own shoe skates.

A whistle blew, directing attention to a shadow box signboard in the corner, which announced changes in music tempo. The lights dimmed, and as the music of "What'll I Do?" found its way through the sound system, a silver ball, with its multifaceted edges, slowly began to revolve. Ray looked for Evelyn. Spotting her, he maneuvered around the other skaters to join his pupil in the center of the floor. The signboard read: Waltz Skate. Bragging of only one fall the night before, Evelyn crossed her fingers for good luck. She wanted to do well.

Later that evening, Evelyn waited for Ray to finish his work before locking up the rink for the night. He didn't want her walking home by herself to an empty apartment three blocks away. On the way, they chatted about the events of the evening and how excited she was to have learned to skate backwards. Ray listened and smiled to himself. He, too, was pleased and would keep pictures she gave him, as well as the memory of a quick kiss.[8]

On March 28, 1940, Evelyn penned another letter to Glenn.

Our weather has been perfectly outrageous, today was terrible, rain and hail. You remember me telling you that we lived across the street from the Old Airport?

Well, something told me to look out the window and what should I see but a yellow Cub on its nose. I tore across the road, under a fence and over a mesh, five-foot fence and to the plane. The pilot and I were both hanging onto it when help got there in a car. After struggling with the plane in the high wind, we finally got to the hangar. One wingtip dug into the ground during the time we were trying to make it to the hangar. Both wingtips were slightly bent and one prop blade broken and a bewildered pilot from Avoca, Iowa. He came to our house and waited three hours, then took a bus to Omaha. He is going to send out a prop and let me fly his plane for a month. It's only a 40-HP Cub—not much power, but it's something to fly. I don't know how I got over that five-foot fence so fast. I tried it later and could hardly make it.[9]

When the wooden propeller blade for the Piper Cub arrived, Ray's mother asked her older son to help Evelyn put it on. The task of tightening bolts while keeping the prop positioned properly required two people. Wayne Jorgensen obliged.[10] On April 18, 1940, Evelyn flew the Cub into Lincoln, probably for an inspection. She spent the next two days getting some dual instruction and practicing commercial maneuvers at Lindbergh and Arrow Airfields in Lincoln. Her license was to expire on May 15, 1940, and she needed to be sure her flying skills were honed before taking the flight test.

In the late spring of 1940, Evelyn made a decision. With all contacts to secure a flying job exhausted in the Grand Island area, she packed up Scottie and moved into Lincoln, thinking her connections would be better there. Myron Larkin, a former flight instructor while she was working on her transport license, was still with Lincoln Airplane and Flying School. She was counting on him to help her prepare for an instructor's rerating. Upon her arrival in Lincoln, Evelyn told the school she needed a job that would pay board and room. Ruby Nichols, known to most people as Nick the Cop, heard of Evelyn's predicament through the student services' director and offered to help. A thirty-nine-year foot-patrol officer near the 12th and O Streets intersection, he had a reputation for befriending others. Ruby Nichols often let young boys in the back door of the local prize-fighting events, and instead of issuing a ticket, would plug an expired meter with a coin of his own.[11]

Nick the Cop knew Valda Hoehne, owner of the downtown Dotty Dunn Hatshop, was looking for someone to help with her children. That very same day, he walked into her store at 1220 "O" and told her about "this young woman who had come to town."[12] An agreement was reached whereby Evelyn would do light housework and chauffeur fifteen-year-old Dorette, and her thirteen-year-old brother Jack, in exchange for board and room. It looked like the perfect plan until the subject of Scottie came up. He could not stay at the house because of Jack's asthma. For the next several weeks, Scottie made his bed at the airport. But he slept in a favorite old place, the wide, rear wicker seats of the brown and yellow Curtiss Robin.

In the May 3, 1940, issue of the *State House News*, an employees' weekly, Evelyn was once again the subject of a poet's admiration.

EVELYN SHARP

What eagle circles yonder lofty peak,
Now vanishing into the morning mist,

Now gliding earthward seemingly to seek
Some treasure its discerning eye had missed.

Ah, now the fog has lifted and I see
More plainly through the fastly clearing skies,
And smile to think I could mistaken be;
It's Evelyn in her morning exercise.

T'would seem her dauntless spirit cannot rest
upon an ordinary couch of ease;
No doubt to her some feathery cloud is best,
So off she goes to race the morning breeze.

— Harry E. Mendenhall[13]

The same issue published an announcement of a meeting to form a local aeronautics club. Its purpose would be to inform the general public of aviation's importance to "all of us as citizens of a city, a state, and a nation."[14] Evelyn and Valda Hoehne were included in a listing of the organizers.

The *State House News* and the *Capitol City Guide* sponsored Evelyn's appearance on stage at the Nebraska Theater on Friday, May 3. She spoke of women's roles in aviation and ideas for aviation opportunities. The *State House News* had organized a contest among the Lincoln Business and Professional Women's Club members to give Evelyn a professional flying name. It was to have been announced that evening, but men felt discriminated against and were able to force an extension of the original deadline. That seemed to dampen interest, and the idea and name simply faded away.[15]

Evelyn made presentations about the proposed aeronautics club to the Lincoln Co-operative Club, the Chamber of Commerce, and a Department of Aeronautics meeting. *The Lincoln Sunday Journal and Star* did a feature story on Jane Tucker's informal radio visits, a program which drew one of the largest-listening female audiences in Nebraska. Tucker's list of guests included Evelyn and Scottie. The dog, with his brass-studded collar, seemed to capture the heart of the newspaper photographer. Sitting on his hind legs in a begging position, Scottie appeared to be speaking into the KFAB microphone, while Jane Tucker and Evelyn looked on with admiring approval.[16]

The Hoehne children loved to go to the airport with Evelyn because it afforded them an opportunity to ride in an airplane as well as a chance to play with Scottie. It was hard to tell whether the children or the dog received more pleasure from the visit. Dorette (nicknamed Dur) also remembers feeling a sense of responsibility helping Evelyn push old NC551N behind the hanger on those days when the Civil Aeronautics Authority inspector was scheduled to arrive. Evelyn showed Dur that when slight pressure was exerted on the canvas fabric, it did not return to its original contour as quickly as it should. If the inspector saw this, he might remove the airworthiness certificate. Dur understood and did not betray Evelyn's confidence.[17]

Evelyn continued to study for the advanced rating, writing and rewriting descriptions of how to do spins and spirals, figure eights, vertical 720-degree turns, steep and shallow 180- and 360-degree turns, and power-off spot landings. She took cues other flight instructors used in getting their students to relax. In the actual test, the examiner pretended he was the student pilot, knowing nothing about flying. Without touching the controls, Evelyn would have to recognize mistakes in flight maneuvers, telling him what he had done wrong and what he must do to correct them.

After a long morning with the books, Evelyn set them aside and leaned back against the metal spindles of the curved headboard bed to rest her eyes. She was tired, but reflected on how lucky she was to have found a family who grew to care for her. John Hoehne had partitioned off a portion of the southwest basement room, where a newly Kemtone-painted chest of drawers sat in the corner. Valda Hoehne grew to embrace Evelyn's clearly focused drive to teach flying. Some years later, a picture of Evelyn in her military flying gear was delivered to 3011 Ryons. The inscription read:

You helped me get my start.

You've been a wonderful friend.

My sincerest for your continued health and happiness.

As ever,
Evelyn[18]

Evelyn in tire tube swing,
circa 1925

"Chalky Gets A New Home,"
Richard Burrows on Chalky, circa 1934

"Campfire Comics," Summer Camp, North Loup River, Wilma Krikac, Irene Whiting and Evelyn, August 1934

"The Garter Girls," pictured from left: Jane Ferguson, Mae Klein, Virginia Klein, Evelyn, Irene Whiting, November 1935

BESS WILSON

"A Landing On The Frozen North Loup River," pictured from left: Thomas "Buck" Williams, Evelyn and John Sharp, January 1936

MARY FARMER PALMER

"Evelyn Solos At Sixteen," pictured from left: Jack Jefford, instructor; LaVern Duemey, classmate; Evelyn, Contact (dog) March 4, 1936

DOROTHY AUBLE HARDISTY

Six Friends On A Truck," pictured on top from left: Jack Janssen, Evelyn, Lillian Kusek, Dorothy Auble; bottom row from left: Scottie (dog), Norma Mae Snell, Armona Beth Achen, circa 1936

Ord High School Girls' Glee Club. Evelyn is in the first row, sixth from right, circa spring 1936

MARY FARMER PALMER

"A Smile For The Photographer, "Evelyn and LaVern Duemey, North Loup River, circa 1936

"Pickin' Posies,"
June 1936

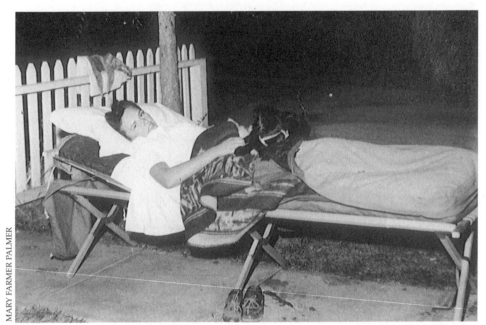

"Fresh Air Remedies Asthma Attack," circa 1936

"Afternoon At Anderson's Island," pictured from left: Virginia Clark, Josephine Romans, Harold "Pud" Garnick, Evelyn, Don Cole, June 1936

"Adventurous And Assured,"
Evelyn, Bonnie (horse) and Scottie
(dog), September 1936

MARY FARMER PALMER

MARY FARMER PALMER

"Evelyn And Her Best Friend, Scottie," October 1936

ROY L. MAXSON

DONNA STEVENS

MARY FARMER PALMER

ROY L. MAXSON

MARY FARMER PALMER

HELEN OSENTOWSKI

ROY L MAXSON

IRENE AUBLE ABERNETHY

POST CARD

FOR CORRESPONDENCE

Evelyn received her student's permit at
the age of 16. Before she was 17, had her
amateur license. A few days after she
was 17 she obtained her private license.
Now, she is nearing 250 hours of solo flying and has carried some 300 guest passengers. She expects to get her transport
license before her 18th year expires. This
is the earliest date the government will
permit anyone to get a transport license.

Many thanks for
the music at my
dance
Evelyn Sharp

LINCOLN
JAN 6
5.30 PM

Mr. Arthur Mason
Ord,
Nebr.

DIANA L. SMITH

MFD. BY FORT WAYNE PRINTING CO., FORT WAYNE, IND.

HELEN OSENTOWSKI

Ord High School Chanticleer Marching Band, Valley County Courthouse, Evelyn is in the second row from bottom, sixth from left, 1936-1937

LILLIAN KUSEK HOMINDA

"Let's Have A Snow Fight," December 1936

Merry Christmas

Evelyn Sharp Sky Rider

Evelyn Sharp

PRESENT THIS CARD FOR AUTOGRAPHING

"A Christmas Memory" December 1937

"Commercial License,"
Lincoln Airplane and Flying
School, May 1938

CORRIGA Curtis

Miss EVELYN SHARP

Nation's Youngest Aviatrix   Government Com License 34711

"Wrong-Way Corrigan--Right-Way Evelyn," 1930 OX-5 Curtiss Robin, August 1938

*"Evelyn And Her
'Sweet Companion,'"
September 1938*

MARY FARMER PALMER

HELOISE CHRISTENSEN BRESLEY

Evelyn And Annabelle, Lexington, Nebraska, August 1939

"A Photo For A Friend,"
To: Ray Johnson,
Evelyn's skating teacher,
circa 1939

"Having Fun!"
The Smoke Signal-Pioneers Park,
Lincoln, Nebraska, circa 1940

Evelyn and Douglas B-18 Crew. Emblem: Tojours la Danger *(Always Danger), Black Hills Airport, Spearfish, South Dakota, 1940*

Evelyn: "Pilot In Command," John and Mary Sharp, Los Angeles, California, June 1942

WAFS "Standardized Attire." Pictured from left: Barbara Poole, Evelyn, Esther Manning, Barbara Erickson, New Castle Army Air Base, Wilmington, Delaware, 1942

"Welcome To Ord, Nebraska, 'This Ship OK'" colored picture hangs at Sharp Field, Fixed-Base Operations building, C-47, circa 1943

Flying The Boys

*I*n Grand Island, John was preparing letters of introduction to sponsors of Civilian Pilot Training Programs. Postdated June 15, 1940, to allow Evelyn time to finish her instructor's rerating, the correspondence included a summary of Evelyn's professional and personal qualifications and the expected salary. Excerpts from individually typed letters included the following:

If in need of an Instructor or Superintendent, what have you to offer me above three hundred a month averaging six to eight hours flying a day.

I can take full charge of quoto students and would like $350 a month or if they would run three quotos a year would like $4000.00 a year. I have been flying five years with 800 hours to my credit and have carried over 5000 passengers with no mishaps and seven forced landings. I hold renewed instructors rating on both classes up to 4000 pounds.

If you have a location in your state that can and wants to set up a unit and will furnish the equipment will go fifty-fifty above operating expenses.

Good standard equipment must be furnished.

CHARACTER: First class. Do not smoke or drink.

REFERENCES: I.V. Packard—Nebr. St. Aeronautics Lincoln, Nebr.

If interested send contract in return letter as I have so many offers I want the best as soon as possible.

I know my profession and am all business. With my publicity the quoto will be filled all the way through.

> Yours truly,
> Miss Evelyn G. Sharp

By J.E.S. Father Secy[1]

Typed on the stationery used in the 1938 Commemorative Air Mail Flight, the letters were addressed to departments of aeronautics across the country. They would be mailed when Evelyn passed the exam.

On June 9, 1940, Evelyn was one step closer toward reaching her goal, that is, making a living through flying. She had passed her flight instructor rerating test, officially qualifying her to teach others to fly. No longer would she have to worry about the vagaries of Nebraska weather, the payments on an old airplane which was forever breaking down, or the scarcity of a Depression dollar whose owner would think twice before spending another for a second ride. Though her personal register would show "hopping" over five thousand people (including Scottie sometimes), there just wasn't an economic future for Evelyn in barnstorming.

Through the grapevine, word had reached Lincoln Airplane and Flying School that a temporary flight instructor was needed in South Dakota. The next day she and Scottie were on their way to Mitchell where she would finish teaching a primary flight training class whose teacher had become ill. Once more, press coverage picked up: "AGAIN YOUNGEST," "Evelyn Sharp is believed to be the youngest woman flying instructor in the country," "Civilian pilot training is likely to be more popular at Mitchell...than most other places," "pretty, 20-year-old, brown-eyes, 5 feet 4," "AIR SCHOOLMA'AM," "Girl Flying Veteran, Busy Teaching for U.S," and "Yes, Teacher—We Have Our Lessons"[2] were all headlines for feature articles in area newspapers. Pictures with male student pilots and sometimes with Scottie often supplemented the stories.

Amid the details of one publicity shot, Evelyn backed up near a caged lion, a friendly beast named Duke. However, Duke became impatient and, thrusting his paw through the bars, took an unfriendly swipe across her back. Although the injury was not serious, a doctor said there was danger of infection from the claws.[3] Beneath a picture of Evelyn and Duke in her photograph album, she wrote, "Just a second before the lion 'loved me up.'"[4] Perhaps Evelyn decided she got along better with dogs than with cats.

At the end of two weeks, the Civil Aeronautics Authority added the names of eight newly licensed private pilots to its registry. With a recommendation from Professor Knox, ground school director at Dakota Wesleyan College in Mitchell, Evelyn collected her $80, hopped an Inland Airlines commercial plane,[5] and flew three hundred miles to the west. Here, at Spearfish, South Dakota, she would work for Professor Guy Jacobs, the developer and director of a recently approved Civilian Pilot Training Program. Jacobs, dubbed the "flying professor" because of his early barnstorming days, teamed his ground school class taught at Spearfish Normal School with his aviation flying service at the Black Hills Airport.[6]

On June 26, 1940, the contract was drawn. Evelyn agreed to flight-train fifteen summer CPTP students "...so that they may receive their private certificates of competency or until they have received fifty hours of flying in accordance with the CPTP regulations." The second party, Guy A. Jacobs, owner and operator of Spearfish Sky Services, agreed to pay the first party (Evelyn G. Sharp) the sum of $900.[7] Because Evelyn was a minor, the paperwork was forwarded to Grand Island where John affixed his signature. He did not hesitate. Evelyn proudly showed the signed contract to Ordites Helen and Joe Osentowski who were at the Black Hills vacationing the first part of July.

On the same day as the dated contract, Evelyn flew nine of her fifteen students to initiate Stage A of the program, but not before familiarizing herself with the flying characteristics of NC2193 in a ten-minute flight. Nicknamed the "flying beer can" because of its malle-

"A Flying Beer Can,"
Evelyn at Black Hills
Airport, Spearfish,
South Dakota, 1940

able aluminum construction, the 50-hp Luscombe was a small mono-plane which wrinkled and popped when put into a spin.[8]

Raymond Kolb remembers the sound well. A twenty-year-old man from Date, South Dakota, he and Evelyn boarded with the Guy Jacobs family at 541 First Avenue in Spearfish. Desperately wanting to be able to fly, Raymond worked as a handyman for Professor Jacobs so as to have money for tuition and books at the Normal School. Flight instruction in CPTP was free.[9]

Evelyn began Raymond's instruction with a thirty-minute ground school lesson. He tried to listen carefully. She covered brake usage, throttle position, the gravity fuel system, seating arrangement, and safety belts. She pointed out extinguisher and first-aid kit locations, followed by the warnings of propeller danger and running an engine with an empty cockpit. Having no starter, the Luscombe, like most early airplanes, needed to be hand-propped. She concluded with a summary of local traffic rules and instruction signals, those hand motions given by instructor to student when one's voice could not be heard because of propeller, engine, and cockpit vibration noise. Under "Remarks" in Raymond's logbook, Evelyn wrote: "Absorbs instruction readily."[10] Raymond remembers being somewhat confused with all the information.

With an almost negligible four mile-per-hour wind from the east, Raymond taxied the Luscombe out to Runway 31 at the Black Hills Airport. He was in the left seat, and his instructor, who was nearly eight months younger, was in the right. A timepiece read 6:30 p.m.

Evelyn directed Raymond to place his feet lightly on the left and right rudder pedals, and wrap the fingers of his left hand loosely around the stick. With Evelyn on her own set of controls, Raymond felt how the movement of those controls caused an airplane to pitch, roll, and yaw about its three axes. As the Luscombe broke ground and gained some altitude, she motioned toward the right, the designated practice area about five miles northeast of the airport. Here, in open country, there was no need to fear shotgun pellets from an irate rancher's shotgun. Low-flying airplanes and a rancher's prized livestock were, more often than not, incompatible.

During Stage A, the period of time prior to a student's soloing, Evelyn averaged seven-and-one-half to eight hours of flying each day, there being some weeks when she had no day off. Arising at four o'clock in the morning, she and Scottie pulled up to the hangar by four-thirty. She did not leave until seven-thirty or eight most evenings. While Evelyn flew thirty-minute lessons throughout the working day, Scottie waited patiently for his mistress on the steps of the airport administration building. Although there were a number of planes coming and going, the dog seemed to know which plane his mistress was flying. He would be waiting for her each time her plane taxied to the ramp. It amazed Howard Ice, also a pilot, that the dog was smart enough to stay away from the invisible, moving prop. Little did he know that Scottie had 150 hours in his own logbook.[11]

Evelyn logged the following on July 12, 1940: "Did over 100 spins today with at least one and a half to two and a half turns in each spin." Regulations stipulated no more than three turns in a spin. Because of an inherent danger in recovery and the negative effects on gyroscopic instruments, spins are prohibited in general aviation today. In 1940, mastery of spins was a required maneuver.

On July 16, Raymond Kolb soloed and moved on to Stage B. Under "Remarks" in his gray-green student pilot logbook, Evelyn wrote, "Made fairly good landings." She was eager for the rest of her students to solo; flight instructors did not get paid until they had done so. In a letter written to her parents in Grand Island, Evelyn asked her mother to tell Clerk 35 at Brown McDonald dry goods store to be sure and keep her cute dress on layaway. "Well, write soon, and I'll get some money to you as soon as possible,"[12] the letter concluded. Employees at Ben's Grill had given Mary a going-away picnic at Ord's Bussell Park on June 28; she had since moved to Grand Island to be with John.[13]

Evelyn made arrangements to fly stunts in the Seventh Annual Black Hills Airfair at Spearfish on July 20, 1940.[14] Working for the same promoter at the Grand Island and Columbus air shows the previous year, she was put in charge of flying a stunt parachutist to altitude for her death-defying fall.[15] The bulky chest and back parachute packs which Dorothy Barden wore barely left room in the narrow confines of the Luscombe 65 cockpit for the parachutist and her pilot.

A low-lying layer of smoke hanging over the Black Hills Airport the night before the Airfair, caused Laura Ingalls, a member of the Tex Rankin Flying Circus, to lose her bearings coming into Spearfish. To show her the way, airport personnel lighted wick-burning kerosene pots set out along the edges of the runway.[16] These "lighthouses" were not unlike the bonfires tended by Nebraska's public-spirited citizens in February of 1921. There, they marked the airway for North Platte native Jack Knight on the first night air mail flight across our country.[17]

On the morning of the air show, Crystal (nicknamed Crys) Thode, the mandatory female in the Civilian Pilot Training Program, made her solo flight. An elementary grade school teacher attending summer school at the Normal School, she had to borrow $10 from her brother-in-law for the required government insurance. To this day, Crys has never regretted that "halcyon time"[18] in her life.

As Crys Calamity, so named by herself, taxied to the ramp, she breathed a sigh of accomplishment and perhaps, one of relief. She had finally soloed; in fact, she had been the last of her class to solo. Evelyn, dressed neatly in her usual faded pants was waiting to offer warm congratulations. Was there any doubt she was thinking about that $300 paycheck? Crystal, four years older than Evelyn, understood why the "men adored her." Not only pretty, she "listened and genuinely cared about those people around her."[19]

Taking top billing at the Airfair that afternoon was Tex Rankin, an ace, stunt pilot from California. In his aluminum Great Lakes airplane with its inverted Menasco engine, he "really showed his stuff with red smoke."[20] The upside down power plant allowed Rankin to do acrobatic maneuvers which were not possible with a factory installed gravity-fed engine. Before Rankin left, Evelyn asked him to help her find a job on the West Coast, there being more opportunities to fly for big oil companies.[21]

As the last of the 1940 Airfair stunt planes touched down on the runway, the CPTP men decided it was time for a party, a long awaited solo party for Crys. With a decision to meet at Iron Creek Lake, several cars headed south to the beautifully wooded forest in Spearfish Canyon. When Evelyn asked about food, there was a noticeable silence. Finally someone said, "Oh, a couple of the guys are going to pick something up." Probably not until Evelyn bit into that first ear of corn, which turned out to be popcorn, did she realize only part of the story had been told.[22] Evans Lane in the Spearfish Valley was well-known for its commercial gardening farms, and although none of the CPTP students can remember who went into one of the fields that day, they undoubtedly agreed they had sent the wrong ones.

Iron Creek Lake, a popular recreation area surrounded by woods of sweet-smelling pines, offered a pleasant break from the flat and unprotected, sun-baked airport. In attempting to build a pyramid with human forms along the bank, the young people decided their expertise lay in maneuvers performed further above the ground. They could never quite hold the position long enough for a camera to record the shot.[23]

As Evelyn crawled into bed that night, there was little doubt as to why she was tired. A fifty-five-hour week of flying and evening classes at the college to upgrade her Red Cross Senior Life-Saving Certificate to a Water Safety Instructor's Certificate had taken their toll.[24] The few hours of laughter and relaxation at Iron Creek were just what she needed. Before another air show tomorrow, she would fly more students and later squeeze Dorothy Barden and her bulky safety-chutes into the tiny Luscombe again.

Evelyn welcomed several Nebraska vacationers to the Black Hills that summer, giving them a bird's eye view of its many famous landmarks. When a woman, writing under the pen name of Agricultural Edith, returned home, she shared the following in the *Burt County Plaindealer*:

> Bob and I probably had the thrill of our life while away on our trip. While at Spearfish, we went to see Evelyn Sharp.

> ...she took us up in an airplane and we saw the Black Hills from the air. We could see Wyoming on one hand and Bear Butte on the other and Harney Peak in front of us. The fields made a checkerboard and some of them were carpeted in the deep brown of pine trees and here and there a break occurred where a river or stream tumbled down the rocks. ...it was really a thrill, especially with Evelyn at the controls.

"Four Presidents And A Pilot," Mount Rushmore, South Dakota, 1940

After the ride, she showed us her scrapbooks and presents she had received from people all over the country. She is probably the most unaffected and level-headed girl I have ever met even though she has received national and international publicity.[25]

"Evelyn On Sioux Holy Ground," Black Hills, South Dakota, 1940

A Luscombe, a B-24, and a '37 Olds

*I*n the early morning hours of Sunday, July 28, 1940, the Grand Island Airport Inn Nightclub and an adjoining hangar at the Old Airport burned to the ground. John Sharp had once managed the cafe, but he and Mary had since moved to Spearfish. Inside the hangar, near the south end, the metal skeleton of a Curtiss Robin stood amidst ashes and smoldering ruin. The night club proprietor, Ernest F. Hemmerling, also a casualty of the blaze, was lying nearby.[1] Although the Van Hoosens, an entertainment skating duo employed at the club, were initially held as material witnesses because of thoughts of foul play, a coroner's jury was unable to fix blame and they were released. A final investigation concluded a highly intoxicated Hemmerling had fallen, causing an electric fan to short out.

John Sharp had been trying to cut a deal to sell both Curtiss Robins to a man in White Lake, South Dakota. Evelyn still owed $221.50 and Coburn Campbell, a lawyer in Lincoln, was not sure how long Chase Investment Company would let the matter of non-payment ride. At the bottom of the lawyer's letter, John wrote to Evelyn. "I am negotiating with a man...on both planes for $275. So if he takes them it will be cleaned up-his name is Harley Thomas."[2]

An agreement was never reached. Instead, the slate-blue Curtiss Robin purchased in Des Moines sat amid the ruins of the flame-blackened hanger, its metal fuselage warped by the heat. Her first Robin,

NC551N, with the newly rebuilt engine, would likewise suffer death, but one of a different nature. Sitting behind a hangar in Lincoln, it was eventually cannibalized, but not before someone removed the wooden propeller and returned it to the Ord Airport.

A second tragedy occurred less than two weeks later, when a Luscombe 50 owned by Guy Jacobs made its last flight. George Karinen, one of Evelyn's students, left the airport vicinity and made an unauthorized pass over his uncle's farm near Fruitdale, South Dakota. Coming in from the east at a dangerously low altitude, Karinen flew too close to a ten-foot embankment just west of the house. Catching the landing gear on a barbed-wire fence stretched atop the bank, the plane slammed into the ground. Karinen was thrown through the windshield, fifteen feet ahead of the plane; his shoes were left beside the rudder pedals inside.[3]

When Karinen did not return to the airport within the usual time, Evelyn became alarmed and initiated a search by herself. By the time she returned, word had reached the airport of his death. Her students remember there was no need on her part or theirs to discuss the crash. They all knew why it had happened. A daredevil attitude and youthful sense of immortality are a fatal combination.

Instruction in 180-, 360-, and 720-degree turns continued, as well as entry into and recovery from spins. Satisfied with Walt Hermansen's fine progress, Evelyn scheduled her first dual cross-country with him on August 10. A few days later, she accompanied Hermansen to Alliance, Nebraska, where he passed his private test and was eventually accepted in the Naval Air Training Program at Pensacola. Walt Hermansen was the first of Evelyn's primary flight students to fly for the military.[4]

Evelyn tried to schedule her dual, cross-county flights from Spearfish to Rapid City, South Dakota, around noontime, giving her a chance to have "scenery with lunch."[5] On August 27, 1940, she arranged such a flight with Lloyd Petersen, a student from Avon, South Dakota. As the plane left the runway, Lloyd recorded the time; it was 12:30 p.m. While he navigated his previously-plotted course along the eastern edge of the Black Hills, his instructor, sitting on an old cushion which raised her to a height to see over the instrument panel, seemed

"Scenery With Lunch," Spearfish, South Dakota, 1940

to enjoy her sack lunch. When the hour and forty-five minute flight was completed, she wrote in his logbook, "Kept on course very well. Kept field to land in in [sic] sight."[6] With a total dual time of seventeen hours and fifty-five minutes and a solo time of twelve and one-half hours, Lloyd Petersen would eventually rise to the rank of Air Force Lieutenant Colonel, logging over three thousand hours.[7]

By the evening of September 14, Evelyn had checked out all her students for the private pilot exam. There was nothing more for her to do but wait the results of their rides with the CAA Inspector. Within a few days, all fourteen students received notification they had earned their licenses.[8]

The next day, Wilson (Willy) Shafer, her Burwell High School boyfriend now stationed with the Fourth Cavalry at nearby Ft. Meade, drove over to Spearfish. On this day, Evelyn and Willy would take a scenic flight. While standing on the ramp at Black Hills Airport, Clyde Ice, the other primary flight instructor, warned Willy that even with the longest runway in the state, it was sometimes not enough for Evelyn to get her plane off. But he should not worry. The hills beyond the end of the runway would stop them and, besides, Clyde said, pointing to the government-required Red Cross ambulance truck, "I'll send out the 'meat wagon'."[9] Willy, who was not that enamored with flying, probably laughed the least.

Their two-hour-and-fifteen minute flight took them over Devil's Tower, the most conspicuous landmark in northeast Wyoming. The huge monolith, resembling a stone tree stump, rose 867 feet from its base and was 1,267 feet above the Belle Fouche River. Having made a complete circle around its perpendicular sides with fluted-like columns, Evelyn banked Luscombe NC28629 to the right and established a heading slightly north of east. This brought them back by Bear Butte, a volcanic bubble rising 1,400 feet above the plains. Continuing south, they passed by Fort Meade and flew on into Spearfish. Though Willy much preferred the back of a horse to the seat in an airplane, the views were spectacular and he enjoyed the company of a special high school friend.

Evelyn's second class of CPTP at Black Hills Airport began flight instruction on October 1, 1940. Edward Ellington, one of ten new male students, who lived across the street from Evelyn, had noticed this good-looking woman during the summer. She always seemed happy and pleasant when friends stopped by to pick her up. At the airport, however, Edward sensed a difference in demeanor. She was very business-like and matter-of-fact. As Evelyn banked the airplane toward the northeast practice field, he wondered, like most men of his day, if she knew what she was doing. It was not long, however, before he came to recognize and respect her competence.[10]

Evelyn made sure the men understood and remembered the teacher-student relationship. Special feelings can evolve when you are learning to fly, and sometimes student pilots transfer that love and exhilaration to their instructors. Evelyn Sharp did not date her students.

Maintenance at airports where flight instruction was offered kept the owner and mechanics busy. Pilots in training were hard on their ships. On one particular day, a newly soloed student pilot and Evelyn came in fast and hard. Hitting a cross rut in the oiled 300-foot wide runway, the landing gear sustained too much of a shock. It took three more landings before Evelyn realized the gear was bent. Guy Jacobs wired for parts, and he and Raymond Kolb spent a whole day taking the broken gear out of the ship.[11] On another occasion, a pilot on his first solo flight who had had no recent difficulties in "finding" the runway, also came in hot, or too fast. As his wheels hit the hard surface, the airplane responded with an equal and opposite force. The forty-foot-high bounce caused an estimated $300 to $500 worth of damage, but more embarrassing than that, it received print in the 1941 *Eociha* college yearbook.[12]

Evelyn did not chew out either of these students, that being her nature. Perhaps she remembered similar landings in the old pasture by the North Loup River and, from personal experience, knew her students already felt badly.

On October 20, 1940, a student pilot from Marcus, South Dakota, soloed. He later recounted his remembrances of that day in an article published in *The Anemone*, the college newspaper:

"Sprouting Wings"
By Kenneth Pittman

Place—Black Hills Airport

Weather—Wind NW 5 CAVU

Instructor—Miss Evelyn Sharp

Student Pilot—Pittman, speaks:

The day for my solo flight had come. My log book showed eight hours of dual flying and I had successfully written an examination over CAR [Civilian Air Rules], the minimum requirements for solo flight. The weather was exceptionally fine, CAVU, which means: ceiling and visibility unlimited: I had arrived at the airport early. The day was an important one to me.

The little silver plane had just landed and was taxiing back to the hangar. My instructor, Miss Sharp, and I climbed into the cockpit, slipped into the parachute harness and fastened our safety-belts.

"O.K. Go ahead," ordered Miss Sharp.

I applied enough throttle to give power to taxi down to the end of the runway, where we stopped headed with wind, to see if any planes were coming into land. Everything was clear. A little more throttle and left rudder turned us into the wind.

"This morning," said my instructor, "I want you to practice spot landings. On your takeoff, keep her headed down the runway. Remember, a ground loop means a smashed airplane and probably both of us in the hospital." If this last remark was intended to help me relax and concentrate I'm afraid it didn't serve the purpose for which it was intended.

Again, she signaled. "O.K. Go ahead—Full throttle, neutral rudder." We were gaining speed. As I pushed the stick forward, the tail of the plane raised into the air. A bit more speed. I eased back on the stick and the Luscombe was flying.

Everything I did seemed to be wrong: bounced landings and attempted ground loops were my main offenses. Many thoughts flashed through my mind as I tried again and again to correct these mistakes. Would I be "washed out," not able to continue flying? My determination and love of flying said "NO" with plenty of emphasis; but—here my thoughts were interrupted by the instructor again. I had just landed and was attempting another take-off.

"You can fly this thing as well as anyone else once you get it in the air, but the way you are doing this morning, you'd never live to get it off the ground if you were flying alone. See if you can get it back to the field and land."

"While taxiing back to the hangar I tried to figure out what was wrong. Suddenly, I felt the rudder pedals kicked from beneath my feet, as my instructor took over. We were heading back to the end of the runway. Again we stopped to look for incoming planes. Miss Sharp unfastened the chute-harness and safety-belt, climbed out and said with a grin, "Well, do you think you can take her up alone?"

After the way I had been flying that morning, I wasn't too sure.

"Go up, circle the field, land and do the same thing again. Keep headed straight down the runway in taking off and get the tail down when landing. O.K. go ahead! And watch out for other ships."

I applied full throttle for the takeoff. This one had to be good, as my instructor was back on the field. A slip now meant my own neck. The feeling of nervousness gradually left me and by the time I had completed my fifteen-minute flight, the self-confidence of being able to fly alone was reward enough for the work and sweat the morning's lesson had caused me. Next time it would be easier, but, it was quite a relief to be back on the ground again.[13]

Kenneth Pittman became another of Evelyn's students who joined the ranks of the military. For a while, he flew two-engine PBY 5-As on search-and-rescue near India. Then when B-24 pilots were needed, he transferred to that duty. One day in April of 1944, while on a low-level bombing mission over Bangkok, Thailand, his B-24 was hit by anti-aircraft fire. With the plane in flames, Kenneth Pittman shoved throttles forward, hoping to gain altitude for a safe parachute drop. Some of his crew jumped, and later credited the pilot for saving their lives. Kenneth Pittman and several others went down with the plane. The man who could not "find the runway" at the Black Hills Airport was awarded the Distinguished Flying Cross, posthumously.[14] Evelyn would have been proud.

On October 25, 1940, Evelyn typed a letter to Glenn Buffington on her newly purchased typewriter. She hoped it would "snap up" her letter writing.

I have about 1270 hours now, and have all of my students soloed now and they are all doing fine. Clyde Ice has a unit of 10 students, and out of his 10 and my 10, 11 are football players. After a game, there are so many banged-up boys that we don't have much of a flying class for a few days. They are sure a good bunch of kids, though.[15]

Scottie, too, was nursing some injuries. A cut under his neck had healed over, sealing a serious infection inside. Evelyn had it lanced four different times, but his condition was not getting much better. "I sure worry for fear I will lose him."[16]

While flying the previous summer, Evelyn had often seen deer in the nearby hills and hoped to get one that fall. Scottie, evidently recovered from the infection, decided he could not wait for his mistress to go hunting. Seeing an open door on a 1937 dark-blue Oldsmobile, the airport mascot jumped in the front seat and vaulted over the back. Howard Ice, on his way out to the country to help his brother dress a deer, returned to the vehicle, slammed the door, and sped away from the airport. Scottie crouched quietly on the back floorboard.

As the car began to slow down, Scottie poked his head over the seat and yipped. Now Howard had a problem. Should he take the dog back or leave it in his father's car? Already late, he decided his uninvited guest could stay where he was. After cracking a window, Howard headed across the field; and, as he disappeared over the rise, Scottie felt abandoned. Though he had slept in airport cars before while waiting for his mistress to return, this was much different. His only company now was a herd of cows on the other side of a barbed-wire fence. Yapping at those strange four-legged creatures, he dug his claws into the seat upholstery. In a matter of moments, the felt ripped. As Scottie became more excited, the claws dug deeper and the white cotton padding began to shred. Finished with the bench and back rest, the dog's claws and sharp teeth ripped the side panels. When those were shredded, Scottie began jumping up, nipping the headliner. Soon bits and pieces of material were everywhere while the headliner hung in long, uneven strips.

About that time a nearby farmer and his family, on their way to church, came along. They slowed down as would any neighbor upon seeing an abandoned car beside the road. Stopping parallel with the car, they simply could not believe their eyes. It was not clear whether they let the dog out to save the car, as most of the front seat upholstery was still intact, or to save his life when the owner came back. With the door wide open, Scottie jumped out and took off for the airport.

Sometime later, Howard approached the car, his face registering curiosity, the first of several emotions he would feel. How'd the door get open? Where was Scottie? His second reaction was disbelief. How did the inside get shredded? And the third was pure hostility as he turned and shouted down the now-vacant road. "Scottie! Scottie! I'm going to kill you!" Fifty-two years later, Howard Ice acknowledges, "If I had, Evelyn would have never spoken to me again."[17]

With the approach of the winter solstice, the hours available for daylight flying decreased. At the airport by seven o'clock, Evelyn usually finished flight instruction by four-thirty in the afternoon. Depending on how she felt, she might go skating or hiking, practice shooting, or ride horses. Sometimes she just went home to her trailer, a twenty-four-foot Covered Wagon, which she had purchased and now shared with her mother and father since the end of September.[18]

After dinner, if Evelyn was not recopying logbooks, as directed by the CAA, she would hop a ride downtown to the Valley Cafe on Main Street for some hangar flying with the students. Sometimes, they would take in a movie at The Vita, the local theater, also on Main.

Everyone in the CPTP unit looked forward to Friday nights at the Pavillion. Located in Spearfish City Park, the rectangular building with its hardwood floor offered an inexpensive evening's entertainment for aviation-minded college students and their young flight in-

"Too Deep To Fly," Black Hills Airport, Spearfish, South Dakota, 1940

structor. The Esquires, a band of some renown in the towns of western South Dakota, played the country's Big Band favorites.[19] In November of 1940, the Number One hits were "Blueberry Hill," "Ferryboat Serenade," and "Trade Winds," while in December "Frenesi" topped the charts, holding on to first place for thirteen weeks.[20]

Evelyn, who was "bright, alert, and lively," had no difficulty in filling her dance card.[21] Here was an opportune moment for student pilots to put their arms around their favorite teacher, something they'd never have tried between the flight line and the cockpit. Evelyn enjoyed the company of these young people, too, writing about them in her letters as a "grand bunch of kids."[22] When they went home to their families for Christmas vacation, she was lonely.

On the twenty-eighth of December, Evelyn wrote to Glenn Buffington:

> I'm rather lonesome the last few days. Only a few of my students are here....How did you spend Christmas? I flew 'till 11 AM and then I drove to Rapid City & then Philip. I took in the dance at Philip and then drove back to Spearfish.
>
> I told you I had a trailer house, didn't I? We sure enjoy being in it. We've got things now so it doesn't seem like were [we're] in a coop.
>
> I got word the other day that several more of my students are in the air corps. Isn't that grand? I am so proud of them. One of my students went to Pensacola & he is doing just fine.
>
> Let me hear from you and I'll try to become a better correspondent.
>
> > Your very good little friend,
> > Evelyn
>
> Scottie sends his special "Arf." Scottie is a proud papa.[23]

Wings In The West

*O*n December 27, 1940, Evelyn flew her last flight as a CPTP instructor at the Blackhills Airport, as each of her students was now ready for the CAA check ride. Three months earlier, just after signing a second contract with Guy Jacobs, she had received a job offer from Glen S. Roberts, secretary at Les Buchner's Flying Service in Bakersfield, California. She had been recommended to Buchner by Tex Rankin, the stunt pilot at the Spearfish Airfair the previous summer, as being a "capable instructor."[1] He also understood she wanted to qualify for an advanced flight instructor rating. In this offer Evelyn probably saw an opportunity to upgrade her skills while, at the same time, provide an income to support herself and her parents.

On January 16, 1941, Evelyn stopped by Spearfish Normal School to get her logbook notarized. Mildred G. Menard, school librarian and secretary to Guy Jacobs, affixed her notary seal to 1393.10 hours of flying in Evelyn's third logbook and wished her good luck. It was not long thereafter when a 1938 Chevrolet, pulling a Covered Wagon trailer, drove south out of Spearfish. Inside the car were Evelyn, her parents, and Allen Marek. Allen had a new temporary private license carefully tucked away in his billfold. Scottie and two men, who like the rest of the party were each looking forward to a new beginning in California, rode behind in the trailer.

Allen Marek liked Evelyn. Their relationship grew into a special friendship. One of Allen's contemporaries says, "He was sweet on her,"[2] while another offers this description, "He squared around with her."[3] Allen reflects upon it in another way. "Evelyn was a good friend. She liked lots of people. Although she enjoyed having a good time, not far beneath the surface was a sense of determination to make things work."[4] Her new life in California would not be an exception.

When Allen had heard of Evelyn's plans to go West, he offered to help her drive straight through, as none of them had money to spend on hotels. Early in the trip it was fortunate for everyone that Allen was along. Miles northeast of Rawlins, Wyoming, on a blustery windswept day, they ran into ice. The mountain highway was steep with a precipitous drop-off on the right. Evelyn, who was driving, pumped the brake pedal. The car slowed, but the trailer did not. She had forgotten to manipulate the handle for the electric trailer brakes which was located on the steering column. Within seconds, the rear end of the car was being pushed to the right; the wheels were not turning, and the car was

Allen Marek and his "Good Friend," Spearfish, South Dakota, 1940

sliding. Quickly, Evelyn turned the wheel right, trying to straighten out the car and the trailer. Now they were headed for the edge of the very narrow road. As Allen grabbed the wheel, forcing it back to the left, the car and trailer jackknifed, skidding to the right. Evelyn applied the trailer brakes, and ever so slowly the car and the Covered Wagon trailer eased to a stop.

Allen could hardly believe what he saw. The trailer wheels were off the pavement, stopping inches from the edge of the cliff. In the trailer, one of the men opened the door...into the emptiness of space.

The front of the trailer was over the edge. With trailer brakes on and Allen giving hand signals, Evelyn turned the front wheels to the right, then drove a few feet to straighten out both car and trailer. Once the vehicles were aligned, Allen grabbed the hands of the men inside and helped them onto firm ground. Scottie jumped into Evelyn's arms, licking her face.[5] Somehow he sensed this was more than one of her tricks she had pulled when flying.

By the grace of God, good luck, or both, everyone was alive. Several minutes later, they were back on the road, continuing down into Rawlins at a snail's pace. There, they got repairs for the twisted hitch.

As the morning beams of sunrise became the bright, reflections of sunlight on snow, they drove into Salt Lake City. Night found them in southern Utah. Another day dawned and miles of pavement passed beneath their tires before the purples and pinks in the western sky silhouetted the Sierra Nevada behind Las Vegas. With headlights on, they drove through the night to Mojave. Here they said their good-byes.

Allen, hoping to earn enough money for advanced flight instruction, would stay with his brother in Trona, California, until he found a good job, while Evelyn and the others went on to Bakersfield. It was January 20, 1941.

In letters to Glenn Buffington, Evelyn wrote:

Surprise! I sneaked out on you. Finished my unit at Spearfish and will start another here soon. In the meantime, I have some private students. Quite the deal—lots of ships here, 60 Army planes and oodles of civilian planes. I'll soon develop a pivot neck watching for airplanes. We have our trailer house in a lovely, little trailer camp [Adobe Autel] about one and one-half miles from the airport. I'm sure I'll like it here.[6]

Enclosed is an article full of hooey about me, as I thought you'd like to have it....I've been instructing Commercial Refreshers while waiting for my CPTP unit to start.[7]

The article, entitled "GIRL TRAINS PILOTS: Noted Aviatrix Coaches Fledglings," appeared in the February 24, 1941, edition of *The Bakersfield Californian*. "Kern County, leader in many aviation activities and known as one of the most air-minded counties in the state, today boasted of another distinction which placed it in the 'nation-wide' category. Evelyn Sharp, the youngest of the ten women flight instructors in the United States, was now on the staff at Les Buchner's Flying Service at Kern County Airport."[8]

When the newspaper reporter asked Evelyn if she had ever had any narrow escapes in 1,450 hours in the air, she smiled shyly. "No," she replied. "I don't remember any. I suppose I've been very lucky. I hope it'll keep on that way."[9]

Evelyn's primary unit flew the first week in March. Instructing in Porterfields, a tandem, 65-hp trainer, she hoped for a chance to fly back to the Kansas City factory and pick up a new one. Her friend, Glenn Buffington, lived there. "You know I'm getting anxious to meet you,"[10] she wrote.

That same week, Billy Lachenmaier, a local pilot from Shafter who had about twenty hours of solo time, was out practicing at Kern County. Trying to get his private license before induction by the Selective Service Board in May, he was flying

"Pilot Training In Porterfields," Kern County Airport. Bakersfield, California, 1941

every day the weather permitted. Evelyn and Billy had become friends soon after she started working for Les Buchner. Several times they picnicked at beautiful Shaver Lake in the Sierra Nevada and hiked in wooded areas of the Kern River Canyon.[11]

As Billy lifted the Hammond airplane off the runway at Kern County, observers on the ramp saw its left wheel fall to the ground. Unaware of the situation, he continued to the practice area, while those on the field made plans for his return. Inbound for a landing, Billy noticed a car parked crossways on the active runway. The parking lot was noticeably full and he could see a string of cars coming down the airport road. He continued the approach, keeping the pattern at a higher altitude than if his intention had been to land. As he flew over the runway, Billy saw people's arms waving him off. "Firetrucks were parked beside the runway, and to make things a little more exciting, they put an ambulance next to the fire equipment. They even encouraged me more by having the stretcher out and waiting."[12] On the third go-around, Les Buchner, owner of the Hammond, joined Billy in the pattern, flying close enough for him to read white-chalked printing scribbled on the fuselage of the dark-blue airplane. "Left wheel gone, land in lake." Buchner motioned for Billy to wait. Flying ahead and across Billy's flight path, he returned with the opposite side of the fuselage in view. It read, "Left wheel gone, land with right wing low." Billy thought for a moment and decided he was not dressed for swimming. Coming around once more, he brought the Hammond in for a single-wheel touchdown. Keeping the right wing low, he landed on the right gear, and when the left wing finally lost lift, it scraped the runway causing the plane to make a gentle turn to the left. Bill Lachenmaier still remembers every detail of that flight. "I probably made the best landing possible,"[13] he reflects. No doubt Evelyn agreed.

In May, Evelyn wrote to Glenn telling him how excited she was with her new car—"it is a 4-door, Plymouth Sedan, a pretty gray. Brand new, too, radio, spotlight, seat covers, etc. I'll take a picture of it and send to you."[14]

How different life was for Evelyn. Those old barnstorming days, while exciting, were filled with economic woes. One day was great, the next just O.K., or bad. There was no financial security, rather debt and doubt. Then, as a flight instructor in South Dakota, a regular income bought a trailer, plus being able to support her mother and father. Now, in California, her new job brought in even more money. Evelyn never had it so good. The new car was evidence of her ability to pay.

Three of her students at Kern County Airport had passed their private exam, and the others were ready. With a break before the next unit began, she looked forward to driving her new car to Yosemite National Park for a few days of rest. "Then I have to practice and everything for my advanced rerating. I sure hope I get it, but darn it, I suppose I'll flunk."[15] That rating would allow Evelyn to teach acrobatics, the next level of flight instruction.

In June of 1941, Allen Marek came to Bakersfield; he and Evelyn went ice-skating, something they had enjoyed doing together in Spearfish. Evelyn had made arrangements to get Allen in Buchner's advanced flight training unit, but when his money ran out, he enlisted in the Navy. In later correspondence sent to the *U.S.S. Astoria*, during World War II, Evelyn told Allen she had no "heart throbs."

> I always have plenty of dates but nothing serious. No danger of me getting married yet. Mother and dad often ask if I heard from you. I keep your blanket on my bed all the time beside my favorite Indian blanket.

Evelyn hoped they would not wait so long to answer each other's letters. "It will make me feel better if I hear from you. I'll know you are still safe."[16] Evelyn and Allen would never see each other again.

On August 22, 1941, "WINGS," a pen name for a *Lodi News-Sentinel* columnist, wrote another of his aviation articles entitled, "Get Up in the Air." Offering readership to residents of the Sacramento Valley, the *News-Sentinel* was published some 235 miles from Bakersfield. That morning, "WINGS" gave his "vote" to a top-ranking aviation personality—a twenty-one-year-old woman with two thousand flying hours.

An ambitious soul, who rose literally by her own boot straps, the diminutive miss who was determined

"Evelyn Earns 'Top Vote' From 'WINGS,'" Bakersfield, California, 1941, (Evelyn and Scottie)

to succeed "or else," lays much of the credit for her present success to the whole-hearted co-operation of her parents... Disapproving neighbors solemnly threatened the foresighted father that his 15-year-old daughter surely wouldn't live to finish high school, being engaged in such a very hazardous pastime, and what was he thinking of, anyway?[17]

Surely Evelyn and John must have chuckled as they read this latest publicity.

"WINGS" also wrote of the Ninety-Nines, an international organization of licensed women pilots whose Nebraska chapter Evelyn helped charter during an Omaha blizzard in 1937. On September 6 and 7, Evelyn and Miss Kay Van Doozer, secretary of the Southwest Section of Ninety-Nines, played host to seventy-five women flyers from California, Nevada, and Arizona. A photo, appearing in the September 9, 1941, issue of *The Bakersfield Californian*, showed the two women and Cecil Meadows, superintendent of Kern County Airport, welcoming Ninety-Nines to their annual fall business meeting.[18]

One of the pilots Evelyn welcomed was Patricia Thomas, a CPTP instructor at Gardena Airport in Los Angeles. The two women, nearly the same age, were fascinated with each other. Both had received their amateur licenses in 1935, earned instructor reratings, and were teaching CPTP units. And although each had arrived in California within a month of the other, neither had met any other Ninety-Nines. At the Ninety-Nines meeting, Pat remembers Evelyn being "so friendly. We spent a lot of time around the Motel Inn pool. She was a good swimmer. I remember her father coming to the hotel and giving me a Rotogravure newspaper feature."[19] Pat thought Evelyn was somewhat embarrassed by John's promotion of her.

Later that fall, Evelyn drove over to Gardena to see Pat. Living in a one-room apartment, she had a bed which pulled down from a closet. "We would spend hours, lying in that wall-to-wall bed, talking about our students, the common mistakes they made, and how we could be better instructors. Evelyn told me of how the people in Ord had helped her. All we talked about was flying. We did have fun yacking."[20]

In a letter dated September 11, 1941, Evelyn apologized to Glenn Buffington for not answering his letter.

Terribly sorry about my laziness, guess everyone is having that trouble around here. It is so easy to jaunt down to the pool and lie on the lawn and talk to everyone with an occasional dip to drive away the heat. That's about how I spend my free hours in the middle of the day. The days have shortened quite a bit now and I fly from 5:45 A.M. until noon and from 3:00 P.M. to 6:15 P.M. I have a gorgeous tan from swimming so much. Yesterday I dove too deep and really skinned my face, my forehead, the bridge of my nose, the end of my nose, upper lip, chin, and right shoulder so everyone teased me today—quite a sight![21]

In another letter written to Glenn just eight days later, she shared a logbook entry with her good friend in Kansas City.

I've passed the 2000th hour mark, have exactly 2,007 hours and 45 minutes.[22]

I have a swell boss. He has good equipment. They are just finishing some swell new runways on our field here. Plenty of Army traffic in here....[23]

Les Buchner had an equally high regard for Evelyn, too. "She was an A-1 pilot, very sharp. You could show her something once, and she would have it. She got along with everyone."[24]

Evelyn's letter continued. "Have been swimming, and ice skating and horseback riding a lot since I've been here. Still wanting my instrument rating—a stickler to get."[25] Very few planes had radios and instruments in those days, and not until the Link Trainer (a simulated cockpit) was invented did most pilots have an opportunity to work on this rating.

On November 17, Evelyn wrote there wasn't much flying, but with a three-day-old license renewal in her billfold, she was enjoying the change. She took Stinson NC32284 out for a one-hour-and-forty-minute "pleasure trip." Flying northwest for sixty-some miles, she scouted Lost Hill territory looking for places to hunt ducks. Commercial duck clubs put levees up, pumped water in from wells, and waited for migrating Mallards, Pintail Sprigs, Blue-wing Teal and the Spoonbill Shovelers. Perhaps this year her schedule would allow her to hunt. A 1938 Nebraska newspaper article, picturing her in hunting clothes with a shotgun, described her as a crack shot, bringing in her limit of pheasants each fall.[26]

On another day, sitting in the shade of a hangar on the airport ramp, Evelyn waited patiently. She had purchased a new camera and was trying to get pictures of "big ships, little ships, odd-shaped ships, everything."[27] The heavy movement of Army and Navy traffic through Bakersfield was exciting to her. Perhaps she, like many other Americans, wondered what it meant for her country. In less than three weeks, they would know.

On the morning of December 7, 1941, Cornelia Fort was monitoring landing and takeoff practice at John Rodgers, a civilian airport right next to Pearl Harbor.

> Coming in just before the last landing, I looked casually around and saw a military plane coming directly toward me. I jerked the controls away from my student and jammed the throttle wide open to pull above the oncoming plane. He passed so close under us that our celluloid windows rattled violently. I looked down to see what kind of plane it was.
>
> The painted red balls on the tops of wings shone brightly in the sun. I looked again with complete and utter disbelief. Honolulu was familiar with the emblem of the Rising Sun on passenger ships but not on airplanes. I looked quickly at Pearl Harbor and my spine tingled when I saw billowing black smoke....[28]

Evelyn was also instructing on December 7, but Kern County Airport remained open, even though airports on the coast were flying red flags of warning. She recorded five hours and fifty-five minutes of dual and twenty minutes of solo time, probably not realizing how profound the changes would be for her and the Les Buchner Flying Service. An Army Air Force directive was soon issued: Kern County Airport would be turned into a bomber base. By the middle of December, two thousand soldiers were tent-camped on the airport premises, and one had to have a pass to get within a half-mile of the field.[29]

Evelyn did not instruct from Kern County after December 19, 1941. Wartime regulations restricted private flying between the coastline and 150 miles inland. That meant all civilian flying, if it wanted to remain in California, had to move into desert country.

In a mood of apparent frustration, she wrote to Glenn:

> Well, everything is such a muddle now. Without private flying, I am practically out of a job, so I am getting mad at the Japs now for almost putting me out of a job.[30]

Evelyn also penned another letter that day, one reassuring a little girl in Eustis, Nebraska, with whom she had stayed when barnstorming off the family's pasture in 1939. Perhaps Evelyn wanted to make sure Patty Baer would not worry about her.

> Hello, Patty,
>
> Just a line to let you know I'm o.k. The war has grounded all civilian flying for the present but I believe we will soon be able to fly again and then I will be o.k. We have lots of blackouts and plenty of guns and soldiers around. That is all you see anymore around here. Well, this is a short letter but it is all I have time for.
>
> Evelyn[31]

Within four days of the Army's directive, Les Buchner had made a decision. He would move his flying school to Lone Pine, California, a beautiful place in the Sierra Nevada where he had spent some time fishing years earlier. On December 26, 1941, Evelyn climbed into NC11490, Buchner's Waco F-2. Taxiing the open cockpit, bi-wing tail-dragger out to the runway, she took a deep breath and thought about the changes this move might bring. World War II, less than three weeks old, would change everyone's life. Her parents, happy with their place in Bakersfield, would be staying behind. When she was sixty or seventy and looking back on her life, would this be the time when she separated permanently from them? That time must come, sooner or later.

Evelyn turned and looked at Scottie. Always ready to fly, he seemed to be smiling. "What does he know?" she thought, and returned the smile. With a steady and purposeful motion, Evelyn pushed the throttle all the way forward. The plane, picking up speed as it roared down the runway, lifted off, responding to the skilled hands of its pilot. Gently banking toward the east, Evelyn would skirt the southern end of the Sierra Nevada as she flew into the beautiful, high desert country of California.

Mary Kathryn Farmer Sharp and John Evans Sharp (Evelyn's adoptive parents), Bakersfield, California, 1941

Beneath Mt. Whitney

*E*velyn loved Lone Pine. Perhaps the small, frame houses with their white picket fences and the beauty of the area reminded her of home—except Nebraska didn't have the Sierra Nevada , snow-capped through most of the year. Looking west, the view was breath-taking.

Evelyn wrote to Glenn: "The little town has a population of 800, and the skiing is wonderful—just 14 miles to snow—beautiful country for horseback riding. Fifteen to 20 movies are made here each year."[1]

Founded in the early 1800s to house ranchers and suppliers of the Cerro Gordo, Kearsage, and Darwin silver mines, Lone Pine had been the location capital of Western movies since 1920. Horseshoe Meadow, Lubkin Canyon, and craggy boulders in the Alabama Hills were settings for such films as the Lone Ranger serials, "Gunga Din" with Cary Grant, Tom Mix's "Riders of the Purple Sage," and the 1943 release of Roy Rogers' "Hands Across the Border."[2] The walls of Lone Pine's Indian Trading Post (at the traffic light corner) still bear the sig-natures of well-known actors, actresses, and directors who stopped in to shop.[3] There was always lots of excitement when the movie people came to town, which seemed to be most of the time.

The relocation of Buchner's Civilian Pilot Training Program to Lone Pine brought about several changes in the community. William Bauer, the local high school principal, went to work implementing ground school instruction for flight training into the teaching schedule.[4] And it soon became apparent to Les Buchner that the present runway was inadequate for his fleet of airplanes. In fact, Evelyn had to wait in Independence, California, with the Waco she was ferrying from Bakersfield until her employer made arrangements to lengthen the runway.

"I just told the farmer who owned the land adjoining the present strip of my problem," Les Buchner relates. "I remember there was no hesitation in his offering to move the fence a bit more to the south."[5] The memories of Pearl Harbor were fresh in everyone's mind. Patriotism ran high; and people, like the farmer in Lone Pine, were eager to do whatever they could to support the war effort.

Evelyn landed at Lone Pine on January 3, 1942, and not long thereafter she received a telegram from Jacqueline Cochran. It read as follows:

NEW YORK NY 23RD VIA BAKERSFIELD

E C SHARP   CALIF 24

DOW HOTEL

CONFIDENTIALLY ORGANIZING BRITISH AIR TRANSPORT AUXILIARY [ATA] I AM WIREING ALL THE WOMEN PILOTS WHERE ADDRESS AVAILABLE TO ASK IF YOU WOULD BE WILLING TO VOLUNTEER FOR SERVICE WITH A NUCLEAS TO CONSTITUTE INITIAL CONTINGENT OF NEWLY FORMED AMERICAN WOMANS SQUADRON OF A T A FOR SERVICE IN BRITISH ISLES REQUIREMENTS COMPRISE REGULAR A T A EXAMINATION INCLUDING FLIGHT TEST AND PHYSICAL EXAMINATION IN MONTREAL IF AFTER I HAVE INTERVIEWED YOU YOU WILL RECEIVE YOUR TRANSPORTATION TO MONTREAL AND MAINTANENCE WHILE THERE IN MONTREAL YOU PAY YOUR FLIGHT TEST AND ALL OTHER REQUIREMENTS. YOU WILL BE SENT TO ENGLAND PAY SAME AS PAID ENGLISH WOMEN ATA—SUBSTANTIAL INSURANCE AND TWO WAY TRANSPORTATION FROM

YOUR HOME TO ENGLAND RANKS WOULD BE SAME
GENERALLY AS ENGLISH ATA WOMEN PILOTS UNI-
FORM FURNISHED BY ATA HOPE WE WILL GET OR-
GANIZED TO LEAVE ABOUT MAR FIRST EVERY
FRONT NOW OUR FRONT AND FOR THOSE DESIRING
QUICK ACTIVE SERVICE SHORT OF ACTUAL COMBAT
BUT INCLUDING FLIGHT EXPERIENCE—I HAVE BEEN
ASSURED BY THOSE IN AUTHORITY THAT WOMEN
NOT USED FOR FERRYING OR ANY ORGANIZED FLY-
ING IF INTERESTED AND SO I WILL KNOW THE NUM-
BER AVAILABLE AND THEIR LOCATION FOR MY
ITINERARY OF INTERVIEWS PLEASE WIRE ME 630
FIFTH AVE NEW YORK CITY AND YOU WILL RECEIVE
LETTER WITH MORE DETAILS. OFFICIAL REQUEST
HAVE BEEN MADE BY THE BRITISH COMMISSION
YOU ARE REQUESTED TO RELEASE NO PUBLICITY AS
A RESULT OF THIS TELEGRAM IF YOU HAVE NAMES
OF ANY PILOTS I HAVE MISSED PLS ADVSE COR-
DIALLY REGARDS

JACQUELINE COCHRANE[6]

It had been Jacqueline Cochran's hope to organize and train
American women pilots to fly non-combat roles for the United States
Army Air Force (AAF), thereby releasing men for war duty. But when
meetings and conversations with Eleanor Roosevelt, her husband,
President Franklin D. Roosevelt, Brig. Gen. Henry H. Arnold, chief of
AAF, and others failed to produce any action, Cochran sent her telegrams to seventy-six women. In a memo, General Arnold directed that
negotiations for hiring women pilots in the United States would not
take place until Cochran returned from England. This would give the
decision-makers an opportunity to study the need for such an organization and then evaluate the women's performance in England.

Evelyn did not join Air Transport Auxiliary, nor did her Ninety-
Nine friend Pat Thomas who had recently moved with her CPTP operation to Lone Pine. There was talk America would soon have its own
women's ferrying squadron. The two young instructor pilots, whose
careers continued to parallel, would wait.

"You can't believe how surprised Evelyn and I were to see each other," Pat Thomas Gladney recalls. Pat had been ferrying Luscombes for Blair Flying Service across the desert from Kingman, Arizona, when she landed at Lone Pine. "As I taxied to the ramp, on the first of several ferrying trips, whom should I see but Evelyn. It was like old home week. We were so glad to see each other."[7]

The only place to stay in town was the Dow Hotel, an old building of Spanish architecture designed for the early movie people. Wartime gas rationing had curtailed recreational driving so the proprietor welcomed the women's business. Most of the male instructors stayed in private residences, while the War Training Cadets had a camp city in tents near the airport.

It was not long, however, before Evelyn found this "cute, little, one-bedroom house with a white, picket fence."[8] Evelyn, Pat, and Kittie Leaming, a former student of Pat's in Gardena, California, all moved in, each trying to carve out some space for one another. Sleeping quarters presented a problem in logistics, especially when Pat's mother came from the East for the winter. The Thomases took the bed, Kittie got the couch in the living room, and Evelyn lugged her sleeping bag and cot outside to the front lawn. Pat remembers Evelyn feeling the fresh air was better for her asthma anyway.

On Sunday, February 15, 1942, the temperature dropped to fourteen degrees. Evelyn probably thought it a bit colder than usual, but she pulled the blanket up over her head and dropped off to sleep. By morning, several inches of snow had fallen not only on the higher elevations of the Sierra Nevada, but also on the sleeping town several thousand feet below. Inside a white, picket fence, the stirring mass of humanity undoubtedly startled any passers-by on their way to early church that morning.

Even after Pat's mother returned to New Jersey, Evelyn continued to sleep outside. By that time, a "lovely black and white cat sort of moved in with us and proceeded to have three kittens."[9] Though Evelyn loved animals, her asthma could not tolerate the fur.

On May 6, 1942, Evelyn wrote to Glenn Buffington, telling him how much she enjoyed the scenery. She swam, hiked, rode horses, and fished in the clear, cold waters of mountain streams. "It's a swell country up here for this."[10] Leaky, and his wife, Ethel, ran the Oliva's Pack Train Outfit in Lone Pine. He apparently was not very ambitious when the movie companies were not on location; the women had to venture into the pasture to catch and bridle the cow ponies themselves. Sometimes the horse took the bit, and other times it waited for the rider to mount, before bucking her off. "Evelyn was a good rider,"[11] Kittie Leaming King remembers. She didn't get bucked off.

Flight training in CPTP at Lone Pine shut down about noon, and the cadets didn't fly again until four o'clock. A combination of high temperatures at an elevation of 3,770 feet above sea level effectively thinned the air, creating less lift on wing surfaces. Known as High Density Altitude, this phenomenon caused risky takeoffs for low-horsepower engines and their young trainee pilots.

Evelyn, Pat, and Kittie enjoyed the break on those days when they just flew until noon. It gave them a chance to cool off at the Lone Pine Country Club in the nearby Alabama Hills. Constructed of railroad ties, the cabin was originally built by cowboy movie star Hopalong Cassidy as a wedding present for his new bride. Its simulated, natural-boulder pool fed by a cold mountain stream offered an opportunity for the three women to catch up on their hangar flying. It also gave Evelyn a chance to work on her suntan. "I'm beginning to get a good tan—take a 20 min. sunbath each day,"[12] she wrote Glenn.

On June 13, 1942, Evelyn took a two-week vacation, but not one from flying. Charles Sumner, the owner of the Whiting Cafe in Lone Pine and a financial supporter of the CPTP at the airport, was working on his private license.[13] Evelyn agreed to give him dual instruction on a flying trip back East because student pilots could fly solo only within a hundred miles of their home airport. The eastern leg of this trip included a route through the southern states of Nevada, Arizona, New Mexico, Texas, Arkansas, Mississippi, Alabama, and Georgia. For their return, Sumner plotted a more northerly course, crossing the states of Tennessee, Kentucky, Indiana, Illinois, and Missouri. Evelyn looked forward to scheduled stops in Lincoln, Nebraska, and Spearfish, South Dakota, where she could renew old friendships.

On Friday evening June 26, 1942, a blue-and-yellow Interstate Cadet turned onto final approach at Union Air Terminal. As NC37421 touched down, memories of earlier flying days at the Lincoln Airplane and Flying School flooded Evelyn's thoughts. On the overnight stop in Lincoln, Evelyn would visit John and Valda Hoehne, the couple who befriended her while she worked on her instructor rerating in the spring of 1940. The next morning, before picking up a northwesterly heading to Spearfish, South Dakota, sixteen-year-old Dorette Hoehne took her first ride in the front seat of a two-place tandem Interstate. Two years before, she had helped Evelyn push the old Curtiss Robin behind a hangar to avoid CAA inspectors. A picture of Dorette, Charlie Sumner, and "Nebraska's No. 1 Aviatrix" appeared on the front page of *The Lincoln Star*. A related article, entitled "Evelyn Sharp, 22, Flies 'Em High, Wide, Handsome" read:

> Miss Sharp has taught five CPTP courses since and has taught more than 20 private students in addition to her government trainees. For herself she has had 2600 hours in the air; she left Nebraska with 760 to her credit. Miss Sharp has trained men for acceptance in the army glider pilot training program and has qualified pilots for instructor positions in the army air force primary training. Men seem to have no hesitancy about taking instruction from a woman even though the woman is only 22 and weighs 117 pounds, and she has had 300 students. They are co-operative, usually not argumentative, attentive. In fact, young men who would be pilots have come to ask for her as flight instructor, saying she had been recommended by someone who had taken the course.[14]

The article concluded with an unhappy story about her dog.

> There was a bit of sadness in Miss Sharp's return [response]. "Scotty," her companion on flights for so many years, practically an aviator in his own proud way, will ride the skies no more. He died as he never would have chosen to die, under the wheels of a car. "Scotty" has no successor although if a little waggle tail in black would present himself, he might be taken on. He never can hope to succeed "Scotty I."[15]

After a two-day RON (Remain Over Night) in Spearfish, Charlie Sumner and Evelyn flew a southerly course that took them through the states of Wyoming, Utah, and Nevada. On June 30, 1942, the Interstate Cadet set down on the high desert, dirt runway at Lone Pine, California.

Although the terrain was beautiful around Lone Pine, the topography produced an unusual, but predictable, weather phenomenon for pilots and their flying operations. Within thirty minutes after clouds formed over 14,495-foot Mt. Whitney, winds funneled down the Owen's Valley, blowing sand off the dry lake bed. The ditches dug in the airport ramp for wheels of the aircraft were often not deep enough to keep the airplanes from "flying." Several times in the night, when the gales were really strong, Evelyn crawled out of her sleeping bag to join her friends at the airport. Hanging onto the wings until winds subsided, Pat Thomas Gladney recalls, "It was great fun!"[16]

Pat remembers another evening, probably the women's first, at the Olancha Steak House some twenty-three miles south of Lone Pine. Famous for its succulent steaks, the simple restaurant provided a Saturday evening setting for cadet pilots and their instructors to compare CPTP operations. There were three government flying school operators at the airport: Bob Blair, Les Buchner, and the newest, Roy Pemberton. Pilots from each enjoyed swapping stories about themselves and each other. Pat also recalls a remark made soon after the women sat down at the Olancha. "Evelyn must have been very poor while in Nebraska because, as we were getting ready to order, she commented she had never had a steak."[17] Most people who knew Evelyn did not understand how poor her upbringing had really been. She was not one to complain.

The war was on everyone's mind. Manzanar, a recently-constructed internment camp capable of housing ten thousand Japanese-Americans, was located nine miles north of Lone Pine on Route 395. Those housed there brought home the reality of war's injustice. Kittie Leaming King still carries very clear images of the displaced people, many native-born Americans who came into Lone Pine with their rocking chairs tied to the fronts of cars. The US Government had decreed the displaced persons could bring anything with them they could carry. With cars so full of personal belongings one could hardly see in, they made their way slowly through the gates of the barbed wire compound just across the road from the Lone Pine Airport. It was not until 1988 that President Reagan issued a formal apology for our government's actions, and Congress legislated payments to sixty thousand surviving internees.[18]

A Birthday Present

That summer, Les Buchner closed his flying operation at Lone Pine and moved it to Cedar City, Utah, where he had hopes and some assurance from the government he could increase the size of his advanced school. Evelyn did not hold the necessary ratings to teach advanced. She would stay at Lone Pine.

On August 6, 1942, Evelyn and two other employees filed a complaint with the State of California Division of Labor Statistics and Law Enforcement against Les Buchner. At a salary of $250 a month, Evelyn claimed Buchner owed her $562.30 in back wages. Apparently there was a lot of paperwork involved in this flight training program and government payments were often slow. Once, when another CPTP operator had used up all his own funds, he shut down the operation and went home. Roy Pemberton recalled, "I had no choice.... We left 40 CPT students stranded, but the Army hand-delivered the money the next day—and was never late again."[1] In a letter dated August 31, 1942, the State Labor Commissioner, H. C. Carrasco, forwarded a check to Evelyn and the two others in full payment of their claims.[2] According to Les Buchner, it was sometimes necessary to file a claim before the government paid up.

By the first of August 1943, Evelyn was working for the new operator, Roy Pemberton. Holding Glider License No. 8 signed in 1930 by Orville Wright, he had something in common with Evelyn. On

May 19, 1938, Pemberton had flown the Twentieth Commemorative
Air Mail Flight out of Bakersfield, California, the same day Evelyn was
flying the air mail out of Ord.[3] In Lone Pine, Pemberton's school was
awarded the contract for the Navy CPTP; Evelyn would have a class
of five and some private students. She wrote Glenn Buffington, telling
him she had soloed all five of her Navy pilots on the same day. By August 25, they were all ready for the test. "Gee, I worry about them. I
hope they will all get through." She closed her note with the following:
"I am supposed to get a little pup about Friday or Saturday. I can
hardly wait."[4]

In an earlier letter, Evelyn shared how lonesome she felt for a "little pooch. A dog is such a sweet pal."[5]

On September 5, 1942, Evelyn and eighty-three other women
who had at least five hundred hours of flying time received a telegram. It read as follows:

> AFATC S938 PERIOD FERRYING DIVISION AIR TRANS-
> PORT COMMAND IS ESTABLISHING GROUP OF
> WOMEN PILOTS FOR DOMESTIC FERRYING STOP
> NECESSARY QUALIFICATIONS...STOP ADVISE COM-
> MANDING OFFICER SECOND FERRYING GROUP FER-
> RYING   DIVISION   TRANSPORT   COMMAND
> NEWCASTLE COUNTY AIRPORT WILMINGTON DELA-
> WARE IF YOU ARE IMMEDIATELY AVAILABLE AND
> CAN REPORT AT ONCE AT WILMINGTON AT YOUR
> OWN EXPENSE RECOMMENDATION PROOF OF EDU-
> CATION AND FLYING TIME STOP
>
>   BAKER END GEORGE
>   ARNOLD COMMANDING GENERAL
>   ARMY AIR FORCES
>   WASHINGTON[6]

Although Jacqueline Cochran had not yet fulfilled her contractual
responsibilities with the Air Transport Auxiliary in England, Harold L.
George, new Brigadier General of the Air Transport Command (ATC),
was apparently not aware of Arnold's directive to wait for Cochran's
return.[7] Day by day, General George became increasingly concerned
about the lack of ferry pilots. There was a small pool of licensed civil-

ian pilots, but the majority of male instructor pilots had secured deferment to teach combat flying to young males.

It was during this time that Nancy Harkness Love, a highly respected commercial pilot, quietly, but assertively, became an advocate of using experienced women pilots for ferrying operations. Use of women in domestic service to ferry airplanes would free men for combat or overseas ferrying. In June of 1940, Love had helped fly new Stinson 105 sport models to the border town of Houlton, Maine. Under the terms of Lend-Lease and United States Neutrality Laws, the planes had to be towed by truck or pushed across the Canadian border before being flown to Europe for the Allied war effort.[8]

On September 10, 1942, Henry L. Stinson, Secretary of War, announced the formation of an experimental women's flying group within the Air Transport Command. Known as the Women's Auxiliary Ferrying Squadron (WAFS), it had as its director Nancy Harkness Love. Jacqueline Cochran, in London with the Air Transport Auxiliary, was livid when she heard the news. Feeling betrayed, she was on a plane "headed for New York within twenty-four hours."[9]

Jacqueline Cochran, holder of numerous aviation speed records, had ready access to the ears of the brass. Her husband, Floyd Odlum, a wealthy investment genius, was a New Dealer and regular contributor to the Franklin Delano Roosevelt presidential campaigns. Not pleased with how events had taken place at ATC, Jacqueline Cochran was appointed Director of the Women's Flying Training Detachment (WFTD) by September 18. In comparison to that of Nancy Love's group, this program took women with less flying experience and prepared them to fly heavier aircraft. Cochran's school also trained women for nonferrying aviation jobs such as flying tow targets for anti-aircraft practice and serving as test pilots for repaired military airplanes.

In Lone Pine, Evelyn and Pat Thomas discussed the telegram of September 5 from Colonel Baker. Both women were interested in this new women's ferrying group, but each felt a responsibility to their employer, Roy Pemberton. Pat writes, "I was the flight examiner and we felt it would leave him in the lurch if we both pulled out at the same time. We decided Evelyn should go and then let me know if it were for

Evelyn and Shanty McTavish, Lone Pine, California, September 1942

real or not."[10] Evelyn did wire Pat later, telling her to come, but by then it was too late. Jobs were frozen and the CAA ordered Pat to Phoenix to teach instrument flying.

On September 24, 1942, Evelyn logged a thirty-five minute flight in a Taylorcraft. Under "Remarks" she wrote, "First ride—went to sleep." No, it was not the pilot. It was Shanty McTavish, Evelyn's new four-month-old Scottie puppy. Logging an additional four hours and forty minutes on an October 7 cross-country flight to Bakersfield and Las Vegas, Shanty slept most of that trip, too. John and Mary Sharp, both now employed at Basic Magnesium, Inc. in Henderson, Nevada, had moved sometime after Evelyn went to Lone Pine.[11] As a member of the Carpenter's Union, John and twenty-five other men had been called to Henderson to help with construction of a new munitions plant. Later, he worked as a machinist preparing shell casings, while Mary became part of the kitchen staff at the plant hospital.

Evelyn's final entry from the Lone Pine area was an October 9 flight to Las Vegas. Phil Livingston, who would ferry the Stinson Voyager back to the high desert country, signed her logbook with the following remark: "First pup I flew with—very quiet and gentlemanly."

In a letter dated October 19, 1942, Evelyn wrote:

I'm on my way back to the East again. This time to the Women's Ferry Command....I don't know what is in store for me, but surely hope I like it and they like me.

My mother came as far with me [on the train] as Des Moines. She's going to visit her mother. She sure deserved it; she hasn't seen her mother for an awful long time. ...my 5 Navy CPT boys all did fine. I started on six new ones and got 3 soloed and then left.

I have a new Scottie pup. At least I think I have if he fairs this trip. I've had him a month. ...and he has already got seven hours' flying time. He's the cutest little fellow you ever saw.[12]

"The perfect combination plane, girl, 'Evelyn', hat and smile — Will you have a smile for me when next we meet? And meet we will so until then, here's best wishes from your 'instructor' Pal." 1942

The first order of business at New Castle Army Air Base (NCAAB) was an interview, conducted by Colonel Robert Baker, commander of the Second Ferrying Group, Nancy Love, director of this experimental women's ferrying program, and several other military personnel. Collectively, they examined Evelyn's logbooks and other official documents which served as proof for the Ferry Command's requirements. And to complete the interview process, she handed them papers showing American citizenship and two letters of recommendation from reputable citizens speaking to her character and flying ability.

Although memoranda from Colonel Baker and the Ferrying Division stated there would be no distinction between male and female civilian pilots, and that women would be employed in exactly the same manner as male pilots under Civil Service Rules, there were explicit differences:

(1) Women were paid $250 a month; men received $380.

(2) Men were employed on a three-month trial basis with the idea of giving those who qualified a commission in the armed forces and permanent appointment to a squadron; these opportunities were not available to women.

(3) Women had to pass the Army "64" medical exam which was not required of men unless they wanted a commission.

(4) Women needed logged time of 500 hours; men were asked to show proof of 200 hours.[13]

Later that day, Evelyn took her flight check in a Fairchild PT19 tandem trainer. Though confident in her ability to pilot a plane, she was very much aware of the power the flight examiner possessed. No doubt she had already heard of several women who had failed the check ride. Evelyn still had that dream of making aviation her career. She did not want to fail.

Evelyn liked the feel of the PT-19A's open cockpit and the 175-hp Range inline engine. For forty minutes, she performed maneuvers and procedures at the direction of Elliot R. Starbuck, a 2nd Lt. Air Corps pilot. He also graded her on relaxation, flying technique, attention to instruments, and judgment in the air. Evelyn made two takeoffs and landings.[14] Then he asked for her logbook and made the following entry:

I consider this applicant qualified for flying with the Air Corps Ferrying Command. Applicant qualified for attendance ACFC (Air Corps Ferry Command) Transition School.

Evelyn's logbook, with an initial entry of thirty minutes on February 4, 1935, now showed 2,968 hours, the most flying time any pilot would bring to the WAFS. On October 20, 1942, she became the seventeenth woman to be accepted into the Women's Auxiliary Ferrying Squadron.[15] If Evelyn had known October 20 to be the actual date of her birth, she might have thought this her best birthday present ever.[16]

A Letter From Aunt Elsie

$\mathcal{T}$he next day, Evelyn was issued a picture ID card which made her employment as a Civil Service pilot official.[1] Although WAFS who had been at New Castle Army Air Base since September were preparing for their first ferry mission, it would be four weeks before Evelyn earned ferrying orders. In the meantime, she would learn to fly, navigate, and march "the Army way."[2]

Evelyn moved into Bachelor Officer Quarters (BOQ) 14, one of many new construction sites on the field at Wilmington. She negotiated the entrance to the two-story rectangular frame building, set off in the boondocks, by "walking the plank." To keep the women from stepping into a ditch with knee-high deep mud, a wooden plank was laid between the BOQ's entrance and a paved road in front. "It took forever for the 'powers that be' to issue us galoshes,"[3] WAFS Kathryn Bernheim Fine remembers.

The furnishings inside the quarters were starkly simple—a sagging regulation Army cot, a chest of drawers, and a bar for hanging clothes. Inside walls were unfinished, with knotholes and unbelievable gaps in boards creating ribbon and round patterns of sunlight on opposite walls or floors. It was not long, however, before the women converted their accommodations into reflections of themselves. Teresa James carried a brand-new chaise lounge up to her second-floor room. Several women turned roughly-cut horizontal wall braces into shelves, displaying pictures of loved ones and mementos from an earlier day. Evelyn tacked up favorite Mexican blankets purchased in California to cover the BOQ walls. Phyllis Burchfield Fulton remembers her liking bright colors, especially red. "Evelyn was always happy when we gathered in her room for some hangar flying. She talked a lot about her experiences in Lone Pine. Shanty, who could forget him? He ruled the barracks. When Evelyn was on a mission, we all looked after him. And even though animals were forbidden, Evelyn's personality won anyone over."[4]

The common bathroom facilities astounded these women who were used to privacy in their own homes. The shower stalls had no curtains and the stools no doors. Above the wash bowls was a short, narrow shelf, and a very small mirror. But the men's urinals attracted the most attention; many women in 1942 had never seen one. Employed by Civil Service, the WAFS paid seventy-five cents a day[5] for this housing, urinals and all.

During the training period, WAFS wore the khaki military one-piece flying suit, helmet, and goggles. Later when the weather turned colder, Evelyn also checked out the "monkey suit,"[6] a bulky, fleece-lined leather jacket and high-waisted, fleece-lined leather pants. Held up by suspenders, the pants zipped from shinbone to sternum. A chin-strapped leather flying helmet, a leather, fleece-lined face mask, and wool-lined boots completed military attire for open cockpit flying at below-freezing temperatures.

During the four-week training period, Evelyn attended Army ground school classes covering meteorology, navigation, courtesies and customs of the service, routing and procedures, and military law. She was taught how to stand guard, handle rifles, and dismantle and assemble a .45 caliber pistol blindfolded.

Another part of the training period was flying the liaisons and trainers they would later ferry. Since these aircraft had no radio equipment, the pilots practiced navigation by using geographical and topographical landmarks — the same skill Evelyn had used while barnstorming back in Nebraska. From October 21 until the end of the month, she trained five hours and forty minutes in the Taylorcraft liaison, a plane very similar to her old Taylor Cub, and seven hours and forty minutes in the PT-19A. All flying was local.

Evelyn had not been at New Castle very long when an indirect reference to her was made in a WAFS meeting. Nancy Love had been discussing Colonel Baker's displeasure with a woman pilot he had seen smoking at Headquarters. It was against the rules for women (not the men) to smoke there.

"And another thing—about joy-riding!" Nancy looked coolly about the room. "I overheard one of you saying a lieutenant invited you to ride along with him while he is taking transition. No matter how great the temptation, you cannot accept rides."

At this point, Evelyn spoke up. "I didn't ask him to take me." Her big brown eyes widened further, while the corners of her mouth turned down.

"I didn't say you did," replied Nancy. "But the boys like to show off."

Betty Gillies, the first woman to sign up for the WAFS added, "Girls, the public does not understand that a mixed crew may work as a flight team. They are suspicious and people aren't ready for mixed crew just yet."[7]

"I remember Evelyn being upset about it," Teresa James recalls. "She was anxious to fly, period, but she didn't know it was strictly forbidden to fly with a male pilot on his transition or be with him in a plane without orders."[8] Evelyn had been jumping into airplanes with male pilots since she was fifteen years old. This attitude was new to her.

Colonel Baker also made it clear the WAFS were not to have flight contact with male ferry pilots who might be going in the same direction. Operations would try to schedule them apart. The women could not hitchhike back from ferrying missions in military planes; they had to return by commercial aircraft, unless the ferrying command sent a special plane for them. All of this was done to protect the WAFS reputation.

It did not take long for Evelyn to catch on. At mess, the women were assigned to tables by themselves; no men were allowed in the BOQ unless they were officers on inspection. Furthermore, a house-mother had been hired for the women's quarters.

The one place where Army Air Force personnel and female civilian ferry pilots could socialize was at the officers' clubs. These privileges were afforded to all civilian pilots in the Air Transport Command. They danced, watched first runs of movies, played Ping-Pong and gin rummy, ate Sunday night buffet, smoked, and drank. In time, many of the restrictions keeping men and women apart would be lifted, but Evelyn waited, as did most of the women, until they were removed. The opportunity to fly was not one she was willing to jeopardize.

In November of 1942, Evelyn continued training in L-2Bs and PT-19As, most of the flying local though some of it into Hagerstown, Maryland, where the Fairchild aviation factory was located. In a letter to her parents dated November 13, 1942, she wrote:

Dear Mom and Pop:

Gee, you don't know how tickled I am that you are in a house. Isn't it much better? Gee, I hope you can make out in it o.k.

I received the box of stuff. But you know I just can't locate those insurance policies. I am going to search everything again & see if I can't find them. This business of moving around sure mixes things up.

Gee, I'm so glad daddy is o.k. Now listen dad, take it easy. Don't work if it's too much for you. We'll manage somehow. Is the CO going to pay the hospital bill?

Yes, I have insurance with the government [this was not true]. But I haven't found out how much.

Oh, yes, Send all the stuff I sent over from Lone Pine. Also the two blankets & coat & panda bear and Scattri. And my formal & the thing to keep it in. Just my winter formal. Remember those boxes I sat beside the bed? Send those. Don't send my cowboy hat or boots or my black boots. Be sure to take good care of the things I leave. Be sure a lot of my hangars are in there. Those boxes from Lone Pine have plenty in them.

Did you get the tire? Also what is new about the rationing and gas rationing?

Also send little cart.

One more week and I'll be ready to ferry. In other words, I'll graduate. Have flown on four practice x-country trips. One to Middletown, Pa. One to Harrisburg, Pa. & two to Hagarstown, Maryland. I don't think you have to worry about me getting into bad weather cause boy we don't even fly unless under certain weather conditions.

In fact, it is too windy today & heck I've flown in lots worse wind.

Boy on those x-country trips in PT 19's they are really cold. We put on those big winter flying suits and the only thing sticking out is my nose. In fact we are so bulky a mechanic has to help us put our chutes on. More fun. We also fly formation. One person leads the group and the rest of us fly formation. At any rate it is more fun than a barrel of monkeys. There are 22 of us now. Two new members. Shanty is here on the floor. He says

> woof, woof, woof
> meaning
> Lots of Luff,
>
> Evelyn and Shanty

Oh, yes Aunt Elsie is coming Nov. 18.[9]

By November 22, 1942, Evelyn had learned to fly "the Army way," thirteen hours and ten minutes in the L-2Bs and L-4Bs and sixteen hours and forty-five minutes in the PT-19As. With the satisfactory completion of ground school, she was eligible to wear the WAFS standard attire as opposed to a uniform which denoted a military connection. Having selected a gray-green gabardine material, Nancy Love sought the services of a tailor who constructed for each of the women a belted jacket, matching skirt and slacks, and an overseas cap.[10] Since

Evelyn Sharp, Civilian Ferry Pilot, Women's Auxiliary Ferrying Squadron, New Castle Army Air Base, Wilmington, Delaware, November 1942

there was no clothing allowance, Evelyn paid for her own. She wore the silver wings of Civilian Pilot, Air Corps Ferry Command, with the stylized radio beacon on the left breast pocket. On its shield border, red and blue enamel spelled out in Morse Code, ATC.[11] On the upper left sleeve, Evelyn sewed the Army Air Force insignia, a sapphire blue disc with yellow wings and a white star with a red center. Beneath it in blue letters was the acronym, WAFS. The silver wings and gold propeller blade worn on the jacket lapel and overseas cap were the insignia of the Army Air Force and the aviation cadets. Elsie Crouse Rick, the woman who had given birth to a daughter in Melstone, Montana, twenty-three years earlier, would be extremely proud.

On the weekend of November 20, 1942, Aunt Elsie came to Wilmington to see her daughter. In a letter to John and Mary, she wrote of feelings and remembrances.

> Dear Folks, I suppose by this time, Evelyn has written you and told you that I was to see her at New Castle Air Base. They sure are a brave bunch of girls to do the things they are doing and they all seem to be happy doing it. It sure was the happiest moment of my life, when she wrote me and told me she was in the east and would like to have me come down and see her. She sure is a grand girl, and thanks to you folks, I don't know how I can ever thank you. We had a

lot of fun together as she introduced me to some of the officers and WAFS, and they would say you sure resemble each other a great deal. Several came up to us and would say Evelyn I take it this is your mother, and we would both pipe up at the same time and say, Oh no, just an aunt. I got a kick out of Evelyn and how much fun she was getting out of it. Of course I still like to dance so we would go over to the Officer's Club and dance.... Whenever I danced with the officers they always told me what a grand niece I had, and how everybody liked her because she was such a wholesome girl, didn't smoke or drink and had such a grand personality. I was terribly disappointed that my visit was cut rather short, I got there on Friday and on Sunday afternoon at three o'clock Mrs. Love came up to the barracks and said she wanted 8 girls to go out on some trips to deliver planes. We were just going out to take some pictures, as Evelyn was all dressed up in her new uniform and did she ever look nice with that figure of hers. Some of the girls are clumsy looking, but she looks just perfect. Even the tailor complimented her and said some of the girls were complaining because their suits didn't fit the girls shape that were out of proportion. He really was right. Hers

"A Grand Girl," proud mother snaps picture of daughter, November 22, 1942, outside BOQ, New Castle Army Air Base, Wilmington, Delaware

fit like a glove. The only trouble Evelyn is going to have is too many officers are falling in love with her. One of the officers had only been there a week and he told me she was the girl of his dreams and she didn't even pay any attention to him just took him as a joke. One Lt. that she dates spent Sunday night with me at the Officer's Club and all he talked about was Evelyn. He is a month younger than she but as handsome as they make them. He thinks Evelyn is just about perfect, and said he had never been so deeply in love with a girl as he was with her, but he knew she had a lot of admirers. He hoped some day he would be the favored one. He said he hoped he could ask Evelyn to be his co-pilot, but he knew she knew more about flying than he did, as she had more flying hrs. Believe me that is no small job those girls are doing and you should see all the baggage those girls have to carry. The next few days after they left it rained so I am wondering if they have returned by now. They sure are a swell bunch of girls and they were all so nice to me. I again want to thank you for doing such a swell job on Evelyn, and I am perfectly happy to be her Aunt Elsie, she seems to get a big kick out of it. Am going to visit around for a few weeks and then I will start out looking for a job again. Hope Evelyn can come to N.Y. soon, so I can show her around. Am staying with friends right now. We had a wonderful Thanksgiving dinner and only hope Evelyn did too. I didn't think much of the eats there, but Evelyn can live on nothing so she doesn't mind. Hope you are both well and happy and write me soon. I think I will be here the rest of the winter.

> Lovingly,
> Elsie[12]

A Letter From Evelyn

O n Sunday afternoon, New Castle Operations received word ten new PT-19As were ready for delivery from the Fairchild factory in Hagerstown, Maryland. Ten WAFS were issued orders to fly; Evelyn was one of them. Visiting family and friends, including Aunt Elsie, said their good-byes, and a line formed at the telephone to break Sunday evening dates.

It took two government-authorized cars to get B-4 bags (the Army's soft-sided, expandable, fold-out suitcase), slide rule computers, brief cases with orders, Transportation Request forms, parachutes, and bulky winter flying equipment to the depot in Wilmington. Fortunately, the train was late. That was not unusual for a Sunday evening when soldiers were returning to their bases from weekend passes, and civilians, who had been visiting servicemen, were going home. There was no room to sit when the women boarded the train, but it was not long until Evelyn, Florene Miller, and Teresa James were favored by three enlisted men who offered their seats to the pretty young women. When the train pulled into Baltimore, it was an hour late. Quickly, Betty Gillies, flight leader for one of the groups, hailed taxis. The women threw in their cumbersome gear and squeezed in around it. But it was too late; they had missed the bus to Hagerstown by two minutes. The pilots would catch an early one in the morning.

The bus from Wilmington made a number of unexpected stops,

and the women ferry pilots did not reach Hagerstown until ten o'clock the next morning. An Army captain assigned to meet them was not happy. He had also met the 4:30 a.m. bus.[1]

Since Hagerstown Airport was socked in due to rain and low ceilings, the WAFS were transported directly and quickly to the Hamilton Hotel. "Sharpie and I went shopping for Christmas cards and long woolen underwear," Teresa James remembers. The women knew the open-cockpit flight would be cold, even with the regulation-issued, fleece-lined, leather flying suit. "Later Sharpie and I went bowling. She did great; the Fairchild aircraft employees wanted to sign her up for their team."[2]

Teresa, who bunked with Evelyn that night, had just fallen asleep when the phone rang. Evelyn, who would awaken to the most subtle sounds, slept right through a ringing telephone. Though half asleep, Teresa finally figured out it was Lt. Walling on the other end of the line wanting to speak with Evelyn. In her address book Evelyn had penciled a rating of D-2 next to the name of Lt. Charles C. Walling. That meant she had dated him and on a scale of 1 to 4, he was good.[3] "I told her later that she would have to bunk with one of the other glamour pusses so I could get some sleep,"[4] Teresa says. A very beautiful woman herself, Teresa could have easily been the recipient of several calls that night; but a few months earlier she and George L. Martin, a B-17 bomber pilot, had been married. Shot down by the Germans, he would not come home to his wife at the end of the war. Teresa would choose not to marry again.

To keep themselves busy until the weather cleared, the WAFS washed their hair, did their nails, shopped, and played cards. Evelyn also provided entertainment for the pilots at the Hamilton Hotel, walking on her hands up and down the carpeted halls. She said she did it to keep herself thin.[5]

Problems with weather minimums continued through Tuesday and into Wednesday morning. Though skies were "soupy" at 1:45 p.m. on November 25, the WAFS with their very first flight of PT-19As were given permission to takeoff. The trip would be short. Visibility was extremely poor, and Teresa James, flight leader of Group II, was not about to continue the mission. Pulling in close to Army 42-33920, she motioned with her chart to return to Hagerstown.[6] Evelyn, raising a hand in acknowledgment, looked to the left and banked her aircraft into a steep 180-degree turn.

After another night at the Hamilton, the women awakened to a much clearer day. It was Thanksgiving. Before sunset, Evelyn and her fellow WAFS had completed the initial leg of her first ferry trip. Using dead reckoning, a method of navigating using landmarks as a visual reference, Evelyn checked off the local rivers, railroads, canals, and roads

"Ready To Fly," first WAFS ferrying mission for PT-19As, Fairchild factory, Hagerstown, Maryland, November 1942

as she flew by. Sometimes the checkpoints were right on the course, at other times they were to the right or left. Evelyn tried to make sure one end of the chart was always firmly secured in the open cockpit. Stories of "flying charts" were not uncommon.

Slices of turkey surrounded by mashed potatoes and gravy, dressing, cranberry sauce, hot rolls, and pumpkin pie with whipped cream awaited their arrival at the Officers' Mess in Charlotte, North Carolina. "We ate until our eyes bulged," Teresa James remembers. "Sharpie had a date with Lt. David Jones from California. Rarely would Evelyn fly into a base where there wasn't someone she knew." She had taught over 350 men to fly before the war, both in CPTP and private instruction. "I can understand why she had hundreds of friends," Teresa reflects. "Everyone loved her. She was a great listener."[7]

The WAFS continued their flight the next morning. Picking up a southwesterly heading, they flew into LaTourneau at Toccoa, Georgia, then on into Chattanooga, Tennessee. Refueled, the planes would fly for an additional two hours and ten minutes, landing at Riddle-McKay Army Primary School at Union City, Tennessee. These pilots, who were part of a military experiment to see if women could ferry Army aircraft, had made history. They had delivered their first fleet of PT-19As.

But Operation's orders were not yet completed:

Upon delv [delivery] of the above aircraft at proper destination the above mentioned Civilian Pilots will return via military, fastest available commercial aircraft, rail, or bus to NCAAB, Wilmington, Delaware, reporting to Gp. Comdr. thereat for further orders.

> By order of Colonel Baker
> Thomas D. Schall
> 1st Lieut., Air Corps
> Asst. Group Operations Officer[8]

Each of these women realized her behavior impacted upon the perceived success or failure of this experiment. Wanting desperately to serve their country and provide similar opportunities for other women, they tried to do what was expected. Without delay, the pilots boarded a bus to Gibbs, Tennessee, where they caught a train to Chattanooga. Female ferry pilots were not allowed to hitch rides on a military plane with male pilots, even if it were going directly to their destination.

At the depot in Chattanooga, Teresa James remembers Sharpie and herself sitting on a bench waiting for the train to arrive. "Ev struck up a conversation with a farmer, Mr. Harper from Hickman, Kentucky. He owned 1500 acres of land. He invited us to send him postcards, and in return, he would send us nuts for Christmas from trees on his farm. Boy, did we get the nuts!"[9] On the first page of Evelyn's brown address book, she wrote:

J.W. Harper   nuts

Hickman Ky.[10]

When the ferry pilots returned to Wilmington, Nancy Love was waiting with a new set of orders. They were to report to Cubhaven in

Lockhaven, Pennsylvania, the following morning. Evelyn laundered her underwear and pressed a few wrinkles from her crumpled cotton shirts. There was no time to wash and get them dry.

On November 29, 1942, Evelyn wrote to her parents from Lockhaven:

> Aunt Elsie had a swell time at NCAAB. She even stayed a couple of days while I was gone.
>
> By the way the gov't has me insured for $10,000 bucks. [This was not true.]
>
> Did you get my letter authorizing you as my agent?
>
> I still can't find those insurance policies. Yours is due in December. Mine too.
>
> Jack Jefford is in Alaska still as a C.A.A. inspector.
>
> One reason the Ferry Command is so much fun is because I have met so many people who knew someone I know. Really fun! Lots of them had heard of me before.
>
> Well, I guess I'll sign off.
>
> > Love,
> > Evelyn[11]

The weather at Lockhaven broke on Monday, November 30, but it did not stay above minimums en route. Forced down at the Marine Base in Quantico, Virginia, the WAFS arrived as unexpected, but not unwelcomed, guests. In a gesture of courtesy, an officer posted an armed guard to escort each of the four WAFS to the common latrine.[12]

The next morning, the flight of L-4Bs flew into Richmond, Virginia, and then on to Camp Pickett at Blackstone, Virginia. As the planes were being refueled, the women grabbed a cup of hot coffee, chatting with the ground crew about the gusty winds and cold temperatures. With several delays on the mission already, they would try to fly another leg before the day ended. Like the rest of the women, Evelyn zipped up her fleece-lined leather jacket with its silver, stylized beacon patch, leaned into the wind and hurried across the ramp. All were seeking the partial protection of an open-cockpit plane. Within an hour, however, four yellow J-3 Cubs were back in the pattern, preparing for another landing at Camp Pickett. Cruising speed of a Cub with a 65-hp engine was rated at 72 miles per hour.[13] Sometimes, strong headwinds made forward progress almost negligible.

That evening, Evelyn, Betty Gillies, Barbara Erickson, and Helen Richards ate dinner at Camp Pickett's Service Club No. 3. They watched a movie, and eventually fell asleep in the nurses' quarters, hoping for better weather the next day.[14] In the morning with more favorable winds, the mission continued. As per orders, Evelyn and another pilot left the group a few days later and continued their delivery to Camp Chaffee at Fort Smith, Arkansas. In terms of time, this was the longest ferry trip Evelyn would make, her flight log recording twelve days. By the sixteenth of December 1942, Evelyn was back at Cubhaven, picking up another J-3 for a return flight to Camp Chaffee. This time she flew a more direct route, west and then south. Delivery was completed by December 19, with only one weather delay.

On December 21, Evelyn was back in Hagerstown for a PT-19A ferry trip to Bellinger, Texas. Weather was still not cooperating. The front page of the December 27, 1942, Charlotte, Virginia, *Sunday Morning Observer* read:

> One-fifth of the feminine detachment of the United States ferry command turned imploring eyes toward the murky heavens above Morris Field yesterday afternoon and begged the sun to break through the pea soup.[15]

Evelyn, Barbara Poole, Esther Manning, and Barbara J. Erickson, standing beside one of their PT-19As, smiled for the captioned press release photo, "GIRLS GROUNDED HERE."

The article continued:

> "They don't allow us to take any chances," explained Miss Erickson. "We are not permitted to fly unless we can have a clear vision of the ground. We must not take off until after official sunrise and we must land not less than one hour before official sunset."

> "Only President Roosevelt and his cabinet members can take seats away from us [on commercial airlines]," one of

them explained. "He has Priority #1. But we're #2. They figure we should get back as quickly as possible."

One of the girls, Evelyn Sharp, ran into a former pupil at Morris Field. "Just think of that," she said. "I gave him his first lessons in flying. And now he's flying a P-40. I wouldn't dare try to fly one of them myself!"[16]

In due time, Evelyn would be flying aircraft with comparable horsepower. But for now, she and her WAF friends would spend a gala New Year's Eve in Jackson, Mississippi, finally delivering their PT-19As to Bellinger, Texas, January 2, 1943.[17]

On January 7, Evelyn and three other WAFS resembling bundled up members of Admiral Byrd's expedition to Antarctica, waddled out to a waiting quartet of open-cockpit PT-19As. The engines had been warming for three hours. A ground temperature of ten below zero would drop another seven-and-one-half degrees by the time the ferry pilots reached cruising altitude. Although wind-chill was not listed as an entry in a 1943 *Webster's Dictionary*, these women knew of its deadly, frost-biting effect.

Dressing for a trip like this, usually accompanied by icy sleet or snow, did have its humorous moments. First came a suit of scratchy woolen underwear, one-piece with buttons. Next they pulled on a pair of long, heavy woolen stockings, slipped into brown oxford shoes, and fastened black wooden buttons on the gray-green uniform. Then the women zipped up the Army's winter flying suit, a leather-covered, fleece-lined, two-piece garment, and a pair of leather-covered fleece-lined flying boots weighing about fifteen pounds. They topped it off with a fleece-lined helmet, a fleece-lined chamois face mask with holes for eyes, nose, and mouth, goggles with fleece around the edges of the eye-pieces to protect the face from metal, fleece-lined flying gloves, and, perhaps, a government-issued Army green woolen muffler. By that time, the women needed help tightening belts and buckles on the twenty-five pound seat parachute. With the winter gear so bulky and cumbersome, all ferry pilots soon learned to strap their navigational aids to a leg. Those who didn't, often watched their charts blow past the Army Air Force white star printed in a big blue circle on the trainer's wing. [18]

Low clouds in the Winston-Salem, North Carolina, area forced the women down early that first day. A front-page newspaper clipping showing Evelyn, Barbara Jane Erickson, Esther Manning, and Barbara Towne seated at a table drinking coffee, read, "Lady Ferry Pilots Spend a 'Ceiling' Furlough in City." Their furlough lasted two nights. When asked why they flew for the military, the unanimous response was "We do this because we want to and because we like it."[19]

As the WAFS flew deeper into the South, the ceilings lifted and weather was more flyable. Completing legs into Spartanburg, South Carolina; Atlanta, Georgia; Selma, Alabama; Jackson, Mississippi; Shreveport, Louisiana; and Dallas, Texas, they delivered the PTs within the next three days to an Army training base in Brady, Texas.

"Sure enjoyed my Texas trip," Evelyn wrote to her parents on January 14, 1943. "Will probably have time for two more trips before I leave for Long Beach. It is definite I'm going out there though. Am sure thrilled about it. Will be able to see you once in a while then."[20]

Plans to divide the twenty-eight original WAFS into four groups had been finalized by January. Gradually, the newly trained ferry pilots from Jacqueline Cochran's Flying Training Detachment in Houston would be added to each cadre, the Second Ferrying Group at Wilmington, Delaware; the Third at Romulus, Michigan; the Fifth at Dallas, Texas; and the Sixth at Long Beach, California.

Evelyn's letter concluded, "Boy, the possibilities of this job are wonderful. We'll soon be flying big stuff. Hot Dog! Oh, yes, one of my boyfriends—a Lt. Walling has been made a captain. Isn't that swell?"[21] This young man was the same one who had awakened Teresa James from her sound sleep in Hagerstown the previous November.

At BOQ 14 in Wilmington, the women gathered in Teresa James' room to talk about their new assignments. Most of them had been placed close to hometowns and loved ones by the Ferrying Division of the Air Transport Command. On this cold, damp evening, the subject of winter flying and drying woolen underwear also came up. Suddenly Teresa remembered those long, cold winters as a child in Pittsburgh and how her mother continually reminded her two daughters to remove the lint build-up in their belly buttons. She started to laugh. "Hey! Let's organize the Belly Button Lint Club. We'll save the lint from our belly buttons and whoever saves the most by spring will become queen of the BBLC."[22] The rest of the club members would do the Queen's chores for a month, cleaning, washing clothes, running errands, and picking up the mail. Teresa recalls it was not easy selling the idea, until someone thought it would be fun to "gas-light" the flying personnel by asking if they were members of the exclusive BBLC. Evelyn liked having a good time, perhaps remembering how much fun she had with a secret club during high school days. Unfortunately, none of the members asked today can remember what the letters M.O.D.R.T. stood for or at least they're not saying.

There was a certain element of ribald humor which raised its head in the WAFS Alert Room at Wilmington. Teresa James had dubbed one particular ferry route from Lockhaven to Wilmington as the "obscene route." Marking off the distance every ten miles on the flight chart, the checkpoints brought forth risqué comments and laughter—Mt. Jay, Bird-In-Hand, Intercourse, and Paradise. Evelyn told Teresa she had an Army mind.[23]

On January 17, 1943, Evelyn climbed into a PT-26, the primary trainer for the Canadian Royal Air Force. With the exception of an enclosed cockpit, it was exactly the same model as the Army's Fairchild PT-17. Evelyn hoped the flight would be warmer as she picked up a northwesterly heading to Toronto, Ontario. Two nights later, from a hotel in Williamsport, Pennsylvania, she wrote a thank-you note to Auntie Pat and Uncle Lobig Lobenstein in Oskaloosa, Iowa.

> I meet so many interesting people. I can't think of a better job. I have shelter, food, clothing, money in the bank, get to travel and meet people, have good times and do the job I want to do & at the same time serve my country. No sir, they don't make better jobs.[24]

Evelyn and Teresa James shared similar feelings about being a part of the Women's Auxiliary Ferrying Squadron. They would fly anything—anywhere—and enjoy it.

Returning from the Toronto delivery on the twentieth of January, Evelyn caught a train to New York for a two-and-a-half day furlough. In a letter to Glenn Buffington on January 25, she wrote, "...visited New York. Sure had fun—Madison Square Garden, Radio City, etc."[25]

Evelyn made no mention of an evening at the Rogers Corner (8th Avenue and 50th) just across the street from Madison Square Garden. But a souvenir photo taken during dinner on January 23, recorded the eventful day.[26] Sitting at the table, Aunt Elsie made a startling revelation. Evelyn's letter disclosed her incredible surprise:

> Dearest Aunt Elsie,
>
> I hardly know how to begin this letter as I've always known you as Aunt Elsie. You see, I've always thought that I was adopted but had never found out for sure. I figured it out that I resembled no one in our family and I could also never get Mother to say anything about my birth. Several people hinted it to me several times. So you see, I really wasn't surprised. What surprised me was who my real mother was. I never really bothered to ask what relation you were to us. I assumed that you were an aunt of some sort of Daddy's. It never occurred to me to ask. I was greatly surprised to find it was you. I'm not at all disappointed. I think you're a real person, and I'm proud that you're my real Mother. I had become attached to you during your stay in North Platte and I had so much fun with you there. I really enjoyed your com-

"Revelation At Rogers Corner," Elsie Haeske Crouse Rick and Evelyn, New York City, January 23, 1943

pany. Little did I realize that you were my own Mother. What did you think of your daughter?

Gosh, there are so many things I'd like to know. Where's my real father? Why I became adopted? Why you haven't told me before? What you think of me. Ever so many things. Write me a big long letter about it all. You know, I don't feel at all bad or anything I guess I've lived with Mom and Dad too long. I certainly owe them a lot, don't I? Everything I have is due to them. I can really never repay them. I am doing all I can to keep them happy the rest of their lives. I would never leave them.

This is all so strange to find you have a new Mother and that the people you've always believed were your Mother and Father aren't even related. It's really just like a story book. I'll never be able to figure out how it stayed a secret as long as it did. Although I'm not sorry it turned out as it has cause

"Memories From North Platte," John Sharp, Evelyn with Scottie, Mary Sharp, Aunt Elsie Rick, Pawnee Hotel, July 1939

I've always enjoyed my life. I certainly hope I can make you proud of me.

As yet, I have no particular near interests. I have so much fun here, going swimming, dancing, bowling. I'm even learning to figure skate. I have different dates all the time. I know almost all the Army Lts. and Officers, and Cadets out at the field and they're swell to me. I date several of the Lts. and they are really swell kids. One especially is Lt. Binkley. I'm very fond of him. I believe more than anyone I know of.

I haven't heard from Lt. Pardee for quite some time. Don't know what happened to him. At any rate, I have oodles of nice friends here and a good job and that's more than most people have. I am going to a Formal Officer's reception to-night. I went to one about a month ago and had a grand time. Lt. Binkley took me to that one and is taking me to this one. We have the most wonderful times together. He has the nicest personality of anyone I know. Even Lt. Pardee doesn't equal him. I'll try and get a picture of me in my formal. Oh, yes I have to have a birth certificate to get my third class ra-dio operator's license, so would you help me get it?

I guess there isn't really much more to say, except I'll try and send you the money I borrowed so long ago and help you in any way I can. Anytime you ever need anything and it is at all possible for me to help you, don't fail to tell me. I want to keep you happy.

All my Love,

Evelyn[27]

Research does not indicate Evelyn ever discussed her adoption with John and Mary Sharp, but she did share her feelings with several WAFS. On February 7, 1943, the night before another ferry trip to Toronto, Ontario, Nancy Batson and Evelyn lay in an old hotel bed in Hagerstown, Maryland. It was late, and Nancy wanted to sleep. But Evelyn was in a mood to talk. She "couldn't get over how her birth had been kept a secret for so many years."[28] Barbara Towne Fasken remembers a similar conversation Evelyn and she had on the airliner to their new ferrying assignment in Long Beach, California. "You'll never believe what I just found out," Evelyn reflected. "The woman I thought was my aunt is my mother."[29]

"BT Knucklehead"

O n February 13, 1943, Evelyn and Barbara Towne moved into one of the barracks at Long Beach Army Air Base. Possibly the most unusual housing occupied by American women pilots during World War II, "...the unpartitioned second floor allowed no means for privacy. At one end, in open space, a row of toilets squatted in full view of God and everybody."[1] The women later learned the place had been used as a psych ward.

"Checked Out In The Basic,"
BT-13 Vultee Vibrator, 1943

Within two days, Evelyn had checked out on the BT-13A and BT-15 aircraft flown in Army Air Force basic training. W. O. Birk, a flight instructor for the Sixth Ferrying Group, rated Evelyn "exceptionally good." The BT-13A Valiant, with its enclosed canopy and 450-hp engine, seemed enor-

mous after flying the primary trainers. Ferry pilots renamed the plane
Vultee Vibrator because of flight characteristics encountered when it
was put into a spin. The plane shuddered as if it would come apart,
falling almost two thousand feet before finding lift and flying again.[2]
But the BT had radios and Evelyn loved that.

In a letter to her parents, she wrote of her enthusiasm.

Well, I'm back from my trip to Dallas. Boy, these ships are
really a dream. Sure are fun to fly. You can trim them up
and just sit there and ride. And the radio in it, gee it's swell.
Over each radio station we have to go through a procedure
like this!

TUSCON RADIO FROM ARMY 454 GO AHEAD!

They answer and then you say—

TUSCON RADIO FROM ARMY 454 2 MI. SOUTH STATION
AT 9000 FT. ON FLIGHT PLAN FROM PHOENIX TO EL
PASO. GO AHEAD!

They answer and repeat what you say & then they say
RODGER! THANK YOU!

Rodger means that its O.K. If you ever answer WILCO, that
means that you will comply. More darn fun!

Evelyn's letter continued:

Almost all the fellows I used to know are in the Ferry Command here. All the gang from Bakersfield. And oodles of
fellows that have met me at one time or another.

Well, guess I haven't any more to talk about. I really like it
here. Boy oh Boy! Hot dog! Saw all our girls who are stationed at Dallas.

At Phoenix, I ran onto a bunch of the fellows who were up
at Lone Pine. They came out to see me off. One—Harry
Conover that I gave a lot of time to.

Well. Bye now.

Love
Evelyn[3]

By March 15, 1943, Evelyn's dog, Shanty, and a new black, Scottie puppy named Tami, were living with John and Mary at 715 N. E Street in Las Vegas, Nevada. Shanty had been sent back from Wilmington some time ago. "He was a little too much trouble to take care of here. Poor little fellow, he hardly knows me," she wrote.[4] In each letter to her parents, Evelyn included "Little Black Sugars" in the salutation, usually asking how the dogs were or hoping they were doing okay. When Tami was in need of a harness, Evelyn asked her mother the size—bought one, and mailed it home.

Evelyn attended ground school classes in the afternoons when she was not out on ferry missions.

> ...I get experience with Emergency equipment (life rafts, etc), Emergency radio—then pistols (Colt & Smith Wesson) then shot guns (skeet and riot) then sub machine gun (45 cal) then 37mm 4 cannon that is on the P-39 pursuit ships. Also had oxygen equipment. And will soon get machine guns and turretts. Most interesting. I am doing this on my own. I don't have to but I get credit for it.[5]

She also continued to work out at the Athletic and Recreation (A&R) Hangar, its specialized physical training program recognized as a model by the Ferry Division.[6]

> Am getting so healthy it is pityful. Every Mon. Wed. & Fri. I appear at the gym for exercises on the table. You know, conditioning exercises like push ups, etc. And then a beautiful luscious steam bath. Really swell. Makes you feel like a million bucks. I also take on a game or two of badmitten or tennis. On the other day I also work out on the tables or on the trapese bars and have a game or two of tennis, ping pong or badmitten. Really swell. Haven't had many trips lately so have had plenty of time for exercise. I think I'll go out tomorrow on a trip. Boy, this is the most wonderful job I could have.[7]

On March 19, 1943, security escorted a photographer onto the ramp at Consolidated Vultee. Five brand new BT-13As were awaiting delivery to an Army Air Force training base in Dallas, Texas. Within minutes, a military ambulance pulled up, the back door swung open, and Evelyn, Bernice Batten, Barbara Erickson, Cornelia Fort, and Barbara Towne hopped out. Sharp, Erickson, and Fort hoisted themselves onto the right wing of one of the new airplanes, while the other two took a position at each end. The picture would appear in a "Meet the Pilots" section of the August *Air-Age*, informing the public of the newer, heavier aircraft the women ferry pilots were now flying. "The girls average 1600 hours apiece,"[8] it reported. In the same article, Jacqueline Cochran "American's No. 1 aviatrix,[9]" was shown climbing into a P-40 Warhawk. She would be inspecting the new Air Force school for women flyers, recently moved from Houston to Sweetwater, Texas.

By the time the pictures were published in *Air-Age*, Cornelia Fort had been killed. Word spread fast, stunning other WAFS in this military experiment. In a letter to her parents dated March 25, 1943, Evelyn wrote:

> We don't know much about the accident yet. As far as we know, she spun in from 7000 from a mid-air collision but don't repeat a word of this as it is military information. If the papers got it, it would make quite a stink. At any rate, its a horrible thing to have happen. We still haven't sent her clothes home and everything is here just as she left them. Makes the barracks a little eerie at night.[10]

At this point Evelyn drew a sketch of the barracks, labeling each of the bunks, including the one that had belonged to Cornelia. The letter continued:

> It is just a big room with six beds and now it seems a little spooky. But her time must have been here. That's the way I feel. Am glad she was killed and not maimed for life.[11]

Evelyn's knowledge of the accident on March 21, 1943, was sketchy, as are details of it even today. But there are some points upon which researchers agree. A group of BT-13s, being ferried by men and women from the Sixth Ferrying Group were in loose formation in open sky near Merkel, Texas. For whatever reason, a young male pilot chose to alter his heading. Moving in on Cornelia in a manner which ultimately proved beyond his control, he hit her plane, tearing off part of the wing. He flew on, his aircraft undamaged. Her plane flew uncontrollably, eventually spinning into the ground. The Flying Safety Section of Ferrying Division Headquarters rated pilot error on the part of Cornelia at zero. "In other words, the accident was not at all due to any fault of the WAF concerned."[12]

After Cornelia Fort's death, there were knee-jerk reactions to the accident. At Romulus AAB, WAFS were told to forget about transition to larger aircraft. Women would not be allowed to fly as copilots on ferrying missions with men, and, whenever possible, WAFS should make deliveries on alternate days from male pilots, so as to keep them separated.

One directive which affected all women pilots came down from Air Transport Command. "No women would be allowed to fly during pregnancy—or from one day prior to her menstrual period to two days after the last day of her period."[13] In effect this ruling grounded every WAF for six to eight days each month. A similar regulation had been issued at Wilmington when the Women's Auxiliary Ferrying Squadron was in its beginning stages. There purportedly had been a 1940 Civil Aeronautics Authority report which showed "women at the controls of planes fainted during their periods and crashed, with fatal results."[14] At Wilmington, Nancy Love had objected strenuously and the regulation disappeared. But with the event of Cornelia's death, the women were grounded once again.[15]

On April 16, 1943, Evelyn wrote:

> And now I'm grounded again because of my monthly sick time. Fine thing. Oh, well, I can really loaf. I've been going into the gym every morning except Sat. I can chin myself 7 times now. A month ago, I couldn't even do one. Hot dog! I also am really getting a beautiful tan. Sure am healthy.[16]

Evelyn was a sun-worshiper. Barbara Erickson London, the commanding officer of WAFS at Long Beach, remembers her good friend's fetish for getting a tan. Taking advantage of the open canopy on the BT's shuttle flights across the desert to Dallas, Evelyn slipped out of her shirt when she reached cruising altitude. But a problem developed. Ferry pilots of the opposite sex had difficulty maintaining their heading. When word of the distraction reached Barbara, she asked Evelyn to at least wear a swim suit top under her clothes. "There was no problem after that,"[17] Barbara recalls. In fact, Evelyn didn't cause problems. She did what she was supposed to do, in the best way she knew how.

John, Mary, and the Scotties came to visit Evelyn the first week in April of 1943. It had been almost six months since Evelyn, on her way to Wilmington to join the Ferry Command, had said good-by to Mary at the train depot in Des Moines. It was less than two weeks since Cornelia Fort had been killed. In a letter to Glenn Buffington, she wrote, "Gee, it was good to see them all. They brought little Tam and Shanty. They enjoyed seeing what Army life was like—they decided it wasn't nearly as bad as they had imagined."[18]

In a May 18 letter to her parents, Evelyn wrote, "Well, we have 5 new WAFS on the field now. Will take them on their first trips the last of the week. We sure hope they will do a good job."[19] When the young women in Jacqueline Cochran's Training Detachment in Houston graduated, some of them were assigned to the Sixth Ferrying Group at Long Beach Army Air Base. Here too, the WAFS had officer privileges, eating in the Officers' Mess and spending evenings at the Officers' Club. Evelyn loved to play cards, especially pinochle, engage other ferry pilots in contests of table games, and join her friends at the piano in song. A favorite was one which several of them had composed after too many trips in the BTs.

"BT Knucklehead"
Tune: "Casey Jones"

Gather round my pilots if you want to hear
The story of the army with a ferry career
He got a Downey bus with his orders in his hand
He was headin' down to Dallas for a one night stand.

Chorus:

Knucklehead, on the left side of the airways,
Knucklehead, with his orders in his hand,
Knucklehead, messin' up the airways
Takin' a BT down to Dixieland.

He got off from Downey accordin' to Hoyle
But once in the air he couldn't change the coil.
Fumbled his way down to Riverside
It was only the beginning of a hectic ride.

(Chorus)

Called Phoenix Tower, said I know I'm late
This is a BT trainer, not a P-38.
Clear the pattern cause I'm comin' in
And in Phoenix I'm goin' to R.O.N.

(Chorus)

Tuscon Tower, comin' to land
Say call that babe at the "Sage and Sand"
Hilltop Pass doesn't look too good
And remember brother this is made of wood.

(Chorus)

El Paso Tower, this is nine*forty
Make one reservation at the Del Norte.
Have a jeep a rarin' to go
Cause tonight I'm goina spend in Ol' Mexico.

(Chorus)

Five thousand feet over Abilene
Engine missin', low on gasoline.
Mixture's back and the pressure is down
But I think I can make it into Dallas town.

(Chorus)

Comin' into Dallas, it was runway three,
But what she said was a mystery to me.
Make a low approach and as I neared the ground,
What I really heard was "Go around."(high feminine voice)

Knucklehead, flying in the pattern
Knucklehead with his flaps rolled down
Knucklehead, flying in the pattern
One more town he'd come spinning down.

(Tune changes to "My Mother Was a Lady")

He went to "Abe and Pappy's", to buy himself a beer
But little did he know it the end was oh**so near.
He stood upon the stairway, his wings shown on his chest
He didn't have a chance poor kid**he fell down all the rest.

Now this concludes our story, our hero now is dead.
But ere will people sing the praise of BT Knucklehead
My BT Knucklehead.[20]

On Deaf Ears

The location of Long Beach Army Air Base in southern California was a ferry pilot's dream, offering opportunities to fly a variety of airplanes manufactured by Lockheed, Douglas, North American, and Consolidated Vultee. There were entertainment advantages many other bases did not have. On several occasions, Evelyn and some of her flying friends left the base to go bowling, catch a movie at a local theater, drive out to Knotts Berry Farm, or go down to the Pike, an amusement park whose roller coaster extended out over the waters of the Pacific. Creating fear in the hearts of its riders, the coaster offered thrills even to pilots, especially at night. With no visual reference to the ground, the members of the Sixth Ferrying Group felt they were flying, without the assurance of wings. This was not the first time Evelyn had ridden roller coasters. On a postcard from Chicago written in 1938 to her boyfriend, Richard Severson, she told him of riding "5 different roller coasters twice last night."[1]

There was also dancing on Saturday nights, if not to Les Brown and his Band of Renown at the Hollywood Palladium, then to other Big Band music on the base itself. "...providing a wealth of features [entertainment] unequalled in the nation," Special Services made arrangements for top radio shows to be broadcast direct from the Athletic and Recreation Hangar.[2] Big-name stars such as Eddie Cantor appeared live on stage, and the bands of Harry James and Tommy

Dorsey played music for listening and dancing pleasure. "I'll Never Smile Again" by the Pied Pipers, the Andrew Sisters' rendition of "I'll Be With You In Apple Blossom Time," and the Song Spinners' very popular "Comin' In On A Wing and a Prayer"[3] brought thunderous applause from the men and women of the Sixth Ferrying Group.

"Things are really looking more encouraging these last few days," Evelyn wrote to her parents. "Believe everything will turn out o.k. We just have to sit tight and hope."[4] Within two weeks Brigadier General W. H. Tunner, Commanding General, Ferrying Division, explained a new classification system for all pilots. No longer would WAFS be restricted to liaisons and trainers; if the women pilots qualified, they could fly the heaviest planes.[5] That was great news to Evelyn, who was eager to fly the Army's pursuits. Getting an opportunity to transition might be slower at some ferrying bases, but there would be no problem at Long Beach. The men and women of the Sixth Ferrying Group displayed a mutual respect for each other.

Evelyn flew another BT-13A to the Army Air Force Training Center at Enid, Oklahoma, on the seventh of May, 1943. It took her five days. Upon return, she checked out in a C-47A, the Army's two-engine cargo and transport carrier.

> And I have news for you. I'm finally co-pilot in a C-47—same as an airliner. And it is very simple. Nothing to it, I put the gear up and down, the flaps up and down, check cowl flaps, tailwheel lock, mixture control, prop control, all the instruments for both engines. Quite a lot of gadgets. More fun! The ship weighs 26,000 lbs. Quite a bit different from a 900 lb Cub. Soon hope to be first pilot on the ship. Things are going a little bit better now. Hot Dog! We had to move off the base to the Villa Riviera until they build us some barracks. So we have a beach now.[6]

In a letter on the twenty-eighth of May, Evelyn wrote to "Mom and Pop, & babies:

> How goes everything. Too bad I didn't know we were going into Boulder City. I would have wired you to meet me. Sure hope you get the trailer house fixed up O.K. so that it is

"A Lady And A Workhorse"
Evelyn and a Douglas C-47, the "skytrain" of the War, Long Beach, California, 1943

comfortable. And if there is anything you want, just let me know.

And how about his [John's] glasses? That is $32 isn't it or more or what? Let me know— [John and Mary had moved again, and Evelyn continued to send money to help out with expenses.]

Under separate cover, I'm sending a little box with gadgets I've picked up around in my travels. One of the service pins is for daddy. You are both entitled to wear one cause I'm in the service. [Officially, that was not true. Like many of the women, Evelyn thought of herself as a military pilot rather than one of Civil Service status.]

We have had pretty good luck here with our new WAFS. Mrs. Love is leaving for duty at Cinncinati and B.J. [Barbara Erickson] and I are in charge.[7]

Nancy Love, WAFS director, had transferred herself from Wilmington to Dallas and then to Long Beach, transitioning into heavier and more sophisticated aircraft at each base. By April 1943, she was pilot-qualified on the C-47, P-51, A-36, and some fourteen other airplanes manufactured near Long Beach.[8] She would ferry her latest transition, the twin-engine B-25, back East to ATC Headquarters in Cincinnati.[9] Each of these transitions would make it possible for other WAFS to check out in those airplanes.

"Nancy Checks Out," Army Air Field, Palm Springs, California, pictured from left: Evelyn, Barbara Towne, Nancy Love, Barbara Erickson, June 1943

On June 1, Evelyn and Barbara Erickson flew another trip together, this time to Baer Field at Ft. Wayne, Indiana. Delivering a C-53D, manufactured by Douglas in Daggett, California, they logged 6.7 hours the first day, 3.3 the second, and 2.3 on the third. On June 4, Evelyn wrote:

Well, we finally got back from our trip. "BJ" and I. We certainly enjoyed it. We went through Boulder City again this morning, but didn't have time to call you. I sure hope we get to go on another one soon.

We have 11 new girls coming in a week from Monday. That will make 21 of us in here in all. Sure wish they would build us a barracks so we wouldn't have to live in town. It's so hard to find a place to live. Although the place we stay is swell. Right on the seashore.

I have the rest of today and tomorrow off so I'm going to take in the beach. Am going to get a good tan. Although I got one already....

Everyone who writes me says to tell "Shanty" "hello." So be sure and tell him "hello."

How do daddy's glasses work? Hope his eyes are o.k. now.

Hope you both wear your star service pins cause you are entitled to.[10]

Along the edge of the letter, she added the postscript, "Be sure to send No. 18 ration stamp back to me as that's the next shoe ration ticket."[11] Because Evelyn was not an official member of the US military, she had to make certain purchases at department stores just like any other civilian. In this case, she wanted stamp #18 from ration book #3, as coupon #17 was only good to June 15, 1943.[12] In this book were stamps bearing pictures of guns, tanks, ships, and airplanes. "...airplane stamps became a commonly heard phrase" at this time and were necessary when civilians bought their three pairs of shoes per person, per year.[13]

On the tenth of June, at Palm Springs Army Air Base, Evelyn and two other WAFS from Long Beach began transition to the "most familiar and numerous Army Air Force plane built during World War II."[14] A large 600-hp engine capable of speeds over 200 miles per hour, the AT-6 Texan was flown by every AAF cadet during advanced training. After 5.3 hours of dual, Evelyn passed the tests to fly the powerful trainer, putting her another step closer to the controls of a pursuit plane.

On June 13, 1943, Evelyn wrote to her parents:

Well, I'm finally a pursuit pilot—I flew the P-51 for the first time today. What a wonderful plane and so easy to fly. Beautiful—

Enclosed is a copy of things to do in the ship. Please return it as it is confidential, but I thought you'd like to know about it. It cruises at 250 miles per hour.[15]

"A Pursuit Pilot," North American P-51, Long Beach California Army Air Field, June 1943

To her friend Glenn Buffington, now in Northwest Territory, Canada, with Air Transport Command, she wrote, "'Wowie' Can you imagine me in a pursuit plane, and the fastest one in the world at that?...What a day!...Guess I told you my best news, so wheels down and locked."[16]

In another letter on stationery embossed with the silver, red, and blue logo of ATC, Evelyn wrote to Patty Baer, her young friend in Eustis, Nebraska.

How have the crops been getting along down that way? Did you get the rain when you needed it? I certainly hope so cause the nation needs all of the food products it can get.... And I have also been flying the P-51 pursuit.... A far cry from the old Curtiss Robin which I hopped passengers in at your farm.

Give your folks my regards and take care of yourself.

Bye now,
Evelyn[17]

Seated in the P-51A's cockpit with its Plexiglas canopy open, Evelyn had studied diagrams in the operations manual, then identified and located various levers, switches, instruments, and gauges in front and to the side of her. Closing her eyes, she touched each one and called out its name: fuel gauge, temperature gauge, oil gauge, airspeed, altimeter, and ball and needle. Again and again, she repeated the self-study until she could do it with no errors. The operating instructions were organized into seven different sections: general information, preliminary check, starting & warm-up, before takeoff, use of power, before landing, and emergency landings.[18] Evelyn read and reread the sequence of procedures, trying to commit the information to memory. The P-51 was a single seat airplane, so there would be no instructor in back when she took the plane up.

Evelyn and the other two WAFS did not finish transition in the P-51A at Palm Springs; no planes of that type were available. The pilots returned to their base in Long Beach to find a flurry of activity. New graduates from Cochran's Training Detachment in Sweetwater, Texas, were already qualified to fly Consolidated's basic trainer, and it soon became necessary to delegate authority so as to monitor everyone's comings and goings. Barbara Erickson, in charge of the WAFS at Long Beach, asked Evelyn to serve as Executive Officer. "I am deputy commander of the group here," Evelyn wrote her parents on June 21. "We now have 20 girls stationed here. We will be commissioned sometime within the next two months."[19] The women pilots were beginning to look more and more like they belonged to the Army Air Force.

Evelyn had only one BT-15 mission in July 1943, and that was near the end of the month. A two-week bout with strep throat and then a recurrence of it after a tonsillectomy grounded her. On July 18, she wrote, "I had a local when I had my tonsils out and I watched them cut them out. It hurt quite a bit before they gave me the hypo to go to sleep.... But I'm back on my feet again and am ok except my throat is still a little sore."

"As for the commissions, we don't know when we will get them. ...you know it just wouldn't be right to do something right off the bat without first quibbling over it in Washington."[20] It had been thought the women pilots would be brought into the AAF when the Women's Auxiliary Army Corps had been militarized as the Women's Army Corps (WAC) on July 1, 1943. But that had coincided with Jacqueline Cochran's appointment as Director of Women Pilots, and "she knew that being part of the WAC would be a bureaucratic hindrance to her progress."[21] When the issue was brought before the House Military Affairs and Civil Service Committees that next year, it was too late. By that time...

> Congressmen from all over the country had been receiving letters and personal visits from representatives of two groups of male civilian fliers demanding commissions—the 900 flight instructors and 5,000 trainees released by AAF's recent termination of the Civil Aeronautics Administration War Training Service (formerly Civilian Pilot Training Program), and the 8,000 flight instructors who had lost their jobs when the AAF closed its civilian-contract primary cadet schools.[22]

Some men who had chosen to stay home and fly airplanes off training fields in Texas, Oklahoma, Nebraska, and South Dakota now realized they could be fighting the war from a foxhole. Suddenly, ferrying open-cockpit airplanes in below-zero weather, towing targets for practice anti-aircraft fire, and test-flying planes out of repair depots didn't seem so bad. Several newspapers and editors also took up their cause, reminding readers that Congress had never authorized the women ferry pilot program in the first place. On the last day of debate, Congressman Karl Stefan from Norfolk, Nebraska, "elicited a gallant speech,"[23] championing the contributions women had made to the war effort. It fell on deaf ears. The bill to militarize the women ferry pilots died on June 21, 1944. They would have to wait until 1977 for congressional recognition of their efforts.

In a July 18, 1943, letter to her parents, Evelyn shared her feelings about the reorganization of the women ferry pilots.

Jackie Cochran is now the head of the WAFS and Nancy is under her. How about that? Isn't that a dirty deal? But you know money talks and Jackie has it. Don't say anything about it though because it is all done now. But I guess everything will be ok anyway.[24]

Loyalty among the WAFS to Nancy Love was strong; and, as with any change at the top, rumors and grievances of a personal nature thrived. On July 5, 1943, General H. "Hap" Arnold had named Cochran Director of Women Pilots within the Army Air Force, and on the same day, Brigadier General William Tunner appointed Nancy Love the Executive for WAFS in the Ferrying Division. Exactly one month later, the WAFS and the Women's Flying Training Detachment, were officially merged into the Women Airforce Service Pilots (WASP). Jacqueline Cochran's dream had finally come true; she was director of all women pilots.

The possibility of militarization was still on Evelyn's mind. "When and if we get commissions we will be treated like Army officers. Our pay will be the same as an officers according to the rank we hold. It won't be any less, I don't think."[25] Evelyn hoped to be treated as an equal, but the differences afforded men and women in the Air Transport Command left some doubt in her mind. The women ferry pilots were paid less than the men. The women's pay was no different if they were ferrying a simple L-2B or a sophisticated pursuit. There was no increase in pay because of additional duties; Evelyn and Barbara Erickson received no extra money for their administrative responsibilities. The women had no housing or uniform allowance as the male pilots did. There were no travel provisions to go home. To stretch their $6 per diem, they tried to stay in nurses' quarters on ferrying missions because they were cheaper than local hotel rates. Extended the privilege of buying meals at officers' mess, the women pilots stopped at the cash register on their way out. But perhaps the greatest inequities were that they flew with no hospitalization, no life insurance (even though Evelyn thought she had some), and no death benefits. Private companies canceled individual policies when men and women signed on as pilots.[26] The men, however, were covered by government insurance. Out of 1,074 Women Airforce Service Pilots, thirty-eight died in the service of their country.[27] Surviving family members received nothing.

P-51s, B-25s, and 'Ahem'

*I*n another letter on the second of August, the question of militarization came up again.

Well, I think we will know where we stand before long. Probably before the end of the month, I'll be in the Army. From what I gather—our uniform will be blue—We just hear rumors so nothing official.

But at any rate, things are popping. Zowie!

Remember my Major friend I wrote about. I must tell you more about him. He is 25 years old. He is from a wealthy North Carolina family. He's been in the Air Corps since about '37 or '38. He flew the first P-38 & B-25 across the Pacific and South Atlantic. He's been across about seven times. He flies anything the Army has. He is a very fine athlete & doesn't smoke or drink. He knows oodles of movie stars. Yesterday we drove up to Hollywood and went swimming at George Raft's place. And I played ball with George Raft. I have met oodles of producers and such. Sure fun. And am getting to see some of the most beautiful homes. Zowie! At any rate, Major Lassiter is a swell person and lots of fun—[1]

By the evening of August 3, 1943, Evelyn had copiloted a C-47A, used by commercial airliners and known as the DC-3, back East. She penciled 13.2 hours in her personal record, a small, brown, spiral notebook. The data would be transferred to the Army's Form 5 when she returned to Long Beach. She wrote to John and Mary:

> Gee, I hope both of you are alright. I haven't done a thing about your birthday yet. I haven't had a chance to go into town. I've been too busy out here.
>
> I would have sent you a card, but I was on the airliner and at Cincinnati that day. Just couldn't get anywhere where they even had cards. But don't worry, I'll get you something as soon as possible.
>
> Don't tell anyone, but perhaps there will be WAFS [WASPs] at Palm Springs & I'll be in charge. Maybe.[2]

Apparently, Nancy Love, now serving on the staff at Ferrying Division Headquarters in Cincinnati, had discussed the formation of a new WASP squadron with Evelyn. In her brown notebook, Evelyn had written "Special Duty-Nancy Love. At ATC Headquarters RON."[3]

When Evelyn returned to Long Beach, she practiced takeoffs and landings in North American's P-51B Mustang, making ten in one day during a two-hour period. On August 14, 1943, she received orders to fly an Army Mustang (43-12406) back to Newark, New Jersey, the debarkation point for European Theater war operations. On the docks of this Atlantic seaboard port, Evelyn watched as some planes were loaded into the mammoth cargo holds of oceangoing vessels, while others were secured to modified deck stands. Navy personnel wasted no time in covering the planes and preparing them for shipping. One WASP felt she would have been "wrapped up with the plane if she hadn't begun her exit before the airplane came to a full stop."[4]

After delivering the P-51B to Newark, Evelyn caught an 8:45 p.m. commercial flight from La Guardia in New York City. She had been flying since early that morning.

The next day, she was ordered to take a basic trainer (BT-13A-8811) to Dallas. On August 18, during a 5.9 hour leg out of Long Beach, she wrote, "I am now on another trip & am flying along at 7000

*"A Mustang To Newark,"
North American P-51,
Army Air Field, Long
Beach, California, August
1943*

ft. over Guadalupe Pass in Texas. There are 23 girls now stationed where I am." [5]

Twenty new WASP graduates from the W-43-4 class in Sweetwater, Texas, came into Long Beach on August 27, 1943. Among them was Kittie Leaming, one of the two women who lived with Evelyn in Lone Pine. Because these pilots had basic, as well as advanced training, it was not long before this new WASP was ferrying the BT-13s. One night, some months later, Kittie shared her boredom with those long shuttle flights between Long Beach and the training fields near Dallas. Evelyn suggested she contact operations at the delivery base to see if they had anything available to ferry east. Always wanting to fly, Evelyn had done that several times herself. "I have to thank Evelyn for a most wonderful trip to Wilmington, Delaware," Kittie Leaming King remembers. "I read the tech orders for the Dauntless Dive Bomber carefully, and took off. I was so proud of myself."[6]

By the end of August 1943, Evelyn had flown 19.1 hours in the P-51B, a newer model with a Rolls Royce V-1650-3 twelve-cylinder, liquid-cooled engine. Although it didn't "get off as well as the A model and landed a little slower,"[7] it was much faster than the one she had flown in Palm Springs. Evelyn had also logged 5.8 additional hours of copilot time in the C-47.

In September of 1943, Hollywood came to the Long Beach Army Air Field. "The base is overrun these days by Universal Studios and Pilots' Loft habitués are going wacky what with Hollywood 'WASPS' Loretta Young and Diana Barrymore coming up for orange juice between scenes."[8] On location for the 1944 release of "Ladies Courageous,"[9] the studio took advantage of several publicity shots with Evelyn, Miss Young, and

"Evelyn Goes Hollywood," Richard Fraser, "Ladies Courageous" male lead, Army Air Field, Long Beach, California, September 1943

Richard Fraser, the actor who played the part of the base commander. Nancy Love expressed doubt as to the authenticity of the "B" grade movie: "Imagine climbing out of an AT-6 after delivery with hairdo perfect and lipstick unsmeared. Only Hollywood can do it!"[10] Perhaps, not true. Florene Miller, a beautiful WASP with the Fifth Ferrying Group at Love Field, Dallas, Texas, had been featured in a *Flying V* cartoon the previous June. In the midst of several nondescript parachutes floating toward earth, a very large canopy embroidered with flowers caught the attention of readers. The caption read, "Must be Florene Miller under that one."[11] Florene Miller Watson remembers crawling across wings to retrieve a pretty high-heeled shoe from each of two ammunition boxes at the end of ferrying trips. You couldn't carry much in a pursuit, and she wanted to look nice for dinner on those nights spent at the officers' clubs.[12]

On September 15, Evelyn sent her parents $60 to cover an insurance premium for her car. The automobile had been with John and Mary since Evelyn helped ferry Les Buchner's flying operation to Lone Pine. "Get this insurance as soon as possible and let me know about it," she wrote.

> I have some news for you. I am being transferred to Palm Springs.... I don't know whether I will be in charge or not, but I certainly hope so. I sure hate to leave my Major friend. He is a very nice fellow. More the type I would like. Oh, well, I guess that is the way it goes.[13]

Apparently Major O. F. Lassiter's interest in physical fitness, and his choice not to drink or smoke were qualities Evelyn admired.

Evelyn reported to the 21st Ferrying Group, Ferrying Division, Air Transport Command, Army Air Field at Palm Springs, California, the twentieth of September. On a post card to Patty Baer, the little girl whose parents owned the pasture strip near Eustis, Nebraska, Evelyn wrote, "Have been transferred to Palm Springs. Am squadron commander here. Am still flying P-51's and C-47's. Been very busy."[14]

Evelyn flew her first C-47 trip as pilot-in-command on September 29, 1943. Another WASP served as copilot. "...a fun trip and am anxious for another,"[15] she wrote. Evelyn had passed the seven page, fifty-seven-question test over the power plant, fuel, oil, and hydraulic systems, normal and emergency operations of gear, flaps, and brakes, electrical system, radio installation, and the location of various controls and flight operations data.[16]

Approximately two weeks later, after checking out as first pilot on a B-25, Evelyn flew the two-engine Billy Mitchell bomber back to Indiana. Twin-tailed, it was powered by two 1,700-hp engines. On this flight, Evelyn's copilot was Claire Callaghan (W-43-1), who later wrote to Jacqueline Cochran, telling her what it was like to be at Palm Springs.

> This, I believe, is going to turn out to be a grand base. Our WASP C.O. is a swell girl—Evelyn Sharp—and is really looking out for us. I went with her as co-pilot...and when we returned here she recommended me for C-47 transition. Unfortunately, if there isn't a shortage of airplanes,

"It's A-OK," Billy Mitchell B-25 (North American), Army Air Field, Long Beach, California, 1943

there is a shortage of instructors...I like the [B-25] very much...at least I have the muscle it requires...We are going to have three hours of calisthenics a week. It's a good thing for me....[17]

Claire Callaghan recalls the 21st Squadron reported to the flight line every morning to await orders. If none were issued, the women pilots returned to their La Paz Hotel quarters to work on physical fitness. In reference to the few planes available for ferrying, Callaghan said, "I think the Ferry Command forgot about us."[18]

Evelyn encouraged the women pilots in her squadron to swim, play tennis, and do push-ups, anything which would increase upper body strength. There were rumors these women, who represented the four ferrying groups from Wilmington, Romulus, Dallas, and Long Beach, had been selected as the best candidates to attend a future ATC pursuit training school in Palm Springs. Evelyn wanted them to be ready. The pursuit airplane fit between the medium bomber and attack plane and the heavy bomber in the Army Air Force Classification List. Planes such as the P-47, P-51, P-40, and P-38 made up this category. Fast and responsive to the controls, the fighters were judged by some to be temperamental.[19]

On November 17, 1943, the same day a new uniform insignia was adopted for the WASPs, Evelyn received a copy of Special Orders #174. She did not understand why all of them were being transferred to Long Beach, even the ones who had not come from there. What about the rumor of a pursuit school? Within less than a month that question was answered. Palm Springs was turned into a pursuit school for ATC, but none of them were in the first class.[20] Apparently, they never knew why.

Evelyn realized if she wanted to transition to more sophisticated aircraft, she would need to get her instrument card. The WASP coming out of Sweetwater, Texas, had more intensive training in the instrument-rated airplanes than the original WAFS who had initiated this program a little over a year ago. As a professional, she realized the ramifications of that. Evelyn wanted to fly. She did not want to be left behind. In Palm Springs, she had picked up fifteen hours and forty-five minutes in instrument-training aircraft and twelve hours of Link. The hood-covered, stubby-winged Link Trainer, mounted on a base which allowed tilting and turning, made it possible for pilots to practice instrument flying with no visual reference to the ground. Reviewing the line graph which recorded the flight path at the end of the lesson was a frustrating, if not humbling experience for many.

On November 29, 1943, Evelyn wrote to her good friend, the originator of the Belly Button Lint Club.

Dear Teresa,

How are you, you old slug. I am finally getting around to doing a little corresponding. Since that movement over Palm Springs and return, I haven't a chance to do any letter writing business. It seems all I get a chance to do any writing on is squadron papers. But now, I am back over here and I think I will have a little more time. I am in instrument school but I get a little tired of always studying about instruments so I will write a few letters.

Several of the girls on the post have gotten married. But not Sharpie. Guess, I will have to be an old maid. Darn it!

The kid I have been dating is from Stockton [California]. He is a LT. on the field here. Very nice too. Ahem! [The "Ahem" she referred to was Lt. Frank R. Moore, an instructor pilot with the 28th Flying Squadron at Long Beach.]

Well, I have to fly at three so I will get this off in the mail. Bye now and write soon.

> Love,
> Sharpie[21]

That afternoon, Evelyn practiced instrument flying in an AT-6, recording two hours under Special Information on the AAF Individual Flight Record. By the first of December 1943, her log read nineteen hours and thirty-five minutes of instrument flight training and thirteen hours in the Link Trainer. She would record another forty-six hours and forty-five minutes by the end of the month.

In a letter to her parents on December 3, 1943, Evelyn copied her schedule.

Have been so busy in instrument transition that I haven't had time to write.

8:00-9:00	Link
9:00-10:00	Study
10:00-12:00	Ground School
12:00-1:00	Fly
1:30-3:00	Study
3:00-4:30	Fly

From 4:30 on, I'm off but I have office work and studying to do. Quite a routine. [22]

The first floor of the WASP BOQ at Long Beach or at least the front part of it, had been converted to a ready room/operations area. On one wall, a large multicolored board listed each WASP by name. As Executive Officer, it was part of Evelyn's responsibilities to keep it current, updating the women's AAF flying classification status, noting pertinent information if assigned to base, or posting their mission if they were out flying. Information from the airplanes (Form 1) and the WASPs (Form 5) also had to be recorded for each ferrying trip. It was time-consuming and paperwork was not one of Evelyn's favorite tasks. She'd rather be flying.

In her letter, Evelyn hoped John had received his birthday gift, and that it was on time. She also spoke of her Major friend who had gone to combat. "He will be in Great Bend, Kansas, for awhile, and then go overseas. Enclosed is a little article about him that I thought you'd like to read." A front-page picture in the *Roger Daily Newsletter*, published by Sixth Ferrying Group Special Services, informed the readership of O. F. Lassiter's reassignment as well as athletic accomplishments. He had broken an Army field record in physical fitness tests by doing 250 sit-ups and 91 push-ups.

In the same letter, she continued: "I also have another fine friend who has been taking me around. Lt. Frank Moore. Very swell fellow."[23] On December 9, 1943, Frank wrote to Evelyn from the Santa Rita Hotel in Tucson, Arizona.

Hi, Squirt,

...the weather has been really stinko east of here, or I would have been home by now. In the meantime, I'm running a transition school over here with my students plus a couple of re-checks I dug up around the field.

Well, here it is 12 PM all ready so guess I'll close and hit the hay for this evening. So take it easy and be a good gal, huh? Incidentally, I've really missed you, but don't breathe a word about it.

Lots of love,
Frank[24]

Show 'Em How To Do It, Sharpie

ancy Love flew into Long Beach around the first of December to check out in Lockheed's new P-38, thereby opening transition opportunities for other WASPs. Evelyn was ecstatic with thoughts of flying one of the most recognizable fighter aircraft of World War II. "Hot dog!"[1] she wrote.

But first she needed to figure out how to fly an airplane on instruments. Getting from one place to another back in Nebraska had been simple; this system of navigating was tough. It took Evelyn two pages of flight record to list the instrument training flights and Link Trainer time in December.

A welcome break from the dials and the gauges came on the thirteenth when she received orders to ferry a P-51B to Dallas. A run on pursuits had created a bottleneck at the North American and Lockheed aircraft factories. Planes were parked everywhere. Ramps were full, some pursuits even spilling onto the taxiways and runways.[2] Low ceilings hanging over the Valley of the Smokes, a descriptive name given to this area by the Native Americans, had kept ferry pilots on the ground for too many days. When the sky conditions finally broke, every qualified pilot, including instructors in instruments and flight training, were on orders. That evening two hundred pilots with their P-51s and P-38s RONed in Palm Springs. Evelyn and Barbara Erickson were the only two women.[3] Earlier that day, they had scratched their

"I'd Rather Be Flying," P-51 Mustang (North American), 1943

names and Sixth Ferrying Group on their P-51s' metal instrument panels. Graffiti were undoubtedly appreciated by war-weary, combat-fighter pilots and their ground crews. Perhaps Roy Maxson, a P-38 mechanic in southern Italy who once had taken a sky-ride with Evelyn back in North Loup, Nebraska, saw some of those messages. On the day of the flight, Roy had no excuse to leave school early, but he knew better than to ask his parents. Instead, Roy told the principal he was needed at a farm sale, and when Evelyn asked him his name for her passenger register, he lied again. Fifty-five years later, Roy recalls fond memories of the flight, but he has forgotten the alias.[4]

The next night from the Hotel Adams in Phoenix, Arizona, Evelyn wrote home:

> Oh, yes, last night at Palm Springs we were sleeping peacefully in the BOQ about a half a block from the Officers Club and we heard the fire siren. It woke us up about 2 A.M. And what do you think. The Officers' Club was on fire. Boy, did it ever go up. You know how flimsy those buildings are. We watched it for about 1 hour. It really blazed. It was brand new and wasn't even paid for. Today it was just a shell. No roof and no floor. You couldn't even recognize it.

Well, tonight I'm having dinner with a gang of the fellows.

Oh, yes, I sent 2 packages. Both to daddy. Don't open them cause they aren't wrapped. I didn't have time to send the rest. I will as soon as I get back. It is all in one box. Each gift is wrapped so you can open the box. I received the box from you but didn't have time to open it as I left on this trip.

By the way, if you have any extra gas stamps, I can always use them cause kids are always taking me somewhere.

Bye now—

Am just going   Love
to Dallas—   Evelyn—[5]

Evelyn flew only as far as Phoenix on the fourteenth of December because it was 11 a.m. before she was cleared for takeoff at Palm Springs. And by the time she landed at Phoenix, they had run out of gas. "We have to wait until tomorrow for gas. Gee, everyone is on the road."[6]

Evelyn wasn't home for Christmas in 1943 either, but her parents sent presents and some homemade cookies. On December 27, she wrote:

Gee, a swell indian rug. I really like it. It goes swell in my room. Thanks oodles. And the cookies were so good...Hot dog!

I hope you enjoy the gifts I sent. There is one more package still coming. It is for mother. I didn't have time to send it before Christmas. Sorry. I also got a string of pearls & some lipstick from B.J. And a nice leather notebook & case from two girlfriends. Really nice. It has my initials on it. One of my boyfriends, Lt. Frank Moore has a gift for me but he's on a trip & I haven't seen him since before Christmas. I also got a box of candy from Mrs.

Hoehne.[7] [Valda Hoehne was the woman in Lincoln, Nebraska, who boarded Evelyn while she was working on her flight instructor's rerating. Evelyn had sent Valda's daughter a wicker basket filled with apricots the previous Christmas, while her son had opened a box to find a salamander, DOA].

Evelyn loved Christmas. Some years later, John Sharp would write a letter expressing recollections of his daughter at holiday time. "We always had a tree just for her."[8]

Near the end of December, Evelyn felt much more secure about her ability to fly instruments. In a letter, she drew a diagram of a true fade and labeled turns, headings, altitude changes, and time. "Boy, I can really follow the beam now," she reported confidently. "You do all this under the hood....There are a lot of other systems, too. More fun!"[9]

In a letter dated January 2, 1944, Evelyn asked her parents to send two photo albums, "My red one & black one. Any pictures of mine that you have in boxes not big ones but snapshots that I haven't put in my albums. Also send me my logbooks and passenger book and anything like that. I would like to have them on hand."[10] From the time she had begun flying as a fifteen-year-old girl back in Ord, Evelyn had kept newspaper and magazine articles, letters, and pictures, notated with personal comments and dates. Perhaps a New Year's Resolution motivated her to work on the project at this time. Perhaps there were other reasons.

On January 4, Evelyn picked up a P-51B (43-7101) at Palm Springs Army Air Field. After a

US Army Air Force logo Christmas card.

fuel stop in Tucson, she continued on into Midland, Texas, both ATC Service Detachments along major ferrying routes. These operations offered AAF cross-country ferry pilots expedited fueling and unforeseen maintenance checks. Her P-51B Mustang had sprung a coolant leak on the leg into Dallas, delaying departure until late afternoon the next day. But on the sixth of January, Evelyn delivered the pursuit to Delta Airlines in Atlanta, Georgia. "Mission completed. Good Weather. Good Flight,"[11] she recorded.

When Evelyn returned to Long Beach, it was back to the sweat box, Link's stubby-winged trainer. She also did instrument work in the North American B-25D and A-27, Cessna's UC-78, and the Douglas C-49, practicing true fade, close-in procedure, fade intercept, and time-turns. "Very poor work today, be more precise, and not so good," were some of the comments recorded in her logbook by flight instructors. There were very few notations indicating acceptable performance. Instrument flying was hard for Evelyn.

On January 19, 1944, Evelyn flew the first of three line checks necessary for her instrument card. With the C-47 windows covered so she could not use ground references, Evelyn scanned instrumentation in the cockpit, making aircraft control and engine adjustments as necessary. Flying on a radio beam, she listened carefully to distinguish the "A" (dot, dash) from the "N" (dash, dot). The "A" was the inbound right side of the beam and the "N" was the outbound.[12] Pilots, wanting to pass instrument flight checks and live to fly another day, did not cross and fly the opposite signal unless they were near the airport where other standard procedures took precedence. Evelyn flew well on January 19. She passed the first line check to Tuc-

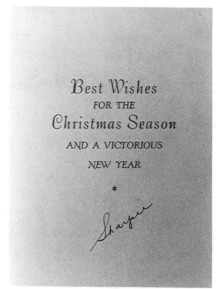

Best Wishes
FOR THE
Christmas Season
AND A VICTORIOUS
NEW YEAR

*

Sharpie

"*Remembering A Good Friend,*"
December 1943

"Instrument Flight Check," Douglas C-47, 1944

son and back. Two days later, she took her second instrument flight test in another C-47, Army 2101024. "The return trip [Ogden, Utah, to Long Beach] was at night. Got back here at 12 P.M. Flew over Las Vegas but couldn't land."[13] John and Mary had moved once again, this time to nearby Henderson, Nevada. Perhaps Evelyn wondered what their new house was like and whether she would ever get home.

Evelyn wrote impressions of her last instrument line check in a January 23 letter to her parents:

> No. 3. A B-17 from here to Oakland, California, and return. The trip back was at night. Boy really wonderful. That is the first time I've been in a B-17. We had passengers...also cargo. More fun! That B-17 is a cinch to fly. Easier than a B-25. Darn thing takes off by itself.[14]

There had been considerable hesitation in allowing women transition to Boeing's four-engine B-17. Powered by Wright nine-cylinder radial engines of 1,325-hp each,[15] the bomber grossed out at approximately 50,000 pounds.[16] Some men concluded women did not have the physical strength to pilot the huge Flying Fortress, but Nancy Love told a favorite story which spoke to at least one man's revelation. Having observed two WASPs execute a proper pattern and skillfully land one of the B-17s, he offered this comment with some humility: "You've found us out at last." Nancy concluded, "There wasn't as much mystery to flying the big boys as has been made out."[17]

Evelyn flew another P-51B back to Newark on January 26, 1944. After a two-night stay in El Paso and a five-night delay in Memphis, she delivered her plane on February 5. Within three days, she was deadheading back east from Long Beach, perhaps on Military Air Transport (MAT). Nicknamed SNAFU Airline, which stood for Situation Normal, All Fouled-Up, their C-47s and C-60s "were never on time."[18] Picking up a Republic P-47D in Evansville, Indiana, Evelyn flew the Thunderbolt west with no weather or mechanical delays. Catching an airliner in Alameda, California, about 9:30 p.m., she fell into bed at the BOQ around two the next morning.[19]

Lt. Frank Moore, whom Evelyn had referred to as "Ahem" in her letter to Teresa James, was Evelyn's check-ride instructor for the Douglas A-20 on February 15, 1944. She printed his name in her logbook after Local Transition—Landings & Takeoffs. At the end of two, one and one-half hour training flights, Frank Moore gave her the "thumbs up." "Boy that A-20 is really some airplane. It is almost as big as a B-25 and has 2 1600 H.P. engines. Opps they just called me for orders for one—See you later."[20]

Evelyn and Frank Moore often spent Saturday nights at the Officers' Club in Long Beach, that is, when both of them were on base. They talked about their ferrying trips, the great places to RON, and the wonderful airplanes they flew. In their conversations, very little was said about the past, and there was nothing about the future. Frank remembers that Sharpie was always ready to fly "at the drop of a hat." He often arranged to instruct on Saturday nights, which excused him from parade dress on Sunday mornings. "When I asked her if she'd like to go along, she didn't hesitate. She'd get her parachute and be ready to go, even if it just meant riding along." Perhaps Evelyn knew Frank would do his best to let her shoot a few takeoffs and landings at the end. "Sharpie, you want to come up here and show these boys how to do it?" he would yell back. "And she usually did," Frank remembers. "Everyone liked Sharpie. She was a kind and warm person."[21]

Evelyn had many friends, and she kept up some type of correspondence with them, even if it was just a postcard from a hotel along the ferry route. One of these friends was Chelys Mattley, who in an earlier March had picked sandburs from her soles after taking a too-early dip in the nearly frozen waters of the North Loup River. On March 5, 1944, Evelyn was grounded because of bad weather at Jackson, Mississippi. She wrote to Chelys:

> My Major friend is training in B-24's for combat so I haven't seen him recently. But I have a 1st Lt. on the string that I like better than anyone I ever met & I'm not foolin'. Don't know if anything will come of it though. Don't suppose so.
>
> I'm flying A-20's now. Better known as 'Havoc' A beautiful ship. I am one of 3 girls in the United States to be checked out in it. You asked how much time I had. I have 3500 hours. I really haven't flown much since I joined. I had 2960 when I joined in October of 1942. But the equipment I'm flying is really wonderful. I also have my instrument flying card [January 24, 1944]. Hot Dog!
>
> Will check out in P-38's after this trip.
>
> Drop me a line,
>
> > Sharpie[22]

An Easter Card

*O*n March 11, 1944, Evelyn penned a note to Glen Buffington. Corresponding with Evelyn since 1938, he had once again remembered the anniversary of her March 4, 1936, solo flight.

Gee, thanks for the "Lady Buxton" [a billfold]. Am on an A-20 trip—have delivered seven of them and am on my eighth delivery. Just returned from a Newark delivery. Now this is an airplane—really wonderful! ...And this coming week I'll get my P-38 check. Isn't that just unbelieveable?[1]

The next day, Evelyn had an A-20 delivery north to Oakland, California. She stopped in Bakersfield, perhaps seeing some old friends from her prewar instructing days.

By the twenty-second of March, Evelyn had logged more time in the Link, ferried a Curtiss RA-25 to San Diego, and made several A-20 deliveries to and from Daggett, California. On that afternoon, she started her transition to the four-engine B-17. Checking out in this heavy bomber would earn her a Fifth Rating, the highest rank in the Ferrying Command. Within the next four days, Evelyn flew an A-20 on a night check, did "airwork" in a Martin B-26B manufactured in Omaha, Nebraska, and made her seventh, forty-five minute delivery of an A-20 for modification purposes to Daggett. She looked forward to her P-38 transition and a longer ferrying mission back East.

On several occasions, Evelyn sat in the narrow confines of the Lockheed P-38 cockpit studying the configuration of the instrument panel. She noted the location of various switches and levers, which would later be committed to memory.

Evelyn's first flight in this pursuit, as in the P-51 and P-47, would be solo. There was no back seat for an instructor. Asking Ground Control for a clearance to an inactive part of the ramp, she practiced taxiing the plane down and back, making turns, and applying the brakes. The first pursuit to feature a tricycle gear handled easily, and the pilot cabin, sitting between and slightly above the twin-engine nacelles, offered good forward visibility. There was "no danger of nose-over or ground loop in this plane should it become necessary to turn sharply or apply full brakes."[2] The P-38 felt good. There must have been moments of reflection for this young woman whose flying career had taken off from the cow pastures of Nebraska in Jack Jefford's bathtub-shaped Aeronca called "Donk."

Evelyn pressed the microphone button, located in the center of the P-38's wheel. She asked Ground Control for clearance to the run-up area where she would go through the airplane's checklist to complete the engine and accessories operation ground test. At an area near the active runway, Evelyn pushed both throttles forward, holding the two toe brakes firmly. As the water-cooled Allison engines approached run-up speed, her toes jumped up and down on the rudder pedals. Shuddering from vibration, the Fork-Tailed Devil[3] wanted to fly. Pulling the throttles back and decreasing rpm to an idle, she made sure all loose material was stowed. Evelyn took a deep breath and depressed the mike key. "Long Beach Tower, this is Army 43-28721 ready to take off." The Tower answered affirmatively.

On March 26, 1944, Evelyn felt the enormous power of the two 1,425-hp engines[4] as her P-38 roared down the runway. Action-reaction forces pressed her body back against the seat and her head into its rest. Adrenalin coursed in her veins. Takeoffs were always exciting, especially those in a new plane. But this one was a magnificent "ride."

As Evelyn throttled back to 160 miles per hour, the best-rate-of-climb at sea level, feelings of pride and accomplishment flowed through her body. There was nothing in this world, absolutely nothing, that was comparable to flight. It was art and skill, inseparable from the human spirit.

For the next three days, Evelyn worked at familiarizing herself with the P-38. At a safe practice altitude, she executed turns and climbs and descents. Visualizing a "runway in the sky," she probably flew a simulated landing pattern and final approach with a make-believe landing. These maneuvers would give her the feel of the P-38 in gear up and gear and flaps down configurations.[5]

On March 29, 1944, after three hours and twenty minutes of logged P-38 flying time, Evelyn signed off on the Army's familiarization form. She agreed to having satisfactorily completed transition flight training, feeling qualified to perform duties as the first pilot, and having an operations knowledge of all instruments, systems, and procedures.[6]

The next day, Evelyn was issued orders to deliver a P-38J to Newark, New Jersey. Because of their long range capability and the capacity to fly all sorts of missions well, the Lightnings were very much in demand in both the European and Pacific Theaters. Their tricycle gear "made landings a piece of cake"[7] on airstrips carved out of jungles in the South Pacific. On takeoffs the counter-rotating propellers dispensed with the torque problem produced by powerful single-engine airplanes like the P-47 and P-51. But the P-38 had its share of problems. Early models had given the fighter a bad reputation. Turbulent air over wings made it virtually impossible to control the craft in a high-speed dive, and the Allison engines had a reputation for quitting from time to time. Losing one on takeoff was the nightmare of every P-38 pilot.[8] The P-38 was more forgiving at altitude.

Evelyn flew into Palm Springs at 2:50 on the afternoon of March 30, 1944. Some ninety miles from Long Beach, the Army air field was protected from coastal fogs and rain by the gigantic Mt. San Jacinto. Long Beach, on the coast of the Pacific Ocean, was often socked in until late morning or early afternoon. For this reason ferry pilots often RONed at the beautiful La Paz Hotel in Palm Springs so as to get an earlier start the next day.[9] And perhaps Evelyn thought she might be able to have dinner with Lt. Frank Moore, who was now instructing at Palm Springs Army Air Base.

With 386 gallons of fuel on board including two forty-gallon wing tanks, Evelyn departed Palm Springs on a northeasterly heading the morning of March 31.[10] Within fifty minutes, the plane touched down at Kingman, Arizona. No doubt she recalled the stories of Pat Thomas and Kittie Leaming who had ferried Luscombes to Lone Pine across the desolation of the Great Mohave Desert a little over two years ago. Yet it seemed so much longer. Was time, too, a casualty of the War?

With more fuel in the tanks, Evelyn flew east across the geographical breadth of Arizona and on into New Mexico. She crossed the Continental Divide some seventy miles west of Albuquerque, her next stop. The alert crew filled the tanks, added six quarts of oil to the No. 1 engine, and checked the communications equipment. The maintenance log recorded forty-four quarts of oil in each tank. She okayed their service and took off due east for the Texas Panhandle. With a checkpoint at Tucumcari, she continued on into Amarillo, Texas, where she would RON. As the wheels of the Lockheed pursuit made contact with the runway at Lunken Field, Evelyn glanced at her watch. It was 3:50 p.m. Before leaving the plane, she recorded in her small, brown spiral notebook four hours and ten minutes of flying.

On April 1, 1944, Evelyn picked up a more northerly heading. With a full load of fuel and the oil in each tank measuring forty quarts, she pointed the nose of her P-38 toward the first checkpoint. Flying abeam of Oklahoma City at 10:38 a.m., she continued on into Tulsa by 11:15. With 161 more gallons of fuel on board, her next stop would be Scott Field in Illinois. The oil level in both tanks was holding at forty.

On the ground for less than an hour, Evelyn wanted to make Cincinnati before sunset. Perhaps she and Nancy Love, the woman who had made female ferry pilots a reality in the Ferrying Command, would spend the evening at the Officers' Club. Many of the original WAFS had much respect for Nancy. Evelyn was no exception.

On April 2, the service crew at Lockbourne Army Air Base in Cincinnati brought each oil tank up to capacity, fifty-two quarts. The Number 2 engine had lost eight quarts. The Number 1 had been holding. At 8:40 a.m. Evelyn lifted off, but within forty-five minutes she had landed in Columbus, Ohio. Perhaps she was waiting for weather to break over the Allegheny ridges dead ahead on her course, or perhaps there was something else. She was on the ground in Columbus for an hour and a half.

Wanting to make her P-38 delivery before the end of the day, Evelyn made the decision to push on. Her weather check showed conditions near Harrisburg, Pennsylvania, were marginal, but perhaps they would clear by afternoon. Using Pittsburgh as a checkpoint, she recorded the time of 11:45 a.m. as she flew by. Just beyond, over the ridges of the heavily forested Allegheny Mountains, lay Harrisburg. As she approached the city, flying due east, Evelyn could see weather up ahead, where the horizon should be. Ceilings were low and visibility was decreasing. Spotting the Radio Range Station on the top of Beacon Hill, she remembered New Cumberland Airport, camouflaged for wartime protection, was just on the other side. And five miles down the Susquehanna River was the Army air field at Middletown, where Evelyn had flown in L-2Bs and L-4Bs when she had first trained with the Ferry Command. That, too, seemed like a long time ago.

Running into a "snow, rain, and sleet storm,"[11] Evelyn flew only a short distance beyond Harrisburg on April 2, 1944. Banking the sleek, twin-boomed Lightning into a skilled 180-degree turn, she touched down within minutes on the runway at New Cumberland. The time was 12:55 p.m. She wired Operations in Long Beach of her intent to RON.

That evening Evelyn wrote several letters from her room at The Harrisburger Hotel. A stack of unanswered mail, which she carried on ferry trips, could include names of special high school classmates, family friends in Ord, contacts made during barnstorming days, Civilian Pilot Training students, Army and Navy pilots who had gone off to war, and new friendships made since becoming part of the Ferrying Command. People were very important to Evelyn. She once wrote: "I try to send them [Mom and Daddy] a card or letter everywhere I stop. They have quite an interesting collection by now."[12]

On the next-to-last page of her worn, brown spiral address book was an entry for someone she had never met. Upon her return from Newark, New Jersey, Evelyn was scheduled to fly an A-20 into Great Falls, Montana; her birth father, Orla Edward Crouse, was planning to drive the 168 miles from Missoula, Montana.[13] The reunion between a daughter and a father, who had probably left Miles City, Montana, before her birth, would never take place.[14]

In a letter (postmarked April 3, 1944, 10:30 a.m., Harrisburg, Pennsylvania), Evelyn wrote to Pat Thomas, her instructor-pilot friend from Lone Pine.

> Seems as tho I finally caught up with a little weather so I thought I'd catch up on my correspondence.
>
> I have a P-38J this trip. A beautiful ship.
>
> My folks plan to come down for a visit soon. I sure hope so. Would like to see them.
>
> Believe it or not I've finally found a fellow but don't know how he feels. Oh well, it will all come out in the wash.
>
> Well, sugar. Lots of good luck. Tell your "Mom" hello.
>
> > Bye,
> > Sharpie[15]

Evelyn addressed another envelope that night in Harrisburg — this one to Lt. Frank R. Moore, 21st Ferrying Group, Palm Springs, California.[16] Since Easter was a week away, she signed the greeting card and tucked it away in her purse. She would mail it later.

"I'll Do Everything I Can"

silver, slightly damaged Lightning, wearing the standard Army Air Force markings of that time, rested quietly on a grassy knoll near the edge of a grove of deciduous trees. Although the two propellers were twisted and there was a slight upward bend in the middle section of the long, twin-tail booms, the aircraft looked pretty much intact.[1] But there was no movement, save for a

"The Lightning At Rest," Beacon Hill, New Cumberland, Pennsylvania, April 3, 1944

small curling wisp of smoke coming from the left engine. There was no sound. It was quiet. Deathly quiet. A short distance ahead and to the right of the cockpit, the P-38's Plexiglas bubble canopy, wrenched from the aircraft, had come to rest on the gently sloping incline. Only a few hundred yards beyond, Yellow Breeches Creek meandered its way to the northeast, skirting the west edge of New Cumberland Airport before emptying into the Susquehanna River.

"Harrisburg Ground Control calling Stinson aircraft N2330. We have reason to believe the P-38 that just took off has crashed somewhere on the other side of Beacon Hill. Can you fly over and confirm?"[2]

John Macfarlane was taxiing his Stinson SR-10 out to Runway 30 when the voice came over his radio. His duties as an inspector for the Pennsylvania Aeronautics Commission would take him out of the Harrisburg-New Cumberland area today, but first, he would make the report. He had seen that pretty WASP chatting with officers on the tarmac just a few minutes earlier and could still hear the unusual whine of those Allison engines as she taxied by. The P-38 was a beautiful plane.

Reflying the path of Evelyn's departure, he swung around the towers atop Beacon Hill. Below, watchmen-observers waved their arms in the direction the plane had flown. They would later report she barely missed the towers while trying to get around.[3] On the west side near the edge of a ravine, John Macfarlane saw the plane. "...seemed to land relatively easily, did not nose into the ground, and skidded only a short distance."[4] Confirming his find, he told the Tower he would circle a few times to determine if he could see the pilot. Within seconds, he saw movement. "The pilot is alive. She's waving her hands in the air,"[5] John reported with a sigh of relief.

As he refocused attention on his flight to Pittsburgh, John could see cars headed up Beacon Hill Road and people running toward the area where they had heard the crash. In the distance, he noticed the men and equipment from the Elkwood and Citizen Volunteer Fire Company were on their way.[6] They would have some difficulty in getting across that muddy, spring-thawed field. And later during lunch recess, children, who had been kept away from the windows by their elementary school teachers, ran to the top of Beacon Hill. Only this time, armed guards from nearby Olmsted Army Air Base kept them away.[7]

John Macfarlane did not realize Evelyn Sharp had been killed until he returned to New Cumberland that late afternoon. The person he had seen walking around the plane was Elmer Zimmerman, a tenant on whose property she had crashed. He and his wife had been in the kitchen of their home, "when they heard the faltering motor of the plane, then a dull thud."[8] They rushed out and saw the crash only several hundred yards away, near the edge of their property line. Fearing fire, Elmer Zimmerman ran to the wreckage. Evelyn lay on the ground about eight feet ahead and to the right of the plane.

> Believing the woman was still alive and in danger of an explosion, Zimmerman without regard for his own safety, picked up the flier and carried her a short distance away. He and his wife then walked toward the center of the field and waved their arms toward the wreckage in the successful hope the (Army) reconnaissance plane would see it.[9] [The man in that plane was John Macfarlane.]

Because Evelyn had crashed just inside Lower Allen Township, Dr. Edward A. Haegele, the Cumberland County coroner, was called to inspect the scene. He reported his view:

> ...Lt. Evelyn G. Sharp, came to her death on the 3rd day of April, A.D., 1944, at 10:30 A.M., by means of severe traumatic shock; compound comminuted fractures of skull and face; broken neck, crushed chest, crushed pelvis, fractures of upper and lower extremities, internal injuries, massive hemorrhage.[10]

The violent impact of the P-38's pancake landing had driven the retracted nose wheel into the cockpit. Breaking the straps on her safety harness, the force catapulted Evelyn out through the bubble canopy. She had died instantly.[11]

"Tears dimmed the eyes of some of the soldiers as they carried her body across the muddy field"[12] to the end of the two-mile road which skirted the towers on Beacon Hill and ended at the Zimmerman

"Bubble Canopy And Twisted Prop," Beacon Hill, New Cumberland, Pennsylvania,
April 3, 1944

farm. Evelyn's body was "tenderly lifted and placed in [the car of] J. Thomas Richardson..."[13] a funeral director from across the Susquehanna River. A lieutenant whose identity was not disclosed said, 'I've seen tragedies before and it's tough to see a boy lose his life but this is the first time I have seen a woman make the supreme sacrifice.'[14]

News of Sharpie's death spread across the country by word of mouth and by front page stories off the wire services. The reaction of those who knew her was one of disbelief. How could this happen to Sharpie? She was an "excellent pilot,"[15] "a superb pilot,"[16] "a wonderful pilot,"[17] "a marvelous pilot, the best."[18] "What a true pilot she was."[19] "I know Nancy Love had complete respect for her."[20] "Her death was a true loss to the Aviation Fraternity."[21]

In Wilmington, Delaware, at the Second Ferrying Division, WASP Squadron Commander Betty Gillies asked Nancy Batson to accompany Evelyn's body back to Nebraska. Original members of the WAFS, Evelyn and Nancy had come to Wilmington some eighteen months earlier and flown several ferry missions together. Dressed in her new Santiago Blue uniform with its matching WASP beret, Nancy boarded a train for Harrisburg. Inside her handbag was an envelope, a collection of some $200 taken up by the WASPs in Wilmington. She would give it to John and Mary Sharp upon her arrival.[22]

As the slow-moving train crossed the rolling plains of Nebraska and neared the small Sandhills community of Ord, Nancy remembered how Evelyn had shared with her pilot friends those simple beginnings. The people back here had believed in the dreams of a fifteen-year-old girl and that was something Evelyn had never forgotten. Slipping her hand into a black leather handbag to check the money collected in Wilmington, Nancy smiled as she reflected on the stack of unanswered letters Evelyn always carried in her purse. One of those had been written by Patty Baer, the little farm girl from Eustis, Nebraska. Later, when Evelyn's personal effects were sent home, John Sharp would write a note to Patty, enclosing it with the unanswered letter.[23] And Mary Sharp would mail the Easter card to the special Army Air Force Lieutenant in Palm Springs.[24]

John, Mary, and Evelyn's birth mother, Elsie Crouse Rick, were waiting in Ord when their daughter arrived. Coming from Los Angeles, they, too, had made the trip home by train.[25] That afternoon, John purchased the north half of lot #39 in the Graceland Division of the Ord Cemetery.[26] Mary and he had decided they would be buried on each side of their daughter.[27]

At the Frazier Mortuary and Furniture store, they selected a vault, keeping the metal-lined casket issued by the military. The Eastern Star would officiate at the funeral in the Ord Methodist Church, with the American Legion conducting services at the gravesite. Lucile Tolen, who had learned to swim when Evelyn taught life-saving classes in the North Loup River, was asked to sing some favorite hymns, and John Sharp chose Edward Petersen, Ellis Carson, Elwin Dunlap, Dillo Troyer, K. W. Peterson, and Curt Gudmundsen to carry his daughter's body.[28] At the funeral service, several of these men, also student pilots of Jack Jefford's, stood and shared early flying memories by the North Loup River and reminiscences of solo parties at John's Town Tavern. There were tears in the eyes of many. Mary would later write "…am so upset and confused. I feel that part of me has left and John is so broken up I don't know what will become of us. Poor Elsie was so brave thru it all and she had planned so much. But its all over now and I know little Picky [Evelyn] was so happy in her work and would want us to keep our chins up but its a hard way. Her things will be shipped from the Air Base at Long Beach and I dread their arrival."[29]

Only twenty-three years old herself, WASP Nancy Batson was unprepared for the outpouring of grief. A man at the funeral home wanted to know if he could drape Evelyn's coffin with an American flag. Nancy was taken aback. None of the WASP were military. They flew with no insurance, no benefits, and certainly no military honors if they died. Batson thought for only a moment and gently whispered, "Of course." Tears of gratitude brimmed in the man's eyes.[30]

"Ord's Favorite Daughter" was buried on Easter Sunday, April 9, 1944. The sun did not shine as the mournful message of "Taps" faded across the rolling fields of the peaceful North Loup Valley. On the following Wednesday, *The Ord Quiz* reported:

> …one of the biggest crowds attended one of the most tragic funerals. Hundreds came in final tribute to Evelyn Sharp, slim, dark-haired Valley County girl…Always a favorite…since the school days when she learned to fly…. Evelyn's funeral was a tremendous tribute to her popularity. Banks of flowers from all the country proved the esteem in which she was held.[31]

Only three years before, Evelyn had been interviewed by *The Bakersfield Californian*. With the war machine on its march in Europe, the reporter asked Evelyn if she would volunteer for war service if hostilities broke out.

"Certainly! There's plenty of things a woman flier can do to help aviation branches of the service. I'll do everything I can."[32] For Evelyn Sharp, that statement of commitment had become prophetic. This twenty-four-year-old woman, who simply loved to fly, could now do no more.

*"I'll Do Everything I Can," Women's Auxiliary Ferrying Squadron,
Women Airforce Service Pilots, Born October 20, 1919, Died April 3, 1944*

Afterword

When the war ended, families and friends turned their attention toward honoring those who made the supreme sacrifice for freedom. It was no different in Ord, Nebraska. Gerald "Bud" Clark, the president of Evelyn's senior high class, had been killed in December of 1944 during the bloody Battle of the Bulge.[1] His body was somewhere in a cemetery across the seas; he had to be brought home. And plans announced at Evelyn's funeral for renaming the airport and erecting a fitting memorial needed to get underway.

Two packages totaling 559 pounds were delivered to the Chicago, Burlington & Quincy Railroad Depot in Ord on April 8, 1947. Addressed to J. E. Sharp, c/o Alfred L. Hill, Postmaster, the $14.50 shipping order had been prepaid.[2] Inside a crate was a war surplus, disassembled, three-bladed P-38 prop from Walnut Ridge, Arkansas; a box held the necessary propeller parts to put it back together.

Alfred Hill, the same postmaster who directed Evelyn's Twentieth Anniversary Commemorative Air Mail Flights out of Ord in 1938, assured John Sharp he would take care of the reassembly.[3]

On September 12, 1948, the bright blue, nearly cloudless skies provided a perfect backdrop for the formation flying and acrobatic maneuvers of P-51s, B-26s, and the Nebraska Air National Guard's new F-80 jets. Thousands of people, who had come to witness the dedication of Evelyn Sharp Field, were welcomed by music from the

Ord High School Band. John and Mary Sharp had also returned, carrying personal remembrances of their daughter's flying career. They would be sealed in a concrete pyramidal monument and placed beneath the silver, six-foot blades of the P-38 propeller.[4]

Dedication of Sharp Field, September 12, 1948, Ord, Nebraska

SHARP FIELD
Ord Municipal Airport.
ORD. NEB.   EL. 2042"

More than two decades later, glass-enclosed cases were built to display a collage of pictures and print at the airport's fixed-base operations building. The primary source materials had been retrieved from an old valise sent by John Sharp to the Nebraska State Historical Society in Lincoln soon after Evelyn's death. No one could remember when or why the suitcase had been returned to Ord, only that it had been gathering dust in a back room at the airport for several years.

Today, a Nebraska State Historical Society highway marker designates the entrance to Sharp Field which is currently listed in *Susan B.*

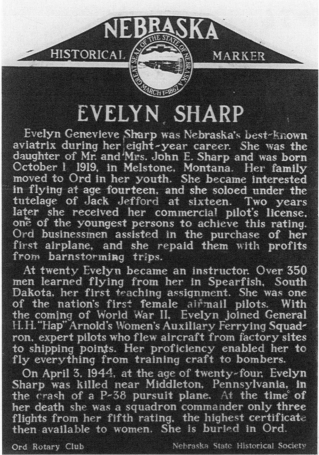

Nebraska State Historical Marker at Entrance to Sharp Field.
Dedicated June 24, 1973, Dr. Glen D. Auble, Project Coordinator

Anthony Slept Here: A Guide to American Women's Landmarks. A gray, granite monument, dedicated at the first Evelyn Sharp Day in June 1996, stands beneath the P-38 propeller. And at the local Pizza Hut across the highway from what was once John's Town Tavern, a framed picture of a young woman standing beside a plane marked US Mail is sometimes the subject of conversation.

One half-mile to the southeast of Evelyn Sharp Field, a simple, white wooden cross marks the gravesite of the only woman to be inducted into Nebraska's Aviation Hall of Fame.

If you were to visit, it would not be unusual to find a mixed bouquet of wildflowers lying on her grave. Once a year a wreath of yellow flowers tied with sapphire blue ribbon is placed against the traditional red granite monument. Beside it is a small wooden plaque carved by a man who also left her a pair of his Air Force pilot wings. For him and countless others, a young girl who grew up in Nebraska and gave her life in service to her country has not been forgotten.

Evelyn Sharp Gravesite, Ord City Cemetery, Ord, Nebraska

Notes

Aircraft and engine logs, pilot logbooks, scrapbooks and other historical documents were used as reference throughout the book.

Hard Right Rudder
Chapter One—Pages 5 - 10

[1] Airway Weather Report, WB Form 1130, Station: Harrisburg, PA Airport, April, 1944, US Department of Commerce Weather Bureau.

[2] *Pilots Manual for Lockheed P-38 Lightning* (Appleton, WI: Aviation Publications, n.d.) 22-24A.

[3] Report to Air Corps Lieutenant E. C. Clemens from Pvt. Frank J. Dougherty and Pfc. Mike E. Lawrence, 3 Apr. 1944, author collection from US Air Force/Sam Parker Collection.

[4] (*Pilots Manual* 31)

[5] "Army Withholds Identity of Pilot Killed In Crash," *Harrisburg Telegraph* 4 Apr. 1944: n. pag.

[6] Description of P-38 accident, author collection from Pateman WASP Collection, vol. XII, US Air Force Academy Archives, Colorado Springs, CO.

Married In Haste
Chapter Two—Pages 11 - 15

[1] Melstone History Class, *Melstone: The Town and Its Times* (Billings, MT: Aztec Printing Company, 1972) 33.

[2] *New Leipzig Sentinel* 9 May 1918: 7.

[3] Winifred Schachterle, telephone interview, 4 June 1992.

[4] WWI draft card, Orla E. Crouse, author collection from SLC Film #1684108, MT, Custer Co. #2309, Salt Lake City, UT Library.

[5] "Married In Haste But All Is Well," *New Leipzig Sentinel* 15 May 1919: 1.

[6] A search of county records in MT, ND, MN, and NE produced no divorce records, though some for that time period have been lost in fires or floods. Elsie married Henry W. Rick on 25 March 1922, Minneapolis, MN. They lived in Augusta, WI, until Mr. Rick died in 1939. Elsie died in Osseo, WI, on 1 March 1981, at 89 years of age. Evelyn was her only child.

[7] Standard Certificate of Live Birth, State of MT, State File No. 91, De-

partment of Health and Environmental Sciences, Cogswell Building, Helena, MT.

[8] Mildred Millard Arvidson, telephone interview, 1 July 1992.

[9] Mary R. Haughian, telephone interview, 14 May 1992.

I Want To Drive An Airplane
Chapter Three—Pages 16-21

[1] Edna Osgood Reiber, telephone interview, 11 Jan. 1992.

[2] "Dry Cedar News," *Ericson Journal* 17 May 1928: 8.

[3] "South Side Items," *Ericson Journal* 2 Aug. 1928: 4.

[4] Robert and Norma Philbrick, personal interview, 9 Oct. 1991.

[5] "South Side Items," *Ericson Journal* 20 Sept. 1928: 4.

[6] "South Side Items," *Ericson Journal* 4 Oct. 1928: 4.

[7] Maxine Severns Eacker, telephone interview, 12 Jan. 1992.

[8] Dale A. Philbrick, telephone interview, 6 Aug. 1988.

[9] "South Side Items," *Ericson Journal* 31 Jan. 1929: 4.

[10] "South Side Items," *Ericson Journal* 28 Mar. 1929: 1.

[11] "South Side Items," *Ericson Journal* 20 Mar. 1930: 8.

Cinders and Double-dip Cones
Chapter Four—Pages 22-29

[1] "Household Equipment" ad, *Ord Quiz* 3 Apr. 1930: 12.

[2] "Laundry Re-opened," *Ord Quiz* 17 Apr. 1930: 7.

[3] "J.E. Sharp Buys Bluebird," *Ord Quiz* 25 Sept. 1930: 1.

[4] "Ord Business Men Sponsor Aerial Rodeo," *Ord Quiz* 9 Oct. 1930: 1.

[5] South School Practical Grade Record, Grade 6, Form G, author collection.

[6] "Stock Is Dying, People Starving In Drought Area," *Ord Quiz* 21 Jan. 1932: 1; "Do It Now! Help Ord's Drought Relief Project As Others Have," *Ord Quiz* 4 Feb. 1932: 1.

[7] "Home Ice Cream Co. Begins Operation," *Ord Quiz* 2 June 1932: 1.

[8] Virginia Klein Cruce, letter to the author, 24 Jan. 1992.

[9] "PERSONAL ITEMS About People You Know," *Ord Quiz* 18 Aug. 1932: 5.

[10] Jim Ollis, personal interview, 6 July 1991.

[11] "NOTICE," *Ord Quiz* 17 Nov. 1932: 5.

[12] "Merry Christmas," *Ord Quiz* 22 Dec. 1932: 1.

[13] "Wanted" ad, *Ord Quiz* 23 Mar. 1933: 8.

[14] "Ord Church Notes Methodist Church," *Ord Quiz* 20 Apr. 1933: 4.

[15] "Children Present Excellent Program At Methodist Church," *Ord Quiz* 16 June 1932: 1, 4.

Messages From The Community
Chapter Five—Pages 30 - 39

[1] Evelyn Sharp related science notes, author collection from Mary Farmer Palmer.

[2] *Oracle* 8 Nov. 1933, author collection from Irene Auble Abernethy.

[3] *Oracle* 23 Sept. 1934, author collection from Irene Auble Abernethy.

[4] "Ord Schools To Offer Carnival Next Thursday," *Ord Quiz* 1 Feb. 1934: 1.

[5] "Something DIFFERENT," *Ord Quiz* 10 May 1934: 4.

[6] "Liquor Law Violators Plead Guilty, Fined," *Ord Quiz* 9 Aug. 1934: 1.

[7] "For Sale Livestock," *Ord Quiz* 9 Aug. 1934: 10.

[8] J. A. Kovanda, "Back Forty," *Ord Quiz* 6 Sept. 1934: 2.

[9] "This Week's Sponsor is Dr. Glen D. Auble, O.D.," *Ord High Oracle*, *Ord Quiz* 4 Oct. 1934: 9, author collection from Virginia Clark Knecht.

[10] "*Ord High Oracle* Will Be Weekly Feature," *Ord Quiz* 27 Sept. 1934: 9.

[11] "Legion Minstrels Please Big Crowd," *Ord High Oracle*, *Ord Quiz* 8 Nov. 1934: 7.

[12] "Amos Harris Dead," *Ord Quiz* 2 Mar. 1911: 1.

[13] Dorothy Auble Hardisty, letter to the author, 12 Nov. 1991.

[14] "Ordites Combine To Bring Xmas Cheer To Needy," *Ord Quiz* 27 Dec. 1934: 1.

[15] "Sophs Shatter Tradition, Win Soccer Tourney," *Ord High Oracle*, *Ord Quiz* 17 Jan. 1935: 9, author collection from Virginia Clark Knecht.

[16] ("Sophs Shatter Tradition 9)

[17] ("Sophs Shatter Tradition 9)

[18] "Editorial," *Ord High Oracle, Ord Quiz* 24 Jan. 1935: 9, author collection from Virginia Clark Knecht.

Taken Out In Trade
Chapter Six⟶Pages 40 ⁄ 45

[1] Journal of flight lesson, author collection from Evelyn Sharp scrapbook.

[2] "1000 Present At Music Festival," *Ord High Oracle, Ord Quiz* 28 Mar. 1935: 9.

[3] "Dust Storm Is Called Worst In Nebraska History," *Ord Quiz* 21 Mar. 1935: 1.

[4] "1,227,022 Tons Of Dirt Left Here By Dust Storm," *Ord Quiz* 18 Apr. 1935: 1.

[5] Journal of flight lesson, 7 May 1935, author collection from Evelyn Sharp scrapbook.

[6] Shirley Dobson Gilroy, *Amelia, Pilot In Pearls* (McLean, VA: Link Press, 1985) 59. Amelia wrote her famous poem while she was a social worker at Denison House in Boston. First appeared in print after her *"Friendship"* flight across the Atlantic in 1928.

> Courage is the price which life exacts for granting peace.
> The soul that knows it not, knows no release
> From little things;
> Knows not the livid loneliness of fear
> Nor mountain heights, where bitter joy can hear
> The sound of wings.
> How can life grant us boon of living, compensate
> For dull gray ugliness and pregnant hate
> Unless we dare
> The soul's dominion? Each time we make a choice we pay
> With courage to behold resistless day
> And count it fair.

[7] "Junior-Senior Banquet Wednesday Evening Was Brilliant Affair," *Ord High Oracle, Ord Quiz* 16 May 1935: 11.

[8] Irene Whiting, telephone interview, 24 May 1992.

[9] "Where You Find One—You'll Find The Other," *Ord High Oracle, Ord Quiz* 24 Jan. 1935: 9.

[10] "Something DIFFERENT," *Ord Quiz* 6 June 1935: 4.

[11] "Fastest Car, Best Driver; They Won $815," *Ord Quiz* 26 Sept. 1935: 1, 3.

A Natural
Chapter Seven~Pages 46 / 52

[1] Journal of flight lesson, author collection from Evelyn Sharp scrapbook.

[2] "'Youngest Girl Transport Pilot' Aim Of Evelyn Sharp, 16, Of Ord," *Lincoln Sunday Journal and Star* 22 Mar. 1936: CD3.

[3] ("'Youngest Girl Transport Pilot' CD3)

[4] "Ord Aviation Club Has 'Solo' Party," *Ord Quiz* 12 Mar. 1936: 1.

[5] "Something DIFFERENT," *Ord Quiz* 26 Mar. 1936: 2.

[6] "Evelyn Sharp, Ord's 16-Year-Old Airplane Pilot, Has Many Hobbies, Is Serious-Minded, Stars in Studies," *Ord Quiz* 30 Apr. 1936: 1.

[7] ("Evelyn Sharp, Ord's 16-Year-Old Airplane Pilot 1)

[8] Edward Nielsen tribute to Evelyn Sharp, 23 Mar. 1936, author collection from Verna Nielsen Wilson.

[9] "Something DIFFERENT," *Ord Quiz* 26 Dec. 1935: 8.

[10] Aviation chart in Evelyn Sharp scrapbook, author collection.

[11] Howard E. Jones, personal interview, 2 July 1988.

Put It Out, Private Pilot, Perfect Evening
Chapter Eight~Pages 53 / 60

[1] "Gov't Grasshopper Poison All Used, No More Available," *Ord Quiz* 9 July 1936: 1.

[2] "Flight of 'Hoppers Passed Over Ord, Gardens Damaged," *Ord Quiz* 16 July 1936: 1.

[3] "Three Are Fined For Intoxication," *Ord Quiz* 2 July 1936: 1.

[4] LaVerne Lakin, "Ord Campfire Girls Enjoy Week's Outing at Mortensen Camp," *Ord Quiz* 6 Aug. 1936: 6.

[5] Irene Auble Abernethy, personal interview, 7 Oct. 1991.

[6] (LaVerne Lakin 6)

[7] "Both Loup Projects Get Funds," *Ord Quiz* 20 Aug. 1936: 1.

[8] "Seniors Hold Class Championship," *Ord Quiz* 17 Sept. 1936: 8.

[9] Irene Whiting, telephone interview, 24 May 1992.

[10] Eleanore Perlinski, telephone interview, 2 Sept. 1992.

[11] "Ord's Irrigation Celebration Was Attended by 8,000," *Ord Quiz* 8 Oct. 1936: 1, 6.

[12] "Ord Seniors Will 'Go to School' In Stores Nov. 8-13," *Ord Quiz* 29 Oct. 1936: 1.

[13] "Evelyn Sharp Youngest Girl In U.S. To Get License to Pilot Airplanes," *Ord Quiz* 19 Nov. 1936: 1.

[14] Mary Wynn, "Hen Party Is Held, by Those Who Flew Coop," *Fort Worth Star-Telegram* 5 Mar. 1939: n. pag., author collection from Evelyn Sharp scrapbook.

[15] LaVern Duemey, personal interview, 4 Aug. 1989.

Don't Forget Me, "Amelia E."
Chapter Nine—Pages 61–70

[1] Belle Hetzel notes, Ninety-Nines charter meeting, 30 Jan. 1937, author collection from Sharon K. Meyer.

[2] "Something DIFFERENT," *Ord Quiz* 14 Apr. 1937: 2.

[3] Wilma Krikac Johnson, personal interview, 9 Oct. 1991.

[4] "Ord High Dramatic Club Is Accepted By The National Thespian Organization," *Ord Quiz* 25 Mar. 1937: 11.

[5] ("Ord High Dramatic Club 11)

[6] Irene Whiting, personal interview, 9 Oct. 1991.

[7] Wilson Shafer, personal interview, 22 Oct. 1991.

[8] "Something DIFFERENT," *Ord Quiz* 14 Apr. 1937: 2.

[9] "Ord's Girl Flier Can't Recall What Train Is Like," *Omaha World-Herald* 16 May 1937: n. pag., author collection.

[10] "Scottie Dog Has Leading Role In Senior Play, 'Growing Pains'," *Ord Quiz* 12 May 1937: 1.

[11] "'Growing Pains' Play Presented Friday By the Ord Seniors, Attracted Big Crowd, Was a Huge Success," *Ord Quiz* 19 May 1937: 3.

12 "Commencement Program Thursday Closes School Year," *Ord Quiz* 26 May 1937: n. pag., author collection from Gerald Clark scrapbook.

13 Senior class will, author collection from Mary Farmer Palmer.

14 Senior class prophecy, author collection from Mary Farmer Palmer.

15 Evelyn Sharp memory book, poem dated 15 Apr. 1936, author collection from Mary Farmer Palmer.

16 Evelyn Sharp yearbook and memory book, author collection from Mary Farmer Palmer.

17 "Two Boys Killed in Car Crash Sunday," *Ord Quiz* 4 Mar. 1937: 1, 3.

18 "'Keep Faith' Is Plea Made to Ord Grads By J. E. Lawrence," *Ord Quiz* 2 June 1937: 1.

City Fathers Buy A Cub
Chapter Ten—Pages 71 - 79

1 "Leaves Air For Water," *Omaha Bee News* 28 June 1937: 4.

2 "Ord Girl Will Study Swimming," *Grand Island Daily Independent* 25 June 1937: 3.

3 "Eddy Employed To Aid In Handling the Swimming Classes," *Ord Quiz* 28 July 1937: 1.

4 "Ord Children Enjoy Swimming Lessons With Competent Instructors," *Ord Quiz* 21 July 1937: 1.

5 Evelyn Sharp, postcards to John and Mary Sharp, author collection from Mary Farmer Palmer.

6 Charles B. Zangger, letter to author, 7 Nov. 1991.

7 "Miss Evelyn Sharp Of Ord Hopes To Be Youngest Transport Pilot In Nation," *Lincoln Sunday Journal and Star* 8 Aug. 1937: CD3.

8 "Plane in Which Chris Hald Was Fatally Injured," *Ord Quiz* 21 Apr. 1937: n. pag., author collection from Evelyn Sharp scrapbook.

9 "Skeleton of Plane After Fire," *Ord Quiz* 28 Apr. 1937: n. pag., author collection from Evelyn Sharp scrapbook.

10 Evelyn Sharp logbook, author collection.

11 Ralph Misko, personal interview, 21 Sept. 1991.

12 "This Week's Sponsor is Dr. Glen D. Auble, O. D.," *Ord Hi Oracle*, *Ord Quiz* 4 Oct. 1934: 9, author collection from Virginia Clark Knecht.

[13] "The Story of Evelyn Sharp's Aeroplane Experience," letter written by Glen D. Auble, author collection from Irene Auble Abernethy.

[14] "Transport License On 18th Birthday Goal of Ord Miss," *Ord Quiz* 25 Aug. 1937: 1.

[15] "Ord Girl Gets Plane Nears Transport Goal," *World-Herald* [Omaha, NE] 19 Aug. 1937: 20.

[16] "1000 Passengers Since Aug. 1st Is Record of Ord Girl Who Just Completed 4 Years Flying," *Ord Quiz* 8 Feb. 1939: 10.

[17] ("Transport License On 18th Birthday 1)

[18] John Sharp, letter to public opinion, author collection from Graydon Dill.

[19] (John Sharp, letter)

[20] "Miss Valley Co. Will Be Selected At Fair Grounds," *Ord Quiz* 11 Aug. 1937: 1.

[21] Evelyn Sharp logbook and passenger register, author collection.

[22] Milo W. Bresley, personal interview, 2 July 1988.

A Lost Cub
Chapter Eleven—Pages 80 - 87

[1] "Evelyn Sharp Will Be First to Land On New Arrasmith Field," *Ord Quiz* 15 Sept. 1937: 1.

[2] ("Evelyn Sharp Will Be First 1)

[3] "Grand Island Gives Hearty Welcome To Evelyn Sharp at Arrasmith Field," *Ord Quiz* 22 Sept. 1937: 1.

[4] ("Grand Island Gives Hearty 1)

[5] "Evelyn Gets Her 200 Hours," *Sunday World-Herald* [Omaha, NE] 26 Sept. 1937: n. pag., author collection from Evelyn Sharp scrapbook.

[6] ("Evelyn Gets Her n. pag.)

[7] "Evelyn's Air Tutor Will Fly in Alaska," *Ord Quiz* 22 Sept. 1937: 1.

[8] "Senator Edw. Burke Principal Speaker At Airport Opening," *Ord Quiz* 29 Sept. 1937: 1.

[9] "Society...Phone 32," *Grand Island Daily Independent* 29 Sept. 1937: 7.

[10] ("Society 7)

[11] Mae Lee Misko, telephone interview, 11 Jan. 1992.

[12] "Evelyn 'Flunks' Transport Exam, Will Try Again in Three Months," *Ord Quiz* 3 Nov. 1937: 3.

[13] ("Evelyn 'Flunks' 3)

[14] "Yule Tide Greetings to You," *Ord Quiz* 22 Dec. 1937: 2.

[15] M. Woodburn, The Alemite Company, Omaha, NE, Re: File #92, letter to Robert R. Reining, Department of Commerce Administration, 3 June 1938, author collection from US Department of Transportation, FAA, Mike Monroney Aeronautical Center, Oklahoma City, OK.

[16] Ruth Lake Armour, letter to the author, 10 April 1992.

A Stairway To The Stars
Chapter Twelve—Pages 88 / 99

[1] "Evelyn Sharp Goes To School; Benefit Dance Raised Funds," *Ord Quiz* 26 Jan. 1938: 1.

[2] Chelys Mattley Hester, personal interview, 22 Jan. 1992.

[3] Evelyn Sharp, letter to Pruda Farmer Lobenstein, 28 Mar. 1938, author collection from Mary Farmer Palmer.

[4] Evelyn Sharp, letters to Richard Severson, 24 Jan. 1938; 30 Jan. 1938; 13 Feb. 1938; 16 Feb. 1938; 1 Mar. 1938; author collection from Gerald Severson.

[5] Dr. W. W. Arrasmith, Western Union telegram to Evelyn Sharp, author collection.

[6] Clark Gable and Myrna Loy, Postal telegram to Evelyn Sharp, 23 Apr. 1938, author collection from Heloise Christensen Bresley.

[7] "Movie Stars Loy, Gable, and Tracy Telegraph Evelyn," *Ord Quiz* 27 Apr. 1938: 1.

[8] "Evelyn Sharp, 18, Of Ord, Gets License As Nation's Youngest Aviatrix—Now She Needs Plane," *Lincoln Star* 14 May 1938: 4.

[9] Chelys Mattley Hester, personal interview, 22 Jan. 1992.

[10] "Evelyn Sharp Wins Her Pilot's License," *Ord Quiz* 18 May 1938: 1.

[11] "Mail Planes Come To Ord Thursday, Circus On Friday," *Ord Quiz* 18 May 1938: 1.

[12] Spencer Tracy, letter to Evelyn Sharp, 23 May 1938, author collection.

[13] Evelyn Sharp, air mail letter to Herman and Winifred Mattley, author collection from Chelys Mattley Hester.

[14] Evelyn Sharp, air mail letter to Richard Severson, author collection from Gerald Severson.

[15] Ralph Misko, personal interview, 21 Sept. 1991.

Off Again, On Again, Gone Again
Chapter Thirteen⁓Pages 100 ⁄ 105

[1] "Fan Letters Do Not Worry Evelyn Sharp," *Ord Quiz* 25 May 1938: 1.

[2] James P. Misko, speech at Rotary Club luncheon, Ord, NE, 23 May 1938, author collection from Evelyn Sharp scrapbook.

[3] (James P. Misko, speech)

[4] "Miss Evelyn Sharp Honored at Rotary," *Ord Quiz* 25 May 1938: 1.

[5] "165 Learning How To Swim," *Grand Island Daily Independent* 30 July 1938: 3.

[6] Lucile Tolen, personal interview, 9 Oct. 1991.

[7] "Swimming Classes End for Season; 178 Were Enrolled," *Ord Quiz* 24 Aug. 1938: 1, 6.

[8] "Local News," *Ord Quiz* 27 July 1938: n. pag., author collection.

[9] "News Of The Neighborhood," *Ord Quiz* 27 July 1938: 10.

[10] William Ferguson, "This Curious World," cartoon, author collection from Evelyn Sharp scrapbook.

[11] "Evelyn Sharp, Sky Rider," *Diller Record* 21 July 1938: 8.

[12] "Some Picnic Notes," *Diller Record* 18 Aug. 1938: 4.

[13] "Some Picnic Highlights," *Diller Record* 4 Aug. 1938: 1.

[14] "Forty-Second Annual Picnic Is History," *Diller Record* 18 Aug. 1938: 1; "The Parade," *Diller Record* 18 Aug. 1938: 4.

[15] ("Some Picnic Notes 4)

[16] 42nd Annual Diller Picnic poster, 11-12 Aug. 1938, author collection.

[17] "Rock County Fair A Successful Event," *Rock County Leader* [Bassett, NE] 25 August 1938: 1.

[18] ("Rock County Fair 1)

[19] "Youngest Woman Pilot Visits New Swimming Pool," *Newman Grove Reporter* 7 Sept. 1938: 1.

[20] ("Youngest Woman Pilot 1)

[21] Evelyn Sharp, letter to H. Glenn Buffington, 19 Oct. 1938, *American Aviation Historical Society Journal* (Summer 1991) : 132.

[22] Evelyn Sharp, letter to H. Glenn Buffington, 19 Dec. 1938, *American Aviation Historical Society Journal* (Summer 1991) : 132-33.

Elevators, Tires, & Rods
Chapter Fourteen⁓Pages 106 ⁄ 115

[1] Jack Jefford, letter to Evelyn Sharp, 18 May 1939, author collection from Evelyn Sharp scrapbook.

[2] "Quartet Lost in Alaskan Wilds Huddle In Plane And Wait for Assistance," n.p. [Nulato, AK] 22 Dec. 1939: n. pag., author collection from Evelyn Sharp scrapbook; "Ex-Nebraskans Play Leading Roles in Alaska Rescue Try," n.p. [Anchorage, AK] 22 Dec. 1939: n. pag., author collection from Evelyn Sharp scrapbook.

[3] Evelyn Sharp, letter to H. Glenn Buffington, 13 Jan. 1939, *American Aviation Historical Society Journal* (Summer 1991) : 133.

[4] "Evelyn Sharp Recounts Experiences as Pilot," *Antelope* [Kearney State Teachers College] 13 Jan. 1939: n. pag., author collection from Chelys Mattley Hester.

[5] Chelys Mattley Hester, personal interview, 22 Jan. 1992.

[6] "1000 Passengers Since Aug. 1st Is Record of Ord Girl, Who Just Completed 4 Years Flying," *Ord Quiz* 8 Feb. 1939: 10.

[7] "Air Show Crowd Rewarded With Daring Feats," *Grand Island Daily Independent* 16 Aug. 1938: 4.

[8] "Youngest Transport Aviatrix Attends Banquet," *Fort Worth Star-Telegram* 4 Mar. 1939: 1.

[9] Mary Wynn, "Hen Party Is Held, by Those Who Flew Coop," *Fort Worth Star-Telegram* 5 Mar. 1939: n. pag., author collection from Evelyn Sharp scrapbook.

[10] Liberty Theater advertisement, Loup City, NE, Feb. 1939, author collection from Evelyn Sharp scrapbook.

[11] Floyd O. Johnson, Ass't Sales Manager, Stinson Aircraft Division, letter to Evelyn Sharp, 26 Apr. 1939, author collection from Mary Farmer Palmer.

[12] Emil Daake, letters to Evelyn Sharp, 23 Jan. 1939; Mr. Sharp and

family, 16 Feb. 1939; 26 Mar. 1939; author collection from Heloise Christensen Bresley.

[13] (Emil Daake, letters)

[14] "Something DIFFERENT," *Ord Quiz* 12 Apr. 1939: 4.

[15] "Dog Taxes Due May 1," *Ord Quiz* 19 Apr. 1939: 10.

[16] Chelys Mattley Hester, personal interview, 22 Jan. 1992.

[17] "Goodland Entertains 'Schoolgirl Aviatrix'," *Sherman County Herald* [Goodland, KS] 11 May 1939: n. pag., author collection from Evelyn Sharp scrapbook.

[18] ("Goodland Entertains n. pag.)

[19] Dana Merlin, "Evelyn Sharp, Famous Girl Pilot, Stops Here Tuesday Enroute to Ord," *Hebron Register* 9 Mar. 1939: 1.

[20] Curtiss Robin Serial No. 567, author collection from US Department of Transportation, FAA, Mike Monroney Aeronautical Center, Oklahoma City, OK.

[21] Evelyn Sharp, letter to H. Glenn Buffington, 12 May 1939, *American Aviation Historical Society Journal* (Summer 1991) : 133.

[22] "FURNITURE FOR SALE," *Ord Quiz* 24 May 1939: 7.

The Grasshopper
Chapter Fifteen—Pages 116 / 124

[1] "Personal Items About People You Know," *Ord Quiz* 7 June 1939: 11.

[2] NC551N aircraft log, author collection.

[3] "Airplane Rides" ad with picture, author collection from Evelyn Sharp scrapbook.

[4] Verna Nielsen Wilson, telephone interview, 24 May 1992.

[5] (Verna Nielsen Wilson, telephone)

[6] (Verna Nielsen Wilson, telephone)

[7] (Verna Nielsen Wilson, telephone)

[8] "Airplane View of Part of Cozad," *Cozad Local* 27 June 1939: 1; "EVELYN GETS READY TO TAKE OFF," *Cozad Local* 27 June 1939: 1; "Another View From the Air," *Cozad Local* 30 June 1939: 4.

[9] "Young Aviatrix Visits In Lexington Again," *Dawson County Herald* [Lexington, NE] 13 July 1939: 1.

[10] Mearl McNeal, telephone interview, 22 Sept. 1991.

[11] (Mearl McNeal, telephone)

[12] "Evelyn Sharp Entertains Crowds Here," *Curtis Enterprise* 6 July 1939: 1.

[13] "Evelyn Sharp Arrived Wednesday," *Bertrand Herald* 14 July 1939: 1.

[14] Edward Nielsen, "Cozad and Vicinity," *Dawson County Herald* [Lexington, NE] 22 June 1939: 7.

[15] Maxine Waters Carlson, telephone interview, 5 Nov. 1991.

[16] (Maxine Waters Carlson, telephone)

[17] Evelyn Sharp, letter to H. Glenn Buffington, 19 July 1939, *American Aviation Historical Society Journal* (Summer 1991) : 133-34.

[18] L. E. Tyson, State Airport Engineer, Nebraska Aeronautics Commission, letter to Evelyn Sharp, 17 June 1939, author collection.

[19] KGNF promotion of "Sky-Rider," 26 July 1939, author collection from Evelyn Sharp scrapbook.

[20] NC551N aircraft and engine logs, author collection.

[21] John A. Clinch, personal interview, 27 Oct. 1991.

[22] Evelyn Sharp, letter to Elsie Crouse Rick, n.d., author collection from Russell and Dolly Zangger.

[23] "17th Massacre Canyon POW-WOW," *Trenton Register* 28 July 1939: 3.

[24] "17th Massacre Canyon Pow-Wow Set For Aug. 3-6; Fine Program Assured," *Trenton Register* 28 July 1939: 1.

[25] ("17th Massacre Canyon Pow-Wow Set 1)

Flippers O.K., Elevators Aren't
Chapter Sixteen∕∕∕Pages 125 ∕ 131

[1] Evelyn Sharp, letter to H. Glenn Buffington, 16 Aug. 1939, *American Aviation Historical Society Journal* (Summer 1991) : 134.

[2] Evelyn Sharp, letter to Civil Aeronautics Authority, Washington, DC, 2 Sept. 1939, author collection from US Department of Transportation, FAA, Mike Monroney Aeronautical Center, Oklahoma City, OK.

[3] Roger Boerkircher, telephone interview, 29 June 1992.

4 Roger Boerkircher postcard, 7 Sept. 1939, author collection from Benita Schmidt.

5 Urcell Baer Bartruff, personal interview, 9 Sept. 1991.

6 Westrope [IA] air show poster, 24 Sept. 1939, author collection from Lawrence Rushenberg.

7 Lawrence Rushenberg, telephone interview, 16 June 1992.

8 Clarke Conway, Civil Aeronautics Authority, letter to Evelyn Sharp, 3 Jan. 1940, author collection from US Department of Transportation, FAA, Mike Monroney Aeronautical Center, Oklahoma City, OK.

9 "Miss Evelyn Sharp, Famous Aviatrix, To Fly During Festival," *Gothenberg Times* 5 Oct. 1939: 1.

10 ("Miss Evelyn Sharp, Famous 1)

11 "Sharp Visits Mattley," *Kearney State College Newspaper* n.d. : n. pag., author collection from Chelys Mattley Hester.

12 Irene Schmale Nesiba, personal interview, 2 July 1988.

13 Evelyn Sharp, letter to Clarke Conway, Asst. Chief Records Division, Civil Aeronautics Authority, 6 Jan. 1940, author collection from US Department of Transportation, FAA, Mike Monroney Aeronautical Center, Oklahoma City, OK.

14 NC551N aircraft log, author collection.

15 Evelyn Sharp, letter to H. Glenn Buffington, 18 Nov. 1939, *American Aviation Historical Society Journal* (Summer 1991) : 134-35.

16 Evelyn Sharp, letter to H. Glenn Buffington, 18 Dec. 1939, *American Aviation Historical Society Journal* (Summer 1991) : 135.

I Wish I Had A Brother
Chapter Seventeen—Pages 132 - 138

1 Evelyn Sharp, letter to H. Glenn Buffington, 17 Jan. 1940, *American Aviation Historical Society Journal* (Summer 1991) : 135.

2 Willard Wiener, *Two Hundred Thousand Flyers: The Story of the Civilian-AAF Pilot Training Program* (Washington: The Infantry Journal, 1945) V, viii.

3 Patricia Strickland, *The Putt-Putt Air Force: The Story of the Civilian Pilot Training Program and War Service 1939-1944* (Washington: US Department of Transportation, FAA Education Staff, n.d.) n. pag.

[4] (Evelyn Sharp, letter to H. Glenn Buffington, 17 Jan. 1940 135)

[5] Evelyn Sharp, letter to H. Glenn Buffington, 17 Jan. 1940, author collection from H. Glenn Buffington.

[6] Fanny M. Leonpacher, ed., "Ninety-Nine News Letter," Jan. 1940, author collection from Ninety-Nines Archives, Oklahoma City, OK.

[7] Ray A. Johnson, personal interview, 7 Mar. 1993; audio tape, 4 May 1992; author collection from Ray A. Johnson.

[8] (Ray A. Johnson, personal)

[9] Evelyn Sharp, letter to H. Glenn Buffington, 28 Mar. 1940, *American Aviation Historical Society Journal* (Summer 1991) : 135.

[10] Wayne Jorgensen, telephone interview, 7 June 1992.

[11] Eugene Masters, telephone interview, 20 Aug. 1988; "Nick, The Cop, Is Dead," *Lincoln Star* 6 Nov. 1954: 1.

[12] Dorette Hoehne Kleinkauf, personal interview, 20 Nov. 1988.

[13] Harry E. Mendenhall, *State House News: State House Employees Weekly* [Lincoln, NE] 3 May 1940: 1, author collection.

[14] "An Aeronautics Club For Lincoln?" *State House News: State House Employees Weekly* [Lincoln, NE] 3 May 1940: 1, author collection.

[15] "Notice To Ladies Contest Closes Monday April 29th," *State House News: State House Employees Weekly* [Lincoln, NE] 26 May 1940: 3.

[16] "Behind The Scenes Of Jane Tucker's Informal Radio Visits...," *Lincoln Sunday Journal and Star* 12 May 1940: 8.

[17] Dorette Hoehne Kleinkauf, telephone interview, 14 Oct. 1991.

[18] Evelyn Sharp picture with inscription, given to Sharp Field, Ord, NE, by Dorette Hoehne Kleinkauf.

Flying The Boys
Chapter Eighteen—Pages 139 / 147

[1] Letters to CPTP sponsors, 15 June 1940, author collection from Mary Farmer Palmer.

[2] "AGAIN YOUNGEST," 10 June 1940: 4; "AIR SCHOOLMA'AM," n.p. n.d. : n. pag.; author collection; "20-Year-Old Girl Head of Aviation Work at Mitchell," *Daily Argus-Leader* [Sioux Falls, SD] 11 June 1940: 1, author collection; "Girl, 20, S.D. Flying Veteran, Busy Teaching for U.S.,"

n.p. n.d. : n. pag., author collection; "Yes, Teacher—We Have Our Lessons," n.p. 26 July 1940: 1, author collection from Crystal Thode Thompson.

[3] "Twenty-Year-Old Girl Pilot Is Instructor Here," *Daily Republic* [Mitchell, SD] 15 June 1940: n. pag., author collection.

[4] Evelyn Sharp photograph album, author collection from Mary Farmer Palmer.

[5] Evelyn Sharp, letter to H. Glenn Buffington, 27 July 1940, author collection from H. Glenn Buffington.

[6] "Flying Hobby of Prof. Guy Jacobs," n.p. n.d. : n. pag., author collection from Don Young.

[7] CPTP contract, 26 June 1940, author collection from Mary Farmer Palmer.

[8] Howard W. Ice, personal interview, 17 June 1989.

[9] Raymond Kolb, personal interview, 21 Apr. 1992.

[10] Raymond Kolb CPTP logbook, author collection from Raymond Kolb.

[11] "AGAIN YOUNGEST," *Lincoln Star* 10 June 1940: 4.

[12] Evelyn Sharp, letter to parents, 14 July 1940, author collection from Dorothy Auble Hardisty.

[13] "Picnic Honors Mrs. Sharp," *Ord Quiz* 3 July 1940: 5.

[14] (Evelyn Sharp, letter to H. Glenn Buffington, 27 July 1940)

[15] (Evelyn Sharp, letter to parents, 14 July 1940)

[16] Lloyd L. Petersen, telephone interview, 9 July 1992.

[17] Jack V. O'Keefe, Chief, Aviation Education/Safety, *Development of Aviation in Nebraska* (Lincoln: Nebraska Department of Aeronautics, 1961) 8, 9.

[18] Crystal Thode Thompson, letter to the author, 5 June 1992.

[19] Crystal Thode Thompson, telephone interview, 30 May 1992.

[20] Guy Jacobs journal, 22 July 1940, author collection from Joan Jacobs Shuey.

[21] (Evelyn Sharp, letter to H. Glenn Buffington, 27 July 1940)

[22] (Raymond Kolb, personal)

[23] Crystal Thode Thompson photograph album, author collection from Crystal Thode Thompson.

24 (Evelyn Sharp, letter to H. Glenn Buffington, 27 July 1940); Red Cross Life-Saving papers, author collection.

25 "Agricultural Edith FARM NOTES," *Burt County Plaindealer* [Tekamah, NE] 22 Aug. 1940: n. pag., author collection.

A Luscombe, a B-24, and a '37 Olds
Chapter Nineteen—Pages 148 - 157

1 "Coroner's Probe Into Death of Ernest Hemmerling, In Airport Inn Fire, Started," *Grand Island Daily Independent* 29 July 1940: 1, 5.

2 Coburn Campbell, letter to John Sharp, 9 July 1940, author collection from Mary Farmer Palmer.

3 "Crash of Plane At Spearfish Is Probed by CAA;" "Spearfish CAA Trainee Dies In Air Crash," n.p. n.d. : n. pag., author collection from Evelyn Sharp scrapbook; Lloyd L. Petersen, telephone interview, 9 July 1992.

4 Evelyn Sharp, letter to H. Glenn Buffington, 28 Dec. 1940, author collection from H. Glenn Buffington.

5 Evelyn Sharp journal, author collection from Mary Farmer Palmer.

6 Lloyd L. Petersen CPTP logbook, author collection from Lloyd L. Petersen.

7 Lloyd L. Petersen, telephone interview, 9 July 1992.

8 Evelyn Sharp, letter to H. Glenn Buffington, 4 Oct. 1940, author collection from H. Glenn Buffington.

9 Wilson Shafer, personal interview, 22 Oct. 1991.

10 Edward H. Ellington, telephone interview, 30 May 1992.

11 Guy Jacobs journals, 26-27 July 1940, author collection from Joan Jacobs Shuey.

12 *The Eociha* [Spearfish Normal School yearbook] (n.p. : n.p., 1941) 70, author collection from Don Young.

13 Kenneth Pittman, "Sprouting Wings," *Anemone* 14 Feb. 1941: 1, 4, author collection from Don Young.

14 Kenneth Charles Marsden, telephone interview, 12 July 1992.

15 Evelyn Sharp, letter to H. Glenn Buffington, 25 Oct. 1940, *American Aviation Historical Society Journal* (Summer 1991) : 136.

16 Evelyn Sharp, letter to H. Glenn Buffington, 25 Oct. 1940, author collection from H. Glenn Buffington.

[17] Howard W. Ice, personal interview, 17 June 1989.

[18] Evelyn Sharp, letters to H. Glenn Buffington, 4 Oct. 1940, 28 Dec. 1940; author collection from H. Glenn Buffington; Guy Jacobs journal, 30 Sept. 1940, author collection from Joan Jacobs Shuey.

[19] Allen Marek, telephone interview, 30 May 1992.

[20] *The History of American Popular Music: Joel Whitburn's Pop Memories 1890-1954* (Menomonee, WI: Record Research, Inc., 1986) 654.

[21] Crystal Thode Thompson, telephone interview, 30 May 1992.

[22] (Evelyn Sharp, letter to H. Glenn Buffington, 28 Dec. 1940)

[23] (Evelyn Sharp, letter to H. Glenn Buffington, 28 Dec. 1940)

Wings In The West
Chapter Twenty—Pages 158 - 168

[1] Glen S. Roberts, secretary Les Buchner's Flying Service, letter to Evelyn Sharp, 26 Sept. 1940, author collection from Graydon Dill.

[2] John Ratigan, telephone interview, 30 May 1992.

[3] I. H. Young, telephone interview, 2 June 1992.

[4] Allen Marek, telephone interview, 30 May 1992.

[5] Allen Marek, letter to the author, 4 June 1992.

[6] Evelyn Sharp, letter to H. Glenn Buffington, 26 Jan. 1941, *American Aviation Historical Society Journal* (Summer 1991) : 136.

[7] Evelyn Sharp, letter to H. Glenn Buffington, 25 Feb. 1941, *American Aviation Historical Society Journal* (Summer 1991) : 136.

[8] "GIRL TRAINS PILOTS: Noted Aviatrix Coaches Fledglings," *Bakersfield Californian* 24 Feb. 1941: 8, 17, author collection from Les Buchner.

[9] ("Girl Trains Pilots 8, 17)

[10] Evelyn Sharp, letter to H. Glenn Buffington, 25 Feb. 1941, author collection from H. Glenn Buffington.

[11] William R. Lachenmaier, telephone interview, 25 July 1992.

[12] William R. Lachenmaier, letter to the author, 8 Dec. 1992.

[13] (William R. Lachenmaier, letter)

[14] Evelyn Sharp, letter to H. Glenn Buffington, 23 May 1941, *American Aviation Historical Society Journal* (Summer 1991) : 137.

[15] Evelyn Sharp, letter to H. Glenn Buffington, 23 May 1941, author collection from H. Glenn Buffington.

[16] Evelyn Sharp, letter to Allen Marek, 3 Mar. 1942, author collection from Allen Marek.

[17] "Get Up in the Air," *Lodi News-Sentinel* 22 Aug. 1941: n. pag., author collection.

[18] "Women Pilots Here;" "County Airport Will Be Host To Fliers," n.p. n.d. : n. pag., author collection.

[19] Patricia Thomas Gladney, letter to the author, 14 Oct. 1991.

[20] (Patricia Thomas Gladney, letter)

[21] Evelyn Sharp, letter to H. Glenn Buffington, 11 Sept. 1941, *American Aviation Historical Society Journal* (Summer 1991) : 137.

[22] Evelyn Sharp, letter to H. Glenn Buffington, 19 Sept. 1941, *American Aviation Historical Society Journal* (Summer 1991) : 137.

[23] (Evelyn Sharp, letters to H. Glenn Buffington, 11 Sept. 1941; 19 Sept. 1941 137)

[24] Les Buchner, telephone interview, 7 May 1992.

[25] (Evelyn Sharp, letters to H. Glenn Buffington, 11 Sept. 1941; 19 Sept. 1941 137)

[26] E. K. Langevin, "All Around Girl," *Sunday World-Herald* [Omaha, NE] 18 Sept. 1938: Rotogravure sec. 1.

[27] Evelyn Sharp, letter to H. Glenn Buffington, 19 Sept. 1941; 17 Nov. 1941, *American Aviation Historical Society Journal* (Summer 1991) : 137.

[28] Cornelia Fort, "At the twilight's last gleaming," *Woman's Home Companion* July 1943: 19.

[29] Evelyn Sharp, letter to H. Glenn Buffington, 22 Dec. 1941, author collection from H. Glenn Buffington; Evelyn Sharp pass to Kern County Airport, author collection.

[30] Evelyn Sharp, letter to H. Glenn Buffington, 22 Dec. 1941, *American Aviation Historical Society Journal* (Summer 1991) : 137.

[31] Evelyn Sharp, letter to Patty Baer, 22 Dec. 1941, author collection from Christine Dunbar.

Beneath Mt. Whitney
Chapter Twenty-one——Pages 169 - 176

[1] Evelyn Sharp, letter to H. Glenn Buffington, 6 Mar. 1942, *American Aviation Historical Society Journal* (Summer 1991) : 137.

[2] Dave Holland, *On Location IN LONE PINE* (Granada, Hills, CA: The Holland House, 1990) 10, 15-16, 31, 33, 42, 61, 82-83.

[3] "Got some 'black hats' in need of a set? Come to Lone Pine," *San Jose Mercury News* 29 Sept. 1991: T13.

[4] William Bauer, telephone interview, 31 July 1992.

[5] Les Buchner, telephone interview, 7 May 1992.

[6] Jacqueline Cochran, Western Union telegram to Evelyn Sharp at Dow Hotel, author collection.

[7] Patricia Thomas Gladney, letter to the author, 27 May 1992.

[8] Patricia Thomas Gladney, letter to the author, 16 Oct. 1991.

[9] Patricia Thomas Gladney, letter to the author, 15 June 1992.

[10] Evelyn Sharp, letter to H. Glenn Buffington, 6 May 1942, author collection from H. Glenn Buffington.

[11] Kittie Leaming King, telephone interview, 7 Nov. 1992.

[12] (Evelyn Sharp, letter to H. Glenn Buffington, 6 May 1942)

[13] "Nebraska's No. 1 Aviatrix," *Lincoln Star* n.d. : n. pag., author collection.

[14] "Evelyn Sharp, 22, Flies 'em High, Wide, Handsome," *Lincoln Star* 27 June 1942: 1, 6.

[15] ("Evelyn Sharp, 22, Flies 'em 1, 6)

[16] (Patricia Thomas Gladney, letter to the author, 16 Oct. 1991)

[17] (Patricia Thomas Gladney, letter to the author, 16 Oct. 1991)

[18] "Convention demands slavery reparations," *Lincoln Journal-Star* 24 July 1994: B2.

A Birthday Present
Chapter Twenty-two——Pages 177 - 182

[1] Bill Wright, "After 90 Years And 40,000 Hours, He's Been Around Longer And Has More Hours Than Almost Anybody," *Pacific Flyer* Apr. 1992: B24-26, B34.

[2] E. B. Daniel, Division of Labor Statistics and Law Enforcement, letter to CLAIMANTS VS. LES BUCHNER, 31 Aug. 1942, author collection from Mary Farmer Palmer.

[3] Brian Pemberton, telephone interview, 11 July 1992.

[4] Evelyn Sharp, letter to H. Glenn Buffington, 25 Aug. 1942, *American Aviation Historical Society Journal* (Summer 1991) : 137.

[5] Evelyn Sharp, letter to H. Glenn Buffington, 24 July 1942, author collection from H. Glenn Buffington.

[6] Betty Huyler Gillies, address to The Ninety-Nines, Inc. International Convention, Baltimore, MD, 27 July 1985, author collection from Betty Huyler Gillies.

[7] Sally VanWagenen Keil, *Those Wonderful Women In Their Flying Machines: THE UNKNOWN HEROINES OF WORLD WAR II* (New York: Four Directions Press, 1990) 111.

[8] "Girl Pilots War Plane to Canada," *Boston Record* 5 June 1940: n. pag., author collection from Nancy Harkness Love Collection, Acc. 1987-0047, National Air and Space Museum Library, Washington, DC.

[9] Marianne Verges, *On Silver Wings: THE WOMEN AIRFORCE SERVICE PILOTS OF WORLD WAR II, 1942-1944* (New York: Ballantine, 1991) 42.

[10] Patricia Thomas Gladney, letter to the author, 15 June 1992.

[11] "John E. Sharp, Former Ohiowan Dies in Nevada," n.p. n.d. : n. pag., author collection.

[12] Evelyn Sharp, letter to H. Glenn Buffington, 19 Oct. 1942, *American Aviation Historical Society Journal* (Summer 1991) : 137.

[13] Requirements to join Ferry Command, author collection from Nancy Harkness Love Collection, Acc. 1987-0047, National Air and Space Museum Library, Washington, DC; Deborah G. Douglas, "WASPS OF WAR," n.p. n.d. : 51, author collection; "HISTORY of the WOMEN PILOTS in the FERRYING DIVISION, ATC, September 5, 1942 to December 20, 1944," prepared by Historical Unit, Intelligence and Security Section, in accordance with AAF regulation No. 20-8 and AAF letter 40-34, completed on 1 Feb. 1945: 68, author collection from Peggy Nigra, MAC/HO. Declassified in accordance with DOD DIR 5200.10.

[14] "Evelyn Sharp Check Flight For Applicants, ACFC Civilian Pilots," 20 Oct. 1942, author collection from National Personnel Records Center, Military Records, St. Louis, MO.

[15] ("HISTORY of the WOMEN PILOTS 72)

16 For reasons unknown to the author, John and Mary Sharp believed Evelyn was born 1 Oct. 1919. MT birth certificate records her birth 20 Oct. 1919.

A Letter From Aunt Elsie
Chapter Twenty-three—Pages 183 - 190

1 Evelyn Sharp ID card, issued 21 Oct. 1942, War Department Ferrying Division, ATC, author collection.

2 Betty Huyler Gillies, address to The Ninety-Nines, Inc. International Convention, Baltimore, MD, 27 July 1985, author collection from Betty Huyler Gillies.

3 Kathryn Bernheim Fine, letter to the author, 9 Dec. 1991.

4 Phyllis Burchfield Fulton, letter to the author, 17 Dec. 1991; telephone interview, 9 Jan. 1992.

5 Libby Lackman, "First of WAFS Go Into Barracks In Delaware for Instruction," *New York Times*, 26 Sept. 1942: n. pag., author collection from WASP Collection, File 03, National Air and Space Museum Library, Washington, DC.

6 "THE WAFS: A squadron of 25 girls is leading the way for U.S. women fliers," *Look* 9 Feb. 1943: 18.

7 Adela Riek Scharr, *SISTERS IN THE SKY: VOLUME I—THE WAFS* (St. Louis, MO: Patrice Press, 1988) 83-84.

8 Teresa James, letter to the author, 23 June 1992.

9 Evelyn Sharp, letter to "Dear Mom and Pop," 13 Nov 1942, author collection from National Personnel Records Center, Military Records, St. Louis, MO.

10 Sally VanWagenen Keil, *Those Wonderful Women In Their Flying Machines: THE UNKNOWN HEROINES OF WORLD WAR II* (New York: Four Directions Press, 1990) 131.

11 Byrd Howell Granger, *ON FINAL APPROACH: The Women Airforce Service Pilots of World War II* (Scottsdale, AZ: Falconer Publishing Company, 1991) 60, A-70/C.

12 Elsie Crouse Rick, letter to "Dear Folks," mailed 27 Nov. 1942 from 35-31-168th St., Flushing L. I., NY, c/o Ira Pfefferkorn, author collection from Mary Farmer Palmer.

A Letter From Evelyn
Chapter Twenty-four—Pages 191 - 203

[1] Teresa James, letter to the author, 23 Jan. 1992.

[2] (Teresa James, letter 23 Jan. 1992)

[3] Evelyn Sharp address book, author collection.

[4] (Teresa James, letter 23 Jan. 1992)

[5] (Teresa James, letter 23 Jan. 1992)

[6] (Teresa James, letter 23 Jan. 1992)

[7] Teresa James, letter to the author, 8 Oct. 1988.

[8] Operations Order CP 297, Flight No. 5688, 22 Nov. 1942, author collection from National Personnel Records Center, Military Records, St. Louis, MO.

[9] (Teresa James, letter 23 Jan. 1992)

[10] Evelyn Sharp address book, author collection.

[11] Evelyn Sharp, letter to "Dear Mom and Pop," 29 Nov. 1942, author collection from National Personnel Records Center, Military Records, St. Louis, MO.

[12] Marianne Verges, *On Silver Wings: THE WOMEN AIRFORCE SERVICE PILOTS OF WORLD WAR II, 1942-1944* (New York: Ballantine, 1991) 53.

[13] Adela Riek Scharr, *SISTERS IN THE SKY: VOLUME I —THE WAFS* (St. Louis, MO: Patrice Press, 1988) 187.

[14] Sgt. Charles Baker, "ILL WIND," n.p. n.d. : n. pag., author collection.

[15] Legette Blythe, "Ferry Command Girls Irked By Bad Weather," *Charlotte Sunday Observer* 27 Dec. 1942: 1, 12.

[16] (Legette Blythe 1, 12)

[17] Evelyn Sharp, letter to H. Glenn Buffington, 25 Jan. 1943, author collection from H. Glenn Buffington.

[18] Capt. Francis A. Tilden, public relations, 3rd Ferrying Group, FD, ATC, Romulus, MI, "WASP Cold Weather Experiences," n.d., author collection from WASP Collection, File 07, National Air and Space Museum Library, Washington, DC.

[19] Annie Lee Singletary, "Lady Ferry Pilots Spend a 'Ceiling' Furlough in City," n.p. n.d. : n. pag. (Original EDITOR'S NOTE: "Publication of this story delayed for approval by army censors."), author collection from Heloise Christensen Bresley.

[20] Evelyn Sharp, letter to "Dear Folks," 14 Jan. 1943, author collection from Mary Farmer Palmer.

[21] (Evelyn Sharp, letter to "Dear Folks," 14 Jan. 1943)

[22] (Teresa James, letter 23 Jan. 1992)

[23] (Teresa James, letter 23 Jan. 1992)

[24] Evelyn Sharp, letter to Jerome and Pruda (Farmer) Lobenstein, author collection from Mary Farmer Palmer.

[25] (Evelyn Sharp, letter to H. Glenn Buffington, 25 Jan. 1943)

[26] Rogers Corner (NYC, NY) souvenir photo, 23 Jan. 1943, author collection from Winifred Schachterle.

[27] John Sharp, letter to Nina Sharp, 24 Aug. 1948, author collection from Russell and Dolly Zangger.

[28] Nancy Batson Crews, telephone interview, 8 Jan. 1992.

[29] Barbara Towne Fasken, letter to the author, 7 Sept. 1993.

"BT Knucklehead"
Chapter Twenty-five—Pages 204-211

[1] Byrd Howell Granger, ON FINAL APPROACH: The Women Airforce Service Pilots of World War II (Scottsdale, AZ: Falconer Publishing Company, 1991) 125.

[2] Sally VanWagenen Keil, Those Wonderful Women In Their Flying Machines: THE UNKNOWN HEROINES OF WORLD WAR II (New York: Four Directions Press, 1990) 173.

[3] Evelyn Sharp, letter to "Dear mom and pop and Shanty and Tam," 22 Feb. 1943, author collection from Mary Farmer Palmer.

[4] Evelyn Sharp, letter to H. Glenn Buffington, 25 Jan. 1943, American Aviation Historical Society Journal (Summer 1991) : 137.

[5] Evelyn Sharp, letter to "Dear sugars and little black sugars," 18 Mar. 1943, author collection from Mary Farmer Palmer.

[6] SIXTH FERRYING GROUP: LONG BEACH, CALIFORNIA (Baton Rouge, LA: Army and Navy Publishing Company of Louisiana, n.d.) 34, author collection from Frank R. Moore.

[7] (Evelyn Sharp, letter to "Dear sugars and little black sugars," 18 Mar. 1943)

[8] "MEET THE PILOTS," Air-Age Aug. 1943: 28.

[9] ("MEET THE PILOTS," 29)

[10] Evelyn Sharp, letter to "Dear Folks," 25 Mar. 1943, author collection from Mary Farmer Palmer.

[11] (Evelyn Sharp, letter to "Dear Folks," 25 Mar. 1943)

[12] "HISTORY of the WOMEN PILOTS in the FERRYING DIVISION: September 5, 1942 to December 20, 1944," prepared by Historical Unit, Intelligence and Security Section, in accordance with AAF regulation No. 20-8 and AAF letter 40-34, completed on 1 Feb. 1945: 117, author collection, from Peggy Nigra, MAC/HO. Declassified in accordance with DOD DIR 5200.10.

[13] Marianne Verges, *On Silver Wings: THE WOMEN AIRFORCE SERVICE PILOTS OF WORLD WAR II, 1942-1944* (New York: Ballantine, 1991) 90.

[14] (Byrd Howell Granger 62)

[15] (Byrd Howell Granger 62)

[16] Evelyn Sharp, letter to "Dear folks," 16 Apr. 1943, author collection from Mary Farmer Palmer.

[17] Barbara Erickson London, personal interview, 28 July 1991.

[18] Evelyn Sharp, letter to H. Glenn Buffington, 16 Apr. 1943, *American Aviation Historical Society Journal* (Summer 1991) : 138.

[19] Evelyn Sharp, letter to "Dear folks," 18 May 1943, author collection from Mary Farmer Palmer.

[20] "BT Knucklehead," author collection from WASP Collection, File 06, National Air and Space Museum Library, Washington, DC.

On Deaf Ears
Chapter Twenty-six—Pages 212 - 221

[1] Evelyn Sharp, postcard to Richard Severson, 10 Sept. 1938, author collection from Gerald Severson.

[2] *SIXTH FERRYING GROUP: LONG BEACH, CALIFORNIA* (Baton Rouge, LA: Army and Navy Publishing Company of Louisiana, n.d.) 58-59, author collection from Frank R. Moore; Jean E. Davis, telephone interview, 19 Mar. 1992.

[3] *The History of American Popular Music: Joel Whitburn's Pop Memories 1890-1954* (Menomonee, WI: Record Research, Inc., 1986) 654-55.

[4] Evelyn Sharp, letter to "Dear Sugars and black sugarsticks," 11 Apr. 1943, author collection from Mary Farmer Palmer.

[5] "HISTORY of the WOMEN PILOTS in the FERRYING DIVISION, ATC: September 5, 1942 to December 20, 1944, prepared by Historical Unit, Intelligence and Security Section, in accordance with AAF regulation No. 20-8 and AAF letter 40-34, completed on 1 Feb. 1945: 108, author collection from Peggy Nigra, MAC/HO. Declassified in accordance with DOD DIR 5200.10.

[6] Evelyn Sharp, letter to "Dear folks," 18 May 1943, author collection from Mary Farmer Palmer.

[7] Evelyn Sharp, letter to "Dear Mom and Pop, & babies," 28 May 1943, 1432 Basic Trailer Park, Las Vegas, NV, author collection from Mary Farmer Palmer.

[8] Byrd Howell Granger, ON FINAL APPROACH: The Women Airforce Service Pilots of World War II (Scottsdale, AZ: Falconer Publishing Company, 1991) 68.

[9] Florence Mitchell, "Women Ferry Pilots Do Man's Job a la Vogue," author collection from Nancy Harkness Love Collection, Acc. 1987-0047, National Air and Space Museum Library, Washington, DC.

[10] Evelyn Sharp, letter to "Dear folks," 4 June 1943, author collection from Mary Farmer Palmer.

[11] (Evelyn Sharp, letter to "Dear folks," 4 June 1943)

[12] "Rationing Afoot," Newsweek 15 Feb. 1943: 36; "Ration Followup," Business Week 27 Feb. 1943: 62.

[13] A. Marjorie Taylor, The Language of World War II (New York: The H. W. Wilson Company, 1948): 16.

[14] Marianne Verges, On Silver Wings: THE WOMEN AIRFORCE SERVICE PILOTS OF WORLD WAR II, 1942-1944 (New York: Ballantine, 1991) 56.

[15] Evelyn Sharp, letter to "Dear folks," 13 June 1943, author collection from Mary Farmer Palmer.

[16] Evelyn Sharp, letter to H. Glenn Buffington, 4 July 1943, American Aviation Historical Society Journal (Summer 1991) : 138.

[17] Evelyn Sharp, letter to Patty Baer, 1 July 1943, author collection from Christine Dunbar.

[18] "Operating Instructions for the P-51A Airplane: HEADQUARTERS 6TH FERRYING GROUP, FERRYING DIVISION, AIR TRANSPORT COMMAND, LONG BEACH ARMY AIR FIELD, LONG BEACH, CALIFORNIA," author collection from National Personnel Records, Military Records, St. Louis, MO.

[19] Evelyn Sharp, letter to "Dear folks," 21 June 1943, author collection from Mary Farmer Palmer.

[20] Evelyn Sharp, letter to "Dear Sugars," 18 July 1943, author collection from Mary Farmer Palmer.

[21] Sally VanWagenen Keil, *Those Wonderful Women In Their Flying Machines: THE UNKNOWN HEROINES OF WORLD WAR II* (New York: Four Directions Press, 1990) 296.

[22] (Sally VanWagenen Keil 291)

[23] (Sally VanWagenen Keil 309)

[24] (Evelyn Sharp, letter to "Dear Sugars," 18 July 1943)

[25] (Evelyn Sharp, letter to "Dear Sugars," 18 July 1943)

[26] (Byrd Howell Granger 128)

[27] (Sally VanWagenen Keil 352)

P-51s, B-25s, and 'Ahem'
Chapter Twenty-seven—Pages 222 - 230

[1] Evelyn Sharp, letter to "Dear sugars," 2 Aug. 1943, author collection from Mary Farmer Palmer.

[2] Evelyn Sharp, letter to "Dear folks," 8 Aug. 1943, author collection from Mary Farmer Palmer.

[3] Evelyn Sharp spiral notebook, author collection.

[4] Kittie Leaming King, telephone interview, 11 July 1992.

[5] Evelyn Sharp, postcard to Patty Baer, 18 Aug. 1943, author collection from Christine Dunbar.

[6] (Kittie Leaming King, telephone)

[7] Evelyn Sharp, letter to "Dear folks," 8 Aug. 1943, author collection from Mary Farmer Palmer.

[8] "Only Hollywood," *WORLD WAR II TIMES* 23 Sept. 1943: 20, author collection from Mildred D. Axton.

[9] Jay Robert Nash and Stanley Ralph Ross, *The Motion Picture Guide*, L-M, vol. 5 (Chicago: Cinebooks, Inc., 1986) 1572.

[10] ("Only Hollywood," 20)

[11] Florene Miller Watson, letter to the author, 16 Mar. 1992.

[12] Florene Miller Watson, telephone interview, 10 Jan. 1992.

[13] Evelyn Sharp, letter to "Dear Mom and Pop," 15 Sept. 1943, author collection from Mary Farmer Palmer.

[14] Evelyn Sharp, postcard to Patty Lou Baer, 23 Sept. 1943, from "The Royal Palms Hotel, Palm Springs, Cal., E. Sharp, WASP, 21st Ferrying Group Army Air Base, Palm Springs, Cal.," author collection from Christine Dunbar.

[15] Evelyn Sharp, letter to H. Glenn Buffington, 23 Sept. 1943, *American Aviation Historical Society Journal* (Summer 1991) : 138.

[16] "Questions on C-47: HEADQUARTERS 6TH FERRYING GROUP FERRYING DIVISION, AIR TRANSPORT COMMAND, LONG BEACH ARMY AIR FIELD, LONG BEACH, CALIFORNIA," author collection from National Personnel Records Center, Military Records, St. Louis, MO.

[17] Byrd Howell Granger, *ON FINAL APPROACH: The Women Airforce Service Pilots of World War II* (Scottsdale, AZ: Falconer Publishing Company, 1991) 199.

[18] Claire Callaghan, telephone interview, 12 Jan. 1992.

[19] Sally VanWagenen Keil, *Those Wonderful Women In Their Flying Machines: THE UNKNOWN HEROINES OF WORLD WAR II* (New York: Four Directions Press, 1990) 250.

[20] (Byrd Howell Granger [November 17, 1943] 216)

[21] Evelyn Sharp, letter to Teresa James, 29 Nov. 1943, author collection from Teresa James.

[22] Evelyn Sharp, letter to "Dear Mom and Pop & Kids," 3 Dec. 1943, author collection from Mary Farmer Palmer.

[23] (Evelyn Sharp, letter to "Dear Mom and Pop & Kids," 3 Dec. 1943)

[24] Lt. Frank R. Moore, 6th Ferrying Group, Long Beach, CA, letter to "Hi, Squirt," 9 Dec. 1943, author collection from Dorothy Auble Hardisty.

Show 'Em How To Do It, Sharpie
Chapter Twenty-eight—Pages 231 - 238

[1] Evelyn Sharp, letter to "Dear Mom and Pop & Kids," 3 Dec. 1943, author collection from Mary Farmer Palmer.

[2] Cassette tape recording, 1986 International Ninety-Nines, Inc. Convention, Pateman WASP Collection, vol. XIIIB, US Air Force Academy Archives, Colorado Springs, CO.

[3] Evelyn Sharp, letter to "Dear folks," 14 Dec. 1943, author collection from Mary Farmer Palmer.

[4] Roy L. Maxson, personal interview, 7 June 1993.

[5] (Evelyn Sharp, letter to "Dear folks," 14 Dec. 1943)

[6] (Evelyn Sharp, letter to "Dear folks," 14 Dec. 1943)

[7] Evelyn Sharp, letter to "Dear folks," 27 Dec. 1943, author collection from Mary Farmer Palmer.

[8] John Sharp, letter to Mary Farmer, 1 Dec. 1944, author collection from Mary Farmer Palmer.

[9] Evelyn Sharp, letter to "Dear folks," 27 Dec. 1943, author collection from Mary Farmer Palmer.

[10] Evelyn Sharp, letter to "Dear folks," 2 Jan. 1944, author collection from Mary Farmer Palmer.

[11] Evelyn Sharp spiral notebook, author collection.

[12] Byrd Howell Granger, *ON FINAL APPROACH: The Women Airforce Service Pilots of World War II* (Scottsdale, AZ: Falconer Publishing Company, 1991) 93.

[13] Evelyn Sharp, letter to "Dear folks," 23 Jan. 1944, author collection from Mary Farmer Palmer.

[14] (Evelyn Sharp, letter to "Dear folks," 23 Jan. 1944)

[15] Sally VanWagenen Keil, *Those Wonderful Women In Their Flying Machines: THE UNKNOWN HEROINES OF WORLD WAR II* (New York: Four Directions Press, 1990) 190.

[16] (Sally VanWagenen Keil 186)

[17] Press Release—AP, 23 Dec. 1943, author collection from Nancy Harkness Love Collection, Acc. 1987-0047, File 07, National Air and Space Museum Library, Washington, DC.

[18] Teresa James, letter to the author, 23 Jan. 1992.

[19] Evelyn Sharp, letter to "Dearest folks," 16 Feb. 1944, author collection from Mary Farmer Palmer.

[20] (Evelyn Sharp, letter to "Dearest folks," 16 Feb. 1944)

[21] Frank R. Moore, personal interview, 25 July 1991.

[22] Evelyn Sharp, letter to Chelys Mattley, 5 Mar. 1944, from Hotel Heidelberg, Jackson, MS, author collection from Chelys Mattley Hester.

An Easter Card
Chapter Twenty-nine—Pages 239 - 244

[1] Evelyn Sharp, letter to H. Glenn Buffington, 11 Mar. 1944, *American Aviation Historical Society Journal* (Summer 1991): 138.

[2] *Pilots Manual for Lockheed P-38 Lightning* (Appleton, WI: Aviation Publications, n.d.) : 25.

[3] Col. Sandy Sansing, "The Scatterbrain Kid II," *CAF Dispatch* Spring 1993: 13. P-38 nicknamed Der Gabelschwanz Teufel (The Fork-Tailed Devil) by German pilots who feared it.

[4] Larry Davis, *P-38 Lightning in action* (Carrollton, TX: Squadron/ Signal Publications, 1990) 31.

[5] Iris Cummings Critchell, personal interview, 19 June 1993; letter to the author, 6 July 1993.

[6] "Familiarization with P-38 Airplane: HEADQUARTERS 6TH FER-RYING GROUP, FERRYING DIVISION, AIR TRANSPORT COMMAND, LONG BEACH, CALIFORNIA," 29 March 1944, author collection from National Personnel Records Center, Military Records, St. Louis, MO.

[7] Mike Blakemore, "Lightning Strikes," *Air & Space* Aug.-Sept. 1987: n. pag.

[8] (Mike Blakemore n. pag.)

[9] "THE DESERT DONS KHAKI," *1942-43 Palm Springs Pictorial* (Palm Springs, CA: Historical Society, n.d.) n. pag., author collection from Palm Springs Historical Society, Palm Springs, CA; Fred Kuster, 28th Ferrying Squadron pilot, telephone interview, 15 Aug. 1992.

[10] Evelyn Sharp spiral notebook, author collection; P-38 accident report, including engineering and flight records, flight plan, and aircraft clearance, author collection from US Air Force/Sam Parker Collection. Author note: Both sources used throughout the remainder of this chapter.

[11] Evelyn Sharp, letter to Pat Thomas, 2 Apr. 1944, author collection from Rita Gladney.

[12] Evelyn Sharp, letter to Jerome and Pruda (Farmer) Lobenstein , 30 Jan. 1944, author collection from Mary Farmer Palmer.

[13] Mary Frances Joy, telephone interview, 14 Aug. 1992.

[14] Orla Edward Crouse was born 19 Feb. 1898, Baltimore, MD. Although he remarried, Evelyn was his only child. He died in Missoula, MT, 1 Nov. 1960.

[15] (Evelyn Sharp, letter to Pat Thomas)

[16] Frank R. Moore, personal interview, 25 July 1991.

"I'll Do Everything I Can"
Chapter Thirty ⁓Pages 245 ⁄ 251

[1] AAF photos of P-38 given to John and Mary Sharp by WASP Nancy Batson, author collection from Mary Farmer Palmer.

[2] John Macfarlane, personal interview, 10 July 1989.

[3] "Army Withholds Identity of Pilot Killed in Crash," *Harrisburg Telegraph* 4 Apr. 1944: n. pag., author collection.

[4] "WOMAN PILOT KILLED ON WEST SHORE," *Evening News* [Harrisburg, PA] 3 Apr. 1944: l, 9.

[5] (John Macfarlane, personal)

[6] "NOTIFY KIN OF WOMAN FLIER'S FATAL CRASH," *Patriot* [Harrisburg, PA] 4 Apr. 1944: 1.

[7] "Young Ferry Pilot Dies In Crash of Army P-38 Near New Cumberland," *Evening News* [Harrisburg, PA] 3 April 1944: 1, 9.

[8] ("NOTIFY KIN 1)

[9] ("NOTIFY KIN 1)

[10] Coroner's view of Evelyn Sharp, Book 5: 119, author collection from Register of Deeds, New Cumberland County Courthouse, Carlisle, PA.

[11.] The official records for airplane accidents during World War II are kept at the US Air Force Inspection and Safety Center, Norton AFB, CA. Much of the P-38, 3 Apr. 1944, accident description is censored. Flight records and flight data logs for service and maintenance are public information from Long Beach AAB through Lockbourne AAB in Cincinnati, OH, but the author was unable to see records for the time spent in New Cumberland, PA, on 2-3 Apr. 1944. Efforts on behalf of the author to secure the complete accident report were filed through Freedom of Information Act. In a letter to Senator J. James Exon, 22 Oct. 1991, Colonel Charles W. Parker, USAF Commander wrote: "portions of the report must be retained only in Air Force safety channels." Author request and appeal of the ruling were denied.

[12] "WOMAN DIES IN SHORE PLANE CRASH: U.S. AIR ARMADA BLASTS BUDAPEST," *Harrisburg Telegraph* 3 Apr. 1944, evening ed. 1, 4.

[13] ("WOMAN DIES IN SHORE 1, 4)

[14] ("WOMAN DIES IN SHORE 1, 4)

[15] Barbara Erickson London, telephone interview, 4 Aug. 1988.

[16] Nancy Batson Crews, letter to Ninety-Nines Archives, 18 Sept. 1986, Oklahoma City, OK, author collection.

[17] Kathryn Bernheim Fine, letter to the author, 9 Dec. 1991.

[18] Barbara Towne Fasken, telephone interview, 28 Apr. 1992.

[19] Barbara Donahue Ross, letter to the author, 8 Jan. 1992.

[20] (Barbara Donahue Ross, letter)

[21] J. G. (Tex) Rankin, Rankin Aeronautical Academy, 4th AAF Flying Training Detachment, letter to John Sharp, 22 Jan. 1945, author collection.

[22] Nancy Batson Crews, telephone interview, 8 Jan. 1992.

[23] Patty Baer, letter to Evelyn Sharp, 22 Mar. 1944, author collection from Christine Dunbar.

[24] Frank R. Moore, personal interview, 25 July 1991.

[25] Itemization Evelyn Sharp funeral expenses, 29 Apr. 1944, author collection from National Personnel Records Center, Military Records, St. Louis, MO.

[26] Ord Cemetery Record No. 2: 98; filed 8 Apr. 1944, 3:30 p.m., $80.00, author collection from Valley County Courthouse, Ord, NE.

[27] Mary Kathryn Farmer Sharp, born 5 Aug. 1889, Atlanta, IL, died 19 June 1971, Henderson, NV; John Evans Sharp, born 28 Nov. 1878, Corning, IA, died 13 Sept. 1960, Henderson, NV.

[28] "EVELYN SHARP WILL FLY NO MORE: ORD'S FAVORITE DAUGHTER BURIED," *Ord Quiz* 13 Apr. 1944: 1.

[29] Mary Farmer Sharp, letter to Pruda Farmer Lobenstein, 18 Apr. 1944, author collection from Mary Farmer Palmer.

[30] (Nancy Batson Crews, telephone)

[31] ("EVELYN SHARP WILL FLY NO 1)

[32] Jim Day, "GIRL TRAINS PILOTS: Noted Aviatrix Coaches Fledglings," *Bakersfield Californian* 24 Mar. 1941: 8, 17.

Afterword ⁓Pages 252 ⁄ 255

[1] "Funeral Services for Gerald 'Bud' Clark to be held Sunday," *Ord Quiz* 16 Sept. 1948: 1.

[2] Burlington Route freight bill, 8 Apr. 1947, author collection from Mary Farmer Palmer.

[3] Alfred L. Hill, letter to John and Mary Sharp, 12 Apr. 1947, author collection from Mary Farmer Palmer.

[4] "Airport Dedication Draws Crowd of 4,000 Here Sunday," *Ord Quiz* 16 Sept. 1948: 1.

Sources

Books:

Caidin, Martin. *FORK-TAILED DEVIL: THE P-38*. New York: Ballantine, 1973.

Churchill, Jan. *ON WINGS TO WAR: Teresa James, Aviator*. Manhattan, Kansas: Sunflower University Press, 1992.

Douglas, Deborah G. *UNITED STATES WOMEN IN AVIATION: 1940-1985*. Washington: Smithsonian Institution Press, 1991.

Fisher, Carmen Jefford and Mark Fisher with Cliff Cernick. *WINGING IT: Jack Jefford, Pioneer Alaskan Aviator*. Anchorage: Alaska Northwest Books, 1990.

Radil, Ronald J. *Scratchtown: A History of Ord*. Ord, Nebraska: Quiz Graphic Arts, 1982.

Valley County Historical Society. *A View of the Valley*. Ord, Nebraska: Quiz Graphic Arts, 1973.

Government Documents:

Final Report on Women Pilot Program to Commanding General AAF by Jacqueline Cochran, Director of Women Pilots.

History of the Air Transport Command by Lieut. General Harold L. George (Ret), Air Transport Command.

USAF History of Women in the Armed Forces: A Selected Bibliography (June 1976) by Eleanor E. Peets, Office of Air Force History, Maxwell Air Force Base, Alabama.

Women Pilots with the AAF: 1941-1944, Army Air Forces Historical Studies #55, March 1946, Office of Air Force History, Maxwell Air Force Base, Alabama.

Research Facilities and Museums:

Albert F. Simpson Historical Research Center, Dept. of the Air Force, Maxwell Air Force Base, Alabama.

Buffalo County Historical Society, Kearney, Nebraska.

Eastern California Museum, Independence, California.

Eastern Star and Masonic Archives, Nebraska and Montana.

Family History Center, The Church of Jesus Christ Latter-Day Saints, Lincoln, Nebraska.

Paul Garber Restoration Facility, Suitland, Maryland.

Hastings Historical Society, Hastings, Nebraska.
Library of Congress, Washington, DC.
Lone Star Museum, Galveston, Texas.
Long Beach Historical Society, Long Beach, California.
Love Library, University of Nebraska-Lincoln, Lincoln, Nebraska.
National Archives, Washington, DC.
The Ninety-Nines, International Women Pilots, Historical Archives, Oklahoma City, Oklahoma.
Palm Springs Historical Society, Palm Springs, California.
William Penn Memorial Museum and Archives, Harrisburg, Pennsylvania.
Smithsonian Institution, National Air and Space Museum Library, Washington, DC.
State Archives, Montana State Historical Society, Helena, Montana.
State Archives, Nebraska State Historical Society, Lincoln, Nebraska.
State Archives, North Dakota State Historical Society, Bismarck, North Dakota.
United Methodist Church Historical Center, Lincoln, Nebraska.
United States National Climatic Data Center, Asheville, North Carolina.
US Air Force Academy Archives, Colorado Springs, Colorado.
USA War College, US Army Military History Institute, Carlisle Barracks, Pennsylvania.
Washington National Records Center, Washington, DC.

Miscellaneous:

Aircraft Registry, Federal Aviation Administration, Oklahoma City, Oklahoma.
The Avenger, AAF newspaper, Sweetwater, Texas.
City and County Records Personnel.
Federal Aviation Administration Records Center, Office of Informational Technology, Washington, DC.
"Ladies Courageous," Universal Studios, 1944.
Lockheed Aircraft, Ontario, California.
Middletown Bureau of Aviation, Middletown, Pennsylvania.
New Cumberland Army Depot, Public Affairs, New Cumberland, Pennsylvania.
"Silver Wings," Public Broadcasting System documentary, 1980.
United States Air Force Inspection and Safety Center, Norton Air Force Base, California.
"Women of Courage," Public Broadcasting System documentary, 1993.
"WORLD WAR II TIMES: Women Pilots of World War II," Indianapolis: Traveler Enterprises, July 1987.

Photo Credits

Photo reproductions made by Robert E. Barrett.

Cover: Mary Farmer Palmer Collection
p. 1   Robert E. Barrett Collection
p. 3   Robert E. Barrett Collection
p. 10   US Air Force/Mary Farmer Palmer Collection
p. 11   Winifred Harke Schachterle Collection
p. 15   Mary Farmer Palmer Collection
p. 16   Mary Farmer Palmer Collection
p. 17   Lois Woodworth Taylor Collection
p. 22   Mary Farmer Palmer Collection
p. 25   Norma Mae Snell Kaufman Collection
p. 35   Mary Farmer Palmer Collection
p. 42   Mary Farmer Palmer Collection
p. 46   Bess Wilson Collection
p. 49   Howard E. Jones Collection
p. 57   Mary Farmer Palmer Collection
p. 58   Barbara Nay Gleason Collection
p. 59   Mary Farmer Palmer Collection
p. 63   Mary Farmer Palmer Collection
p. 65   Ellen Servine Misko Collection
p. 68   Mary Farmer Palmer Collection
p. 69   Mary Farmer Palmer Collection (taken by LaVern Duemey)
p. 70   Milo W. Bresley Collection
p. 71   Barbara Nay Gleason Collection (taken by LaVerne Lakin)
p. 73   Mary Farmer Palmer Collection
p. 77   Barbara Nay Gleason Collection (taken by LaVern Duemey)
p. 78   Dennis L. Wohlers Collection (taken by Jose E. Guevara)
p. 81   Al Baeder Collection (taken by LaVerne Lakin)
p. 82   Mary Farmer Palmer Collection
p. 84   Heloise & Dean Bresley Collection
p. 86   Mary Farmer Palmer Collection
p. 94   Mary Farmer Palmer Collection
p. 95   Mary Farmer Palmer Collection
p. 96   Diane Ruth Armour Bartels Collection (taken by Milo W. Bresley)

p. 97   Mary Farmer Palmer Collection
p. 112   Mary Farmer Palmer Collection
p. 113   Heloise & Dean Bresley Collection
p. 118   H. Glenn Buffington Collection
p. 120   Heloise & Dean Bresley Collection
p. 126   H. Glenn Buffington Collection
p. 127   Mary Farmer Palmer Collection
p. 142   Mary Farmer Palmer Collection
p. 146   H. Glenn Buffington Collection
p. 147   Mary Farmer Palmer Collection
p. 150   Helen Osentowski Collection
p. 156   Winifred Harke Schachterle Collection
p. 159   Winifred Harke Schachterle Collection
p. 161   H. Glenn Buffington Collection
p. 163   Mary Farmer Palmer Collection
p. 168   Mary Farmer Palmer Collection
p. 180   Diane Ruth Armour Bartels Collection
p. 181   Mary Farmer Palmer Collection
p. 188   Mary Farmer Palmer Collection
p. 189   Winifred Harke Schachterle Collection
p. 193   US Air Force/Marty Wyall Collection
p. 200   Winifred Harke Schachterle Collection
p. 201   Heloise & Dean Bresley Collection
p. 204   US Air Force/Mary Farmer Palmer Collection
p. 214   McDonnell Douglas/Barbara Erickson London Collection
p. 215   US Air Force/Mary Farmer Palmer Collection
p. 217   US Air Force/National Air and Space Museum Collection
p. 224   US Air Force/National Air and Space Museum Collection
p. 225   Mary Farmer Palmer Collection
p. 227   US Air Force/Barbara Erickson London Collection
p. 232   US Air Force/National Air and Space Museum Collection
p. 234   H. Glenn Buffington Collection
p. 235   H. Glenn Buffington Collection
p. 236   US Air Force/National Air and Space Museum Collection
p. 245   US Air Force/Mary Farmer Palmer Collection
p. 248   US Air Force/Mary Farmer Palmer Collection
p. 251   Mary Farmer Palmer Collection
p. 253   Mary Farmer Palmer Collection
p. 254   Robert E. Barrett Collection
p. 255   Robert E. Barrett Collection

Index